THE Case FOR Home Schooling

Published by Hawthorn Press, Hawthorn House,
1 Lansdown Lane, Stroud, Gloucestershire, GL5 1BJ, UK
 0044 (0) 1453 757040   E-mail: info@hawthornpress.com
www.hawthornpress.com

Warm acknowledgements and thanks to the home education story contributors: Lara Elliott, Emilie Bailey, Ciaran Sneddon, Nana-Adwoa Mbeutcha, Diane Westland, Ceris Brewis, Simon and Tessa Osbourn, Livvy Leaf-Grimshaw, Tammy Palyo Frances Matthews, Astrid Vijne, Gemma Black, Maria Jones.

The Case for Home Schooling © Hawthorn Press 2020
Cover illustration by Kate Hajducka
Cover design by Lucy Guenot: typesetting by Winslade Graphics
Typeset in Adobe Garamond Pro typeface
Photographs © Shutterstock
Printed by Short Run Press Ltd, Exeter

British Library Cataloguing in Publication Data applied for

ISBN 978-1-912480-28-9
eISBN 978-1-912480-41-8

THE Case FOR Home Schooling

Free range home education handbook

Anna Dusseau

Former teacher turned home-educator'

Hawthorn Press

PRAISE FOR *The Case for Home Schooling*

'If you are considering home education, this book will help you over the bump. If you aren't considering it, this book will lead you to consider it. Anna Dusseau brilliantly anticipates all your questions and concerns and greets them in ways that make sense. Her style makes you feel you are having tea and a chat with her at the kitchen table. My own advice, which also runs through this book in various ways, is follow the lead of your kids. They know what they are ready to learn and how they can best learn it.'

> PETER GRAY, research professor at Boston College and author of *Free to Learn: Why Releasing the Instinct to Play Will Make Our Children Happier, More Self-Reliant, and Better Students for Life*

'So lively, so intelligent, but above all, so RIGHT... Children were never intended to have their learning forced on them. They are learning animals, and they are deeply directed by their inner urges to master the world, in their own unique individual way. The best teachers know this, home educators hold it as their core belief. If you want your child to flourish and be suited to the future, and their childhood to be joyful and powerful preparation for anything life can bring, then this book is a treasure chest.'

> STEVE BIDDULPH AM, author *Raising Boys in the 21st Century*, and *The Secret of Happy Children*

'This book is a joy to read. The author's principled convictions, coupled with her appreciation of children's individuality and her deep respect for their powers, are uplifting and reflect the skills of a very sensitive and imaginative educator. Any child would be fortunate to live in such a rich and responsive environment. The author and other contributors also have lessons for school teachers, encouraging them to bring thoughtful new dimensions to their work in class.'

> WENDY SCOTT OBE, Former CEO of the British Association for Early Childhood Education and Chair of the Early Childhood Forum, and Special Advisor to the DfES

'This book is a beautifully cut and crafted diamond, the voices that lift off the pages giving varied and honest perspectives of homeschooling. Our own children were home-schooled and they are now out in the world, with an unmistakable "can-do" attitude that serves them so well, that others are drawn to. This book will leave you with the feeling, "I can do this".'

KIM JOHN PAYNE M.ED., author of *Games Children Play*, *Simplicity Parenting*, *The Soul of Discipline* and *Being at Your Best when Your Kids Are at Their Worst*

'Over the last 30 years, with the introduction of the National Curriculum, the creation of Ofsted and the incessant testing and accountability regime, the joy of learning has been increasingly sucked out of schools in the UK, which have, with some notable exceptions, instead become a source of increasing toxic stress for many teachers and children. If you are considering home schooling for your children, this is an inspiring book and also a very practical guide. It is packed with invaluable information, with the experiences of many homeschoolers, and with thoughtful answers to all the big questions. It is also full of richly creative ideas about how to properly educate your children in the best possible sense, so that they enjoy their childhood, become life-long learners, and fulfilled, capable and resilient adults.'

DR DAVID WHITBREAD, Retired Senior Member, Homerton College, University of Cambridge; author of *Developmental Psychology and Early Childhood Education* and co-editor of *Teaching and Learning in the Early Years*

'Is homeschooling a concept whose time has come? My social media feed suggests that this may well be the case. After three months of lockdown, some families are observing positive changes within their children, particularly in terms of improved mental health. This has led many to hover on the brink of not sending their children back to school at all, but homeschooling them instead. This book will be a very useful source of information for families in this position. Based on the author's experience and on reports from other homeschooling families, it gives an excellent, in-depth account of what homeschooling is actually "like". Highly recommended for anyone who is curious about the process of homeschooling, written by someone who has been there, done that and worn the T-shirt.'

DR PAM JARVIS, author, chartered psychologist and historian, co-author of *The Complete Companion for Teaching and Leading Practice in the Early Years*

'A timely book given the dramatic rise in learning at home as a consequence of the pandemic. It shows that what children thrive on most of all is an education that is relevant to their lives and which allows them to follow and develop their interests, and the book enables and empowers parents to support that process. In essence it is about home learning rather than homeschooling, and the need to radically rethink how we equip young people to live purposeful and fulfilling lives in these challenging times.'

FIONA CARNIE, educationalist and writer. Author of *Rebuilding our Schools from the Bottom up (2018)* and *Alternative Approaches to Education (2017)* both published by Routledge

'If you're wondering whether it's better to homeschool or have your child go to school, this book is a must read. A comprehensive yet highly digestible look at the case for homeschooling, which thoroughly debunks the previous myths you've probably downloaded from society. Thinking of deschooling your kids? Warning – you'll probably be utterly sold after reading this!'

TALYA STONE, 'Motherhood: The Real Deal' blog

'This tour de force is laced throughout with pedagogical wisdom derived from a rich combination of common sense, emotional intelligence, acute perception and professional insight. It could only have been written by a thoughtful, playful, critically minded teacher who has struggled with the mainstream system, and then compared it with her own experience of home schooling. A landmark text in the evolving history of the home-education movement, it is essential reading for all progressively minded educators.'

DR RICHARD HOUSE, chartered psychologist, editor of *Too Much, Too Soon?*, and *Childhood, Well-being and a Therapeutic Ethos*

'An encouraging, perspicacious, and wonderfully relevant read, The Case for Home Schooling is a must-read whether you're considering home-educating for the first time, or you've already been doing it for years. Dusseau is a rare thing: a passionate homeschooler who seeks to unite rather than divide on the topic of education. I highly recommend it.'

ELOISE RICKMAN, author of *Extraordinary Parenting: The Essential Guide to Parenting and Educating at Home*

For Teenwolf, my long-suffering technical assistant.

For my kids, who inspired me.

And for everyone who wants better for their children.

Me to small boy: 'What do you want for breakfast?'
Small boy sitting sadly on kitchen floor: 'I wanted to have an adventure.'

Jax Blunt @liveotherwise

Acknowledgements

A huge thank you to the people whose personal stories contribute so richly to this book. You have transformed it from a thesis into a tapestry, and for that I am most indebted.

Thank you to Richard, Charlotte, Emilie and Ceris for your help editing the first few drafts; for your time, your experience, and your extensive annotations. You are the best.

Many thanks to Shutterstock for the superb images that have brought the text to life.

And finally, thanks to my family – Oli and the kids – who are thoroughly sick of mummy being a writer. Sorry, guys. You are all so patient and supportive. I love you.

CONTENTS

INTERVIEW: *Memories of Homeschool*
With Lara Elliott

AD: *'You grew up homeschooled, right? Was that a positive experience for you?'*

LE: It's what makes me who I am today. And it's the reason that I now lecture in Geophysics. I was taught to pursue my own goals and I knew more about science at 15 than most people. I was actually once asked to deliver a talk on magnetism at the high school down the road, which was a weird experience. It was also the first time I had ever set foot in one of these places.

AD: *'Did you have brothers and sisters?'*

LE: Actually, I'm an only child. I think my mum and dad worried about that to begin with; I know they had hoped for siblings. But homeschooling wasn't uncommon in our town, even back then. I had a lot of playmates, and I never had a problem getting to know the school kids in our area, too.

AD: *'Did you ever miss school?'*

LE: God, no. Next question.

AD: *'What was a typical day like in your house, growing up?'*

LE: My parents ran a bookstore with a small café on the main street. Some days, I would be at home with one of them, and on others we would all go to the bookstore. When I was little, I would help out, or else find an empty box in the storeroom that I'd crawl into and read. When I was old enough to be a bit more independent, I would cross the road to the local library, or meet another homeschool friend at the park. I was a kid living the life of an undergraduate, though I didn't realise it at the time.

AD: *'Did you have a good relationship with your parents?'*

LE: Of course, they are my inspiration. We were friends and partners all the way through, and I never argued with my parents the way I saw my schoolfriends sometimes do. Everything was a discussion and everything was, ultimately, my choice. I don't recall feeling angry too often and, when I did, we would sit down and figure it out.

AD: *'How did you make friends?'*

LE: Mostly through clubs and classes. We never went to a group looking for other homeschool families; I don't think so. They just sort of 'appeared' along the way. What I wanted to do every weekend was horse-riding and I started helping out at a trekking ranch, which was a bus ride out of town. Some of the friendships I still have today come from this time, but that's just one example.

AD: *'Did you find it okay taking exams and getting a job after growing up home educated?'*

LE: Sure. I took the ACT and went to college, like everyone else.

AD: *'You now have three children. Do they go to school?'*

LE: They don't; they are all homeschooled. But we made a point of enrolling each one of them in Kindergarten to give it a go. We wanted the decision to be theirs.

AD: *'What would you say has been the main advantage of being homeschooled in your life?'*

LE: Honestly, I think it's about how you feel. I've never seen learning as 'work', and neither do my kids. My husband is trying to see the world in that way, too. When you don't learn 'at school', everything is suddenly interesting and worth exploring. That feeling never dies.

AD: *'What do you think is the problem with school?'*

LE: There's too much to say, really. Testing, bullying, poor teaching, the K-12 curriculum. And the accountability grenade of 'No Child Left Behind'; you guys also have that in the UK. Isn't this what you're covering in the book?

AD: *'Well, I'm going to try.'*

FOREWORD
Steve Biddulph

We'd always been very happy with our local primary school, a village school of only a hundred or so children in the mountains of Tasmania. But one day a new teacher arrived, a brash young man with a rather sneering manner, and we learned he was to be our little boy's teacher next year.

Then, in the playground one day, I saw him really put down a child in a most unpleasant way, and I realised – we can't have this man in our children's life. A year is a long time when you are seven, and the right or wrong teacher has an emotional and educational impact that can be lifelong. So when the time came, and evidence mounted that this was a bad person around children (and gossip in Tasmania is a rich grapevine), we bit the bullet. We would homeschool for the upcoming year.

Living on a farm, working from home, and being enthusiasts for children's learning all helped, but we were still daunted. But there was lots of help available, a network of homeschooling parents who were happy to offer advice, and the rather compelling proof of how mature, kind and thriving their children seemed to be.

That was all long years ago. When we talk to our son – now in his mid-thirties – he remembers it as easily the best time of his school life. He flourished. It took time and energy, but then – as anyone reading this book knows – so does school! From the transport hassles, playground bullying and other dramas, homework stresses, and the sheer administrivia that plagues parents and drives teachers demented, school may be far from a happy or easy place. In the UK especially, it's become a bureaucratic nightmare of testing and lockstep learning imposed by governments who seem to be frightened of diversity or variation, and think that you can legislate for human development. That you can frighten people into learning, when we know the very opposite is so.

Homeschooling isn't for everyone, though the COVID-19 virus is making sure we all get a fairly good tryout. In fact, millions of parents are being confronted with how boring, soul-crushing, meaningless and rote much of the curriculum is. And wondering if there isn't something better.

To be clear, I am also a fan of schools. They can be wonderful, with a team of caring adults who enrich, widen and stimulate kids, become more interesting and inspiring than mum and dad can be, and get them into an independent community with their peers and the wider world. If that describes your local school – lucky you!

If not, then in the pages that follow, you're going to experience just how much more alive, more motivating and exciting learning is when you break away not just from school, but from the whole idea of a child as a receptacle. Your child has yearnings, talents and interests, and a huge enthusiasm to understand their world. Unleash that, and see what real education is really like. And find that you, too, are happiest when you are learning, creating, and nurturing those things in your family.

Claim back the power!

Read on!

Steve Biddulph AM

Churchill Fellow, retired psychologist, author of the million-selling *Raising Boys in the 21st Century*, *Raising Girls* and *Ten Things Girls Need Most*

July 2020

Introduction

Earlier this year, I was contacted to be interviewed on a local radio show. It was at the height of the pandemic and the entire world seemed to be homeschooling, with mixed success. I was asked to come on and speak about my experience of home education, and what advice I would give to parents doing it for the first time. Sitting cross-legged on the sofa, I chewed my lip – a habit I still can't shake from childhood – and waited for the call to go live.

Soundcheck. Okay, listen in. 'Hello, do we have Anna Duss-e-o on the line?', barked a stern voice. He did. 'Can you tell me then, in your experience of homeschooling, how you would manage a child who doesn't want to do any work?' And I'll admit, I wasn't expecting that. Where to even begin?.... Not with the reluctant child, but with the problems in the question. I hesitated, then cautiously acknowledged that my eldest was also feeling unsettled since lockdown, and had spent several hours that day doing laps of the kitchen in her new rollerskates. 'Forgive me', the interviewer cut in. 'But I don't think our listeners are interested in letting their kids mess around on roller skates.' And that was that. I put the phone down, frowning at the blank screen of the laptop, listening to my children's tinkling laughter drift in from the garden. It's a shame some people don't want to hear it. Because, in a way, it's all about roller skates.

Let's think back to pre-lockdown. What did your schedule look like? Depending on the ages of your children, a typical day might have involved getting up early when the alarm rang, packing lunchboxes and checking book bags, walking or driving your children to school and dropping them off at the gates. Later on, you would most likely return to collect your child, transport them home, help with their homework, cook dinner, and supervise bath and bedtime. And that was on a quiet night! Over the weeks, your routine might also have included things like swimming lessons, football, ballet, Brownies, and a whole list of other activities and engagements specific to your family. It was, you might recall, a busy schedule. And you have been doing a brilliant job managing it all. But I expect you've also noticed that the focus is almost entirely practical; it is about getting places and making things happen. You might well have occasionally wondered where the time is going and when your child's 'big' questions get answered. In school? Possibly. Still, you might have felt some unease about this. Perhaps, in fact, that's why you're reading this book.

And what does this routine feel like for the child? For many children, their lives are so busy with school journeys, subject changes, after-school clubs and homework that they have little time to think, or to take ownership of the life they are leading. They spend an awful lot of time being 'processed' by well-intentioned adults. In the morning, mum or dad has breakfast ready on the table for them to bolt down and, in the car, they appease their parents' anxiety by answering questions about their day and practising the spellings or tricky formulae that they will be tested on in class. From the moment they step into school, they are herded by authority figures and given an endless stream of instructions along the way; form tutors have 'important' notices, the art teacher wants to know where their homework is, and the science teacher tells them to make notes on the video they are watching because it will come up in a test next week.

But the onslaught doesn't stop at the end of the day, because even the most caring parents often forget what the school day is like and immediately begin shepherding again, reminding the child that they have swimming or perhaps karate later, so they will need to crack on straight away with homework. It is a modern mania that has become progressively worse over the past 20 years or so.

I got this message just the other day from a former colleague. It is a screenshot of an email sent between colleagues about a boy in Year 9 at his school. Many teachers, you see, think the system stinks just as much as I do; confidentiality be damned.

> Dear All,
>
> We have agreed with Santi's form tutor and subject teachers that he must complete all the work that he has missed during Lockdown, within the first two weeks of September. The library has agreed to make provision for a desk to be available for him every morning before school and during break and lunchtimes, as well as an hour of additional study at the end of each day.
>
> I have printed the full list of unsubmitted work (over two hundred pages) and have created a schedule for him to work with, including revision for missed assessments and bullet-point summaries of the material covered during missed Zoom meetings. There will be no excuses. If Santi refuses to engage with his own education, then we will come to him. His mother has verbally agreed to this course of action over the phone.
>
> Thank you for your co-operation.
>
> Miss G, Head of Year

I blinked, and read it again. Santi is 14. Poor guy.

Roller-skating – much like chess, tennis or playing the piano – is a holistic activity that engages both mind and body. Wherever skill and co-ordination are involved, a child is activating neurological pathways that light up areas of the brain connected to learning and memory. After physical exercise, or any 'different' way of thinking, children are also more receptive to engaging with activities that require concentration; hence why the strategic reduction in playtime at most state schools demonstrates a devastating oversight.

More than this, there is an element of emotional development that takes place through play-based learning, which is less readily gained in the classroom, or through textbooks. Gabriel Santos, creator of the first skate-park in Syria, puts this clearly in his observation that 'skating is good for kids because it is psychologically challenging. The philosophy is simple: get up and try again. It's an amazing form of self-development.' (Santos, 2020) The very notion of trial and error, of learning through perseverance as opposed to taught technique, is utterly alien to the school system – and yet without it, we are lost.

To anyone who suggests that five-year olds should be studying The Great Fire of London rather than practising roller-skating or reading comics, I would ask them to cast their minds back to what they were doing at age five. In fact, the national age for starting school has become progressively younger while, at the same time, the legal exit age for full-time schooling has risen to 18. With this, we have shifted our *cultural understanding* of what children should be like and, also, what young adulthood should be like; and this is destructive at both ends of the spectrum.

More and more, we place unreasonable expectations on young children who, only 40 years ago, would have been left in peace to play at home. We feel stressed if they are falling behind in their spelling tests, or aren't showing an interest in extra-curricular clubs. We no longer allow them to spend lazy afternoons catching grasshoppers in margarine tubs; learning patience, mindfulness and mercy. Young adults, too, are strangled in their growth by a system which forbids them to take their own path in life, if they are ready at 15 or 16 to begin an apprenticeship in a skill that they are passionate about. The spectacular failure of the school system seems obvious when you understand *how* school works – and, of course, when you step out of it and look around a little bit. I hope this book will help you to do just that.

Families like yours might be considering to home-educate for many different reasons. Perhaps your child is frequently tearful on school mornings, or maybe you see them too often looking tired and defeated, bringing home piles of homework. Possibly your child is not yet of school age, but you already feel fearful of placing him or her into the school system. In fact, many parents experience this anxiety prior to sending their children to school, and they are right to worry. School is a very tough environment which, contrary to popular belief, bears almost no resemblance whatsoever to the skillset required to succeed in adult life. A great deal of childhood trauma can be connected, directly or indirectly, to school. Many of us, indeed, have to 'unlearn' the damaging habits and defensive behaviours acquired at school over the course of several decades. Some of us never disentangle ourselves from the 'survival mode' of our school days and, as a consequence, fail to thrive in our adult lives.

This book is about helping you and your child to navigate the choice that lies ahead of you: whether to pursue an education at school, or otherwise. Home education is a legal and legitimate choice; and in Part III, we will look more closely at the law surrounding homeschooling in the UK, as well as how to document your child's development and engage positively with your local education authority (LEA), if you choose to do so. By considering home education, you are choosing to reimagine the time spent with your children and to engage with them in a brand new and incredibly liberating way. It is a way which allows room for the 'big' questions to get tackled every day of the week.

Here are some terms for you to bear in mind, as you read on:

i.   This book is founded on the concept of Non-Prescriptive Home Education. If you are educating your child outside of school and they are happy with this choice, then you are home-educating. There are several different approaches to homeschooling, and you are free to select what works for your family.

ii. In Part I, you will be introduced to a new concept: Learning Moments. This will help you to identify when important learning is taking place for your child, and how to 'scaffold' the learning environment in order to best facilitate this. You will form an understanding of when to back off and observe, but also when to offer hints and direction.

iii. Throughout this book, you will recognise again and again what I call the Whole-Family Benefits of home education. This is a broad term to describe the changes that occur for the entire family if you choose to homeschool. These benefits will be outlined more clearly in Chapter 3.

iv. In writing this, I hope to achieve a Simplification of the Learning Process; that is, demystifying the mind-boggling nomenclature of the classroom, in order to show you how children can develop organically and without the need for a framework to which they must adhere. If we scrap the assessment grid terminology and trust our intuition, we will learn more.

v.   This work aims to Depolarise the Debate on school vs homeschool that the media loves to exploit. Teachers and home educators are on the same page when it comes to understanding child development and respecting the importance of safeguarding for all children. There is no 'them and us' when it comes down to the basics.

Part I will look carefully at two very important questions. First, what is the purpose of education? And secondly, how do children learn? By thinking about these questions, you will be able to appreciate how homeschooling fits into a wider understanding of education. As a species, we have evolved over thousands of years, following a natural system of learning based on children being raised and taught by a handful of close adults who love and support them (Biddulph, 2018). School is a modern deviation from this ancient approach, and brings with it a set of human complications which we are still figuring out. By the end of Part I, you will have a clear grasp of the implications of mass schooling, as well as the ways in which children are best placed to learn and grow. We will conclude this section with a summary of the global benefits of home education; an important grounding for the stories you will read later.

Part II speaks for itself, and comprises a series of short personal stories from a wide range of homeschooling families. Each story is written from a single perspective, and as such represents a snapshot only – a glimpse into homeschooling in action. This is a crucial part of the book, as it demonstrates the breadth of practice that exists. Feel free to experiment with your own approach, if you choose to pursue homeschooling, and to 'borrow' from the different voices and methods presented in this book, until you find your own, unique style of home-educating. The stories in Part II range from memories of homeschooling in the early noughties through to current insights into the experience of homeschooling in the UK and overseas. I have also included the reflections of some young adults who were home-educated, as well as the challenging experiences of some families who have 'crisis schooled' through COVID-19. Both are important contributions to the homeschooling discussion.

Finally, in Part III we will look at how to answer the practical questions relating to home education. Moving away from the theory of child psychology and learning, this part of the book will address the concrete information you need to begin your home-educating journey. There is a chapter focusing on concrete activities to try at home, as well as a question-and-answer section, providing responses to any outstanding concerns you may still have by the end of the book. We will be sure to cover the legal side of home-educating here, as well as the very valid queries relating to tracking academic progress, taking examinations, managing socialisation, and identifying the rare situations where home education would not benefit the child.

As a teacher, there is an important concept that I would like you to bear in mind when reading this book, and that is the infancy of the National Curriculum itself. In Britain the first statutory National Curriculum was introduced by the Education Reform Act 1988 – just over 30 years ago – and has since become a doctrine for what happens in all classrooms. It has, as with most government policy, been added to in an unsystematic and reactive way – in many cases simply 'adding content' in order to *do* something with students, as curriculum planning responds to the ever-rising age limit for compulsory schooling. Imperfect though it may be, parents are often drawn to the 'importance' of the National Curriculum, without paying attention to the gaping problems. Answering pages of arithmetic does not form a mathematical mind (Lockhart, 2002). Teaching children about nouns and adjectives is total nonsense, compared to the value of just curling up with a good book.

More than this, there are *dangerous omissions* from the National Curriculum which feed into the social and environmental issues facing us today. Consider the fact that history is taught from a European imperialist perspective, focusing on the British Empire and the World Wars, with Black History Month 'bolted on' every autumn term. Or the way that the history of the planet fails to be addressed in meaningful terms; all the stuff kids *love* such as the Big Bang, dinosaurs, cave men and ancient civilisations are given lip-service at primary-school level only. It is a curriculum that teaches white supremacy and, arguably, human supremacy over the natural world. It is a crutch for the bedrock of narrow-mindedness and toxic entitlement that has poisoned the new millennium.

School has become an increasingly dominant theme in children's lives over the past 50 years or so. The relentless 'upping' of homework, extra-curricular activities and constant testing has created generations of human beings programmed to be self-focused and target-driven, or else shoved into semi-obscurity; the breeding ground for extremism, as we will touch upon later. It seems a plausible link to make that the more all-consuming compulsory schooling has become and, with it, the less time children spend caring for younger siblings and helping around the house, the more we see the rise of *part-time parenting*. This refers to the growing number of people who seem overwhelmed by the task of just being with their own children and relentlessly seek opportunities to hand them over: childminders, babysitters, private nannies, clubs, summer camps, crèche, nursery and school. In many ways, this is the logical conclusion for today's parents – myself included – who were themselves brought up within an increasingly dysfunctional school system. Raised to be egocentric, easily distracted and expecting constant stimulation, this is one of the huge failures of the great 'teaching and learning' concept. Unable to settle into the natural mould of mid-life parenting, many ignore the human significance of our natural life stages, in favour of endlessly seeking life accomplishments.

But let's be frank – there is nothing particularly ground-breaking about another book on the topic of home education. Every year, more and more books are published on this topic, adding to the rapidly swelling chorus of voices from the various worlds of parenting, education and child psychology, all calling out the problems in school, and the positives of an alternative education. So what makes this book different? I will tell you now.

1. This text is the result of over a decade spent teaching and working in schools, marking national exam papers late into the night, and tutoring students of all ages. It is a professional – as well as a personal – perspective on the matter.

2. Within these pages, you will find concrete guidance and 'solutions' to teaching and learning at home, including advice relating to family well-being and your own self-care as a home educator. There is a gentle 'coaching' element here that is absent from many homeschooling books.

3. Importantly, this is not the work of one person. Whilst my voice brings everything together, what you are holding represents the collaborative thinking of many people from the world of home education: parents, educators, researchers and more.

4. The purpose of this book is to unite people. It links the experience of education for families who school and homeschool, and represents people of different beliefs, colours, countries and financial position. There is something to connect with for everyone, as well as a shared underlying concern: the future of our children. In other words, whatever your family situation, the diverse family stories in Part II of the book will almost certainly contain something that will have direct relevance to your particular family circumstances.

And another difference: you will likely notice that I have taken the unusual step of inserting the family stories in between Part I (Chapters 1 to 3) and Part III (Chapters 4 and 5). Why have I done this? Crucially, the family stories are – in themselves – instructive, and will help develop the reader's understanding of home education. The final Q&A section, therefore, and the practical ideas to go forward with in your own home-education practice, feel like they naturally sit at the end of the book. I hope you won't mind my meandering methodology; we'll get there in the end.

The forerunner to this book – *Free Range Education* by Terri Dowty – was published in 2000. I was 14 then – a schoolgirl myself, rolling my skirt up and sticking thumbs through the holes in my chewed sleeves. I was academically very able – always top of the class – but I also spent a lot of time in bed suffering from extreme stomach pain which only disappeared when I was 30; the year I quit my first teaching post in London. I don't know exactly what to make of that now. I suppose I rather wish my parents had read Terri's book which, like the book you are holding now, is packed with useful information, personal stories and practical advice.

But the book I have written here will also tell you a lot about the school system; and in recounting my memories of classroom teaching, I have had to be 'creative' with the truth – with the names and identities in stories relating to former pupils or colleagues of course having been changed beyond recognition. And I guess you might be thinking, 'Yikes! Do I need to be a teacher to homeschool my child?' Absolutely not. In fact, rather than seeing me as a guide here, try to look at it this way: if someone like me – totally ingrained and invested in the system – can do it, then so can you.

But, hang on a minute. I sense you might already have some reservations about this before we properly begin. Am I right? Let me see if I can briefly address those concerns now, so that we can work together through the rest of the book. I don't want to be holding your hand; I want us to be walking side by side as we look into childhood and the learning process.

First – you are right – for some children, school *is* a lifeline; an escape from violence or neglect, an opportunity for a hot meal and some positive connection. You'll be glad to know that this book is not about 'doing away' with school altogether, but rather investigating key principles for learning and growth that are worryingly absent from our current system. Secondly, I wonder whether you might be – as I once was – holding on to the idea that 'children should be in school'. We've certainly all had that drummed into us over recent months; and where the message is a powerful one, it can sweep everyone along with it. Surely, many children enjoy school, don't they? You see them running around playing tag at lunchtime. and the classrooms appear cheerful and brightly decorated on Open Evening. In fact, I don't doubt that there are some fun elements to school; but the fact remains that children are almost universally there by force, not choice. This is problematic in itself, as we will discuss later in the book; but here I will draw your attention to two related facts about childhood which school does not consider.

i.   Children fundamentally *dislike* having their freedom curtailed and being told what to do. It goes against their instinct to be self-directed, to explore the world, and to establish themselves as people. They also thrive on recounting what they *do* know, and find it irksome when they are 'pinned down' on the receiving end of grown-up 'wisdom'.

ii. Children, when they ask for help, prefer minimal guidance. You will notice this any time your child asks for support with cutting, colouring, geometric manipulation or piano notation. You lean down to assist, and your fingers have barely moved across the page before your hand is slapped impatiently away. They actually *prefer* to figure things out independently.

Clearly, a typical school day doesn't come close to satisfying these basic psychological premises, which means that most children are getting through school by employing a coping mechanism. Many primary school children – especially girls – enjoy the 'game' of pleasing the teacher; a demographic which thins significantly at secondary school, where academic pressure mounts and students seeking self-validation from their teachers are batted away like flies. Other students are playing a different game, though. Already bored of adult-led learning, they are using their intelligence to get *out of* doing work and to actually 'avoid' learning at all costs. At either end of the spectrum, it's a sad way to spend 14 years of your life, whether or not you kick a ball around at lunchtime.

Please be patient as you read this. It takes time to change a lifelong perspective on an institution that sits at the heart of our society. And there is no pressure for you to adhere to the educational philosophy which this book presents. You are not at Parents' Evening and your family is not under the spotlight. It's time to sit on the other side of the table – with me – and this time it's school in the uncomfortable plastic chair and we, the parents, arranging our notes and preparing our verdict. Whether your child remains in the public education system or not, I believe the information contained in this book will be useful for you in best supporting your child to learn and grow.

So, welcome to *The Case for Homeschooling*. I'm Anna, a former English teacher and examiner who simply fell into homeschooling by chance one cloudy afternoon, when I decided there *had* to be a better option than our local primary school. We have never looked back (and, by the way, this is a story you will hear again and again in the home-educating community). I live with my husband and our three *Star Wars*-obsessed children in a small village just north of London. This is my first book, and it marks the end of our first year as a home-schooling family. My perspective on child development and the nature of education comes from years of working with children in secondary schools, but my thoughts on homeschooling are absolutely instinctive, like drawing on a glove.

I'm so glad you're here with me. Let's do this together, shall we?

PART I
Quitting the School Run

'There are loads of different activities that you can do and they're quite fun, really. Be creative. You can craft and write stories and stuff, whenever you like. I like riding my bike.

You don't have to wake up early all the time. If you don't go to school you'll be able to choose the things you learn about a bit more.'

Nina, age 9

Chapter 1

The Purpose of Education

There were so many rules that you couldn't do anything without being told off, and there seemed to be tests and exams every week.

Jill Murphy, The Worst Witch

What is an education, and how do we go about getting one? This chapter is going to look closely at both questions. If the *measure* of an education is quantified by assessment results, then it might interest you to know that in the USA, homeschooled students typically score 15 to 30 percentile points *above* public-school students on standardised academic achievement tests (Ray, 2020); or that in the UK, the National Literacy Project assessment results revealed that 80.4 per cent of home-educated children scored within the top 16 per cent (Rothmerel, 2002).

But is education about test-paper scores at all, or is it about something else altogether? Can we really measure the depth of our learning – our 'readiness' for adult life – in this way? And is adulthood the logical point at which our education grinds to a halt? Notably, there is nothing 'special' about homeschool kids. School children are just as bright, witty and complex, but they come into adulthood via a different route – one which represses questions like this. I will point out, too, that this chapter, and indeed the book as a whole, is not a targeted attack on the state sector. The words 'mainstream', 'public' and 'state' are frequently used as a readily identifiable model of education, from which we can distinguish the differences in the practice of homeschooling. Private schools are still schools, though, albeit liberated from the constraints of the National Curriculum. From fee-paying to free schools – and everything in between – these institutions *all* provide an education; the question is simply, 'Is it any good?'.

Teachers and home educators need not be at war, though. With respect to educational methodology, it is refreshing to first observe the areas of natural overlap and shared thinking that exist between the seemingly opposing orbits of school and homeschool. Contrary to popular belief, many home-educating parents follow the National Curriculum closely, whilst in turn, many teachers and senior academics fully support the global benefits of homeschooling. (Indeed, a number of the editors and contributors to this book were, or still are, teachers.) Also contrary to popular belief, there are multiple ways in which mainstream pedagogy and home-education ideology dovetail. For example:

i. **Autonomy:** This is what home educators call 'child-led' learning, and what, back in 2008, teacher training courses referred to as 'radiator teaching'. We all agree that children learn most effectively when it is organic and self-directed.

ii. **Deep Learning:** The idea of allowing children the time and space to fully engage with a topic and pursue that interest without limits. The positive neurological impact of enabling young people to undertake independent research is indisputable.

iii. **Interdisciplinary:** The division of subjects doesn't really correspond to the way knowledge is applied in the real world, and schools are aware of this. The best schools make regular attempts to forge inter-departmental topic links; in home education this is standard practice.

So there are several important areas of common ground, where teachers and home educators are, in fact, in total agreement on what education 'should be like'. The difficulty, of course, is actually implementing this pedagogy in a real and meaningful way in the classroom. The environment of school – with its bells and changeovers, large class-sizes and turbulent student dynamics – makes these educational ideals hard to deliver.

But why are we talking about 'education' in the first place? What are we sending (or not sending) our children to school for? For when we subscribe to an educational approach, we are also subscribing to what we anticipate the 'outcomes' of that process to be. We all quite naturally have hopes and aspirations for our children, ranging from the desire to see them graduate from medical school, to the wish to see them simply live a happy and fulfilling life. In an article published earlier this year, Peter Gray defined an education as 'the sum of everything a person learns that enables that person to live a satisfying and meaningful life' (Gray, 2020). That, I think, will do nicely.

In this chapter, therefore, we will be looking at the 'outcomes' of education, and observing the ways in which a homeschooling method is relevant to achieving this. I use the term 'homeschooling method', as it is important to recognise that many parents who send their children to school nevertheless approach their children's well-being and educational journey with what we could consider to be 'homeschool' values. To use more popular terminology here, we might refer to the 'Growth Mindset' (Dweck, 2012), but it boils down to the same thing; cultivating intrinsic motivation to learn *beyond* the classroom. A self-directed and holistic view of education. And so, as with teaching, *there is no one true path* when it comes to parenting, either; we must therefore seek to nurture the experience of childhood and personal growth for children across the board.

Love of Learning

Children are born with a natural instinct and desire to learn. Babies learn an incredible amount from birth, including movement, communication, social interaction and more refined skills such as humour, playfulness and the appreciation of books and music. In the early 'preschool' years, children go on to explore the world around them with independence and enthusiasm, mastering the more complex business of sharing, measuring, riding a scooter, operating the television and learning to cook. None of this is achieved by sitting the child down and delivering a lesson. In fact, none of this is 'taught' at all. These capabilities naturally arise when learning opportunities are sought by the child and supported by a caring parent or guardian.

Most parents are, without knowing it, experts at this. A six-month-old baby might not yet be sitting up independently, but we would mostly not worry too much. Parental instinct tells us that he or she will sit properly when they are ready – and they do! Similarly, when it comes to toilet training, most parents understand that their child needs to be developmentally at the correct stage to undertake this successfully, and so for a year or so, you will find a wide spectrum of children at different stages of toilet training; some two-year-olds already in pants and some three-year-olds not yet ready to manage without a nappy. This is normal, and we all feel relaxed enough to laugh fondly about these differences. And yet just a year later, the same children enter Reception and start to be measured against their peers for global skills from literacy and numeracy to refined motor skills. Suddenly, no one is laughing. And it's not okay to be different.

Psychologist Peter Gray notes that 'the biggest, most enduring lesson of school is that learning is work, to be avoided when possible' (Gray, 2013). This is a problem. The process of learning – something innate, instinctive and essential for human evolution – is corrupted almost as soon as children enter primary school. Let's look at how this happens.

1. **Learning becomes adult-led.** Once children enter the classroom (or earlier, if they have attended nursery school), adults take over in directing the 'learning' taking place. This almost immediately has the effect of switching at least half the children 'off'. They stop thinking for themselves, lose interest in learning, and stop asking questions. With personal exploration and enquiry firmly squashed, the children who appear to thrive in this environment are those who adapt most quickly to the new expectation: please the adult and get a star on your wall chart. The pure pursuit of learning is gone.

2. **Children are away from home for too long.** The school day is long and, frankly, exhausting for children, especially under the age of ten. Once you add travel time and the 'wrap around' activities of school (preparing uniform and book-bags in the morning, homework and reading logs in the evening) it could be fairly said that the school day consumes almost every waking hour of a child from Monday through to Friday. This is a strain which, naturally, affects concentration and well-being.

3. **The environment of school is exhausting, too.** When you enter a school, the first thing you might notice are the brightly coloured displays on the walls. You might also notice the squeak of your trainers on the rubber-sprung floor, the hum of activity, the constant glare of strip-lights regardless of the weather outside, the sharp drill of the lunch bell and the

smell of disinfectant. It's okay for a visit; but to spend your entire day in this environment is draining, even for the adults who work there.

4. **Same-age classes are a recipe for social tension.** Choosing to teach children in groups according to their age is a mistake and brings with it a whole host of problems. In mixed groups of children, you will notice mutually beneficial roles emerging between the older and younger ones, as we will observe more closely later in Chapters 2 and 3. By teaching children only in narrow age brackets, the lack of natural hierarchy and positive behavioural models leads to an unhealthy environment of competitiveness and 'herd mentality'. This, in turn, affects concentration.

5. **The pressure to record learning ruins the process.** Although most school teachers have received basic training in child psychology and are aware of different learning approaches, the dominant method is still pen and paper. The necessity of 'writing it down' – whether filling in a worksheet or producing a diary entry – is driven by the scrutiny and level of accountability placed on teachers, meaning that your child's 'development folder' for Year 1 is really more like an end-of-year Performance Review for the teacher. Few children, however, enjoy this repetitive clerical work (Robinson, 2006).

6. **Lack of space forces children to behave like adults.** The average class size in British primary schools currently stands at 28 – the largest in the developed world (Turner, 2019). And yes, that's a lot of people to fit in one room! During Key Stage One in particular, many children will spend the entire day learning in this one space, with only breaktimes, PE lessons, and assembly (which happens once a week) to break it up. There simply isn't the space for children to roam freely, and so learning happens, day after day, sat at a desk facing the whiteboard. Even in an office-based job, this is an environment which most adults would only be expected to endure for an hour or so of their day, for a meeting or presentation. How I used to dread the weekly team meeting, when I taught in schools! Yet this is the universal experience of school children, from registration through to home time. No wonder they get ratty.

7. **Testing and levelling destroy learning.** Testing has nothing to do with education. Testing children and recording their 'level' is a purely administrative process, enabling schools to measure teacher performance and compare schools; yet the damage done to our children in the process is immeasurable. Education is a deep and complex process by which human beings shape themselves to function effectively in their society. Testing short-term memory capacity and drilling children in a narrow set of prescribed topics does not serve us well as a species.

It is October. Like all the other Reception-class parents, my husband and I book an evening slot to attended our daughter's first Progress Meeting with Mr C, held in the echoey canteen which also doubles up as a sports hall. I have sat on the other

Parents' Evening WITH **Mr C**

side of this table many times, informing parents on their child's academic progress, but I've never been on the receiving end, and certainly not at primary level. It is difficult to say exactly what we were expecting from this, but what actually happens leaves us rather stunned.

I have grown to quite like Mr C, whose blustering jokes and friendly manner has definitely helped our child to settle in during her first term. Once we sit down at the meeting, however, the tone is different. Our four-year-old's 'progress' is mapped on a chart; she is apparently good at communication, average at reading and below average with her manual skills. This could be because she is left-handed. How can we support her at home?, he wants to know. Sat between us, her small legs swinging, I immediately feel our daughter curl up into her seat, knees to chin. She has never been 'measured' like this before. Soon afterwards, she begins complaining about school work and describing herself as 'not good at' certain things.

Later that year, her best friend Jennie can be found in tears every Friday because she can't stand the shame of the weekly spelling test. Jennie is a confident girl who runs everywhere and has a wicked sense of humour, but she is mostly averaging 3/10 on her spellings. At age four, this becomes the focus of all communication between the teacher and her parents, who are nice people that we get on well with. They are crushed, and feel frustrated for Jennie. It shouldn't, we all agreed, be like this. And yet it is.

So, school kills a child's love of learning as surely as flowers will die without the proper conditions to grow. Even those children who appear to be coping well overall – our daughter included – are almost universally doing so for the 'reward' of adult praise or house points, rather than for the sake of pursuing an interesting topic. At the extreme end (performing at either top or bottom, academically) the pressure is excruciating and damages a child's self-confidence and interest in learning for life. This is not what education should look like.

What education should be – and successful home education undeniably achieves this – is the cultivation of an intrinsic willingness to learn; an engagement with learning as a positive activity to be sought out, rather than avoided. Many home-educating families will refer to themselves as lifelong learners – meaning that both they and their children are learning together in partnership, always looking to deepen and extend their knowledge. Education like this is desperately needed to face the rapid changes and challenges of the modern world.

Emotional Education

Hand in hand with learning about the world around them, children need to learn about their inner world, too. Mental health is better understood now than when I went to school, and there are campaigns and support groups in all schools and youth clubs to encourage young people to take care of their mental health. Yet the source of the problem – namely, the academically competitive and socially stressful environment of school – has only become worse during this time. It is now a tragic normality of modern life that 'five to eight times as many young people today…[have] a clinically significant anxiety disorder or major depression than fifty or more years ago' (Gray, 2013).

From their early years through to adult maturity, a healthy child should develop in many ways through their emotional education. However, I am going to focus on just three points, which we might consider the most essential for that child to become a successful and useful part of the community they live in.

- Self-control
- Good judgement
- Personal well-being

We will talk more about each of these emotional attributes during the course of this book, but I will now briefly highlight the inherent problems with attempting to cultivate them at school. All three aspects of a good emotional education – self-control, good judgement and personal well-being – require a person to spend some time being guided by their own instinct.

We learn SELF-CONTROL by feeling rage or excitement and having the freedom to walk away from the situation, or find the method within ourselves that helps us to calm down. Next time, we might be able to utilise that technique at an earlier stage.

Similarly, GOOD JUDGEMENT usually develops through a process of trial and error, gradually forming a steady confidence in our own judgement. We cannot be 'taught' this skill.

Nor can we be 'taught' PERSONAL WELL-BEING which, again, requires a degree of autonomy and self-directed emotional education in order to determine how we feel at our best. I use music to clear my mind, but perhaps you prefer to go for a run. Either way, we most likely learnt this about ourselves in adult life rather than when we most needed it, in childhood.

In 1964, John Holt published *How Children Fail*, an explosive text which applied Holt's experience as a classroom teacher to conclude that children 'love learning but hate being taught' (Holt, 1964). His

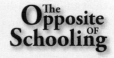

book *How Children Learn* then provides a response to his first book, with insight into the ways children can grow and learn without school. His central message is for us to trust children (Holt, 1967) if we want to see them flourish.

I will summarise Holt's ideas on the education system here:

- Experts agree that it is before children start school that they do their best learning.
- Children use their mind in 'a special way' which school trains them out of. School, Holt asserts, teaches children to 'think badly', or not think at all.
- Because the learning is 'inflicted', school children use their minds not to learn but to get out of learning, causing them to grow up as 'limited versions' of the human beings they might have become.
- Schools have become bigger, more depersonalised, more threatening and more dangerous than they used to be. Learning in schools is also more 'fragmented', i.e. not connected with anything else and therefore meaningless.
- Education and teaching are wrongly modelled on industrial processes, to be designed and planned from above and then imposed on passive teachers, and even more passive students.
- Assessment has increased beyond reason; the weekly test has become the daily, or hourly, or even 15-minute test.
- We are trained to believe that knowledge, skill and wisdom are the products of schooling, and that people should be graded and ranked by the amount of schooling they can consume.
- The oppressive structure of education boils down to a few key beliefs: 1) Children are no good; they won't learn unless we make them; 2) The world is no good; children must be broken into it; and 3) I had to put up with it; why shouldn't they?
- We must break the downward cycle of fear and distrust, and trust children as we ourselves were not trusted.

Holt concludes that the education system is beyond repair and claims that no child with any 'real range of choices in the world' (Holt, 1967) is going to want to spend time in a place where 'only learning happens' and they are constantly made to do things. Reading this book as a classroom teacher myself, nearly 50 years later, I am stunned by the comparisons I can draw between then and now. Learning Objectives. Self-Assessment. Peer Assessment. What are we doing? Didn't anyone in education read Holt's book?

Life Skills

It is such a cliché, but a surprising amount of domestic discord within families, shared houses and adult relationships begins with a pair of dirty underpants on the floor. 'Why are they *there* and not in the laundry basket? Wait, why haven't you loaded the washing machine? It's *your turn!*' We may well roll our eyes and smile at this, but a more serious lack of basic 'life skills' can erode the happiness of a household and lead to a toxic living environment. Nobody wants this for their child – so what can we do to avoid it?

Let me first set out for you what I mean by essential 'life skills' which a comprehensive education should provide:

1. personal hygiene and self-care
2. household chores and basic DIY
3. cooking and nutrition
4. management of finances and budgeting
5. childcare and social responsibility
6. health, well-being and fitness
7. time management and organisation

If we look at this list together, I think we might all be able to think of at least one or two people (perhaps ourselves!) who are lacking in a few of these important areas. It is wearing to live with another person who doesn't know how to cook and clean. Eventually, there will be a dispute and someone will move out – which, even where children are not involved, is a personal loss; a missed opportunity. Far more damaging, though, is the parent whose child is severely overweight because they themselves never learnt about proper nutrition and can't prepare home-cooked meals. Or the husband, who is unable to manage his finances, and creates an unstable environment for his family through debt and gambling. Or even the mother who never learnt about how to parent or relate to young children, and finds herself isolated and depressed when alone with her child. These very real and highly traumatic circumstances arise from a lack of adequate life skills; a fundamental part of any good system of education.

In this respect, home-educated children have one clear advantage in acquiring life skills, and that is *time*. Consider, for a moment, the typical routine for a teenager attending high school. This is the age when we might reasonably expect a certain degree of participation in the running of the home; and it is, according to Peter Gray, the stage at which children in hunter-gatherer cultures begin to take on some of the adult responsibilities, such as childcare and serious hunting. This makes sense on a developmental level. Yet, with the crippling pressure of constant assessment, homework, enrichment activities and hobbies, it can seem like there is barely time for your teenager to make an appearance at the dinner table to gulp down a bowl of pasta, let alone prepare it. Children and teenagers who fit this model are often high achievers and are, *on paper*, doing well. However, the price to pay lies down the line, when these promising young adults go out into the world, academically equipped yet unable to clean up after themselves or understand what activities are beneficial to their own well-being. The child who, for the sake of chasing good grades and an impressive resumé, has foregone the life skills gained by participating in the real world is a loser indeed.

From the word go, home-educated children approach things differently. Alongside their academic studies, leisure activities and social life, homeschooled children typically spend a lot of time with younger siblings or socialising in mixed-age groups. It is not uncommon to see a 15-year-old girl talking to her friends about exam preparation, whilst bouncing a little brother or sister on her hip. Or, as I witnessed the last time we attended our local home educators' group, for a teenage boy to spend nearly an hour painstakingly teaching karate moves to a small tribe of adoring four-year olds. Homeschooled children also learn about cooking, relaxing, making lists, scheduling and budgeting, from spending considerable time with their parents observing how they run the household. Over the age of 16, most will have a part-time job – something actively discouraged by most sixth-form colleges – thereby gaining financial awareness and helping to develop good organisational skills. A child raised like this is ready for life, with any academic achievement a part of – but not the sum total of – the education they have received.

Conflict Resolution

It is also relevant to touch upon conflict resolution at this point – an issue which to some extent affects all of us. The resounding message from our school days was to 'walk away' from conflict; and there is a clear strategic reason for this. School is a very intense environment in which many children struggle to resist the personality-effect of peer pressure, public humiliation, and the constant repression of physical and emotional outlets. As a result, many children are 'on edge', or even 'ready to blow', during a large proportion of the school day, making reasonable and productive attempts at conflict resolution between peers – and even with teachers – a virtual impossibility. Moreover, staff are vastly outnumbered, and classroom fights (if you've never witnessed one) can be a terrifying thing to deal with. Everybody loses their head in a situation like this, and the teacher is desperately trying to consider the safety of all the students in the room – most of whom are up out of their chairs at this point and heckling, or getting involved – whilst signalling for back-up. That's why we are told, time and time again, to 'walk away' from conflict. Only it's a shame, because in the real world it is often better to talk things through.

Many parents bring home this approach to conflict resolution, too, especially if our children attend school. For families who only unite once at the end of the day, it can understandably be heart-breaking to see your children squabbling amongst themselves, or your partner barking at them unreasonably because he's had a bad day. We all say the same thing: 'Oh, you know what your brother is like; just ignore him.' Or, 'Dad's a bit tired tonight; just let it drop.' Which is a sensible measure to take in a high-risk situation, such as avoiding the classroom brawl described earlier, or extracting yourself from a confrontation with an aggressive stranger on the train. But as a long-term solution to managing relationships with family and friends – this is the worst advice. What home education immediately achieves is a safe situation in which conflict can be properly identified and addressed in meaningful terms. Spending more time together means that parents often have a better idea of what's actually 'going on' between siblings, and the steady, supportive 'nest' of the home becomes a secure place to work through conflict and achieve a mutual understanding.

Effective conflict resolution, in conjunction with the other life skills discussed here, forms the basis of a healthy mind and happy home in adult life. We cannot always walk away from our problems, and people with whom we disagree are not always 'the enemy'. We would all do well to bring our guards down and reach out to other people, especially the angry ones. They need it most of all.

Finding Your Strengths

C.S. Lewis famously said of education: 'No one has time to do more than a very few things well before he is twenty, and when we force a boy to be a mediocrity in a dozen subjects we destroy his standards, perhaps for life.' I find this to be true.

Especially at GCSE level, school children are absolutely overloaded with work coming from up to ten different subject areas at once, most of which will serve no purpose in their future lives and career paths. We are expecting more of young people than we would of most capable adults. How many times, as a teacher, have I told Year 11 students that this is 'about as tough as it's going to get' in terms of the spread of subjects? This seems ludicrous, when we consider that this is a developmental and hormonal phase which in fact benefits from plenty of sleep, physical exercise and regular contact with positive adult role-models. The current framework for education presents a 'sink or swim' dichotomy; failing children who are unable to cope, and strangling development for more able students by over-stretching them in terms of content rather than depth. One step forwards for the school league table, two steps back for the real pursuit of knowledge.

Ask a young person what they want to be when they grow up, and you will most likely receive the answer that they 'don't know'. Here's why:

1. The sheer amount of time school children spend in lessons, completing homework and preparing for assessments means that most students haven't even got as far as thinking about the future.

2. Schools typically offer a limited range of traditional subjects, with more diverse areas such as Film Studies and Philosophy only available at sixth form. It is rare for a school to offer Photography, Ethics, Archaeology or Chinese to a ten-year old.

3. A child's school career is broken down into a series of short-term goals, ranging from the next assignment, to mock exams, to the first draft of their UCAS statement. In this way, they are constantly kept 'busy', and rarely have an opportunity to figure out the bigger picture.

4. Career advice offered in schools is notoriously limited, presenting leaflets on traditional career paths which now constitute largely outdated advice. Almost universally, students are counselled to apply to higher education, regardless of aptitude.

5. The delivery of the National Curriculum is entirely adult directed, with knowledge 'fed' to students based on a department-prescribed schedule. It is no wonder many young people emerge from this unsure of their real interests and strengths.

The overwhelming feeling for students leaving the school system is of being 'lost' and unsure how to place themselves in the working world. The vast majority of students go on to university and emerge with degrees which, not uncommonly, become redundant in the actual job they end up doing. How could it possibly be that children spend 14 years in compulsory education and emerge without a real sense of what engages them? Because passing exams is not, in itself, a typical job requirement.

Let's look at the last item on the list and consider what happens when the shaping of education moves from being entirely adult-directed to being child-led and responsive to individual interests and goals.

When children are given the autonomy from an early age to explore the topics which they find interesting, a pattern emerges. It might be clear that they have an artistic talent, or a mind that is wired for logistics and problem solving. Without curbing their enthusiasm for the limitless learning across all areas of knowledge, home-educating parents can observe their child's development and support them in channelling a path that nurtures their interests and strengths. A homeschooled boy who loves reading, for example, may be able to indulge that interest far beyond the scope of one whose childhood is dominated by school bells, subject changes, homework assignments and a generally adult-directed agenda. This boy might have read more stories by the time he is twelve than most adults have read in a lifetime; he would make an ideal writer, editor, publisher, or perhaps something that hasn't occurred to his adult mentors. In any case, he will soon be ready to refine those skills and consider what exams – if any – or work experience would be useful to develop this key area, whilst also maintaining a natural balance with other subjects which he enjoys, such as airplane modelling and tennis. He is extremely good at each of these things because he enjoys them, and has been given the freedom to develop his abilities over time. This is a boy who knows what stimulates his mind and is on the way to finding a place in the world where he will be able to make a real contribution.

The world needs more young people like this. The economy needs more children who grow up with real skills to offer born out of genuine interest, rather than a mushroom of sameness. In every ecosystem, diversity is the key to success, and it is no different in education. Children should be allowed to discover who they are and what their strengths are, rather than being branded like cattle. And school could be *so* different... But when we look back to the concerns raised by C.S Lewis nearly a century ago, we might well ask, 'What really has changed?' Not much.

Engaging with the World

How do I know when I've spotted another home-educating family? It's the nine-year old with the litter-picker that gives it away. There's no high-visibility jacket, no school project to complete – in fact, no personal gain at all; it's just the right thing to do. There is a quiet etiquette to being a homeschooling family which I am still on a learning curve with. People remember each other's birthdays and celebrate in style, they share books and resources, and always ask you to stay for lunch. Liberated from the painful self-focus to which many children are driven by traditional schooling ('When is my essay due?' 'What percentage do I need to pass?' 'Is so-and-so still my friend?' 'Why does Miss T always ignore my questions?'...), children educated outside this are often fully engaged with the world around them, both local and global. They are, we might say, mindful.

This is, in fact, the way that most young children operate through to school age. A typical three-year old will stoop to pick up a dead butterfly, or instinctively go to put an empty Coke can in the bin. They will also ask you with genuine

Marissa is small for her age, with bone-white skin and hair that envelops her in a cloud, like a Renaissance painter's muse. She is the only girl in her class who wears trousers for non-religious reasons and still manages to look feminine; more

Marissa's Big Idea – Off-Script AND Teaching

than that, she looks like she means business. Dragons' Den kind of thing. Today she certainly does, as she marches up to my desk on the bell and stands with her hands on her hips, waiting to be asked what's up. I raise my eyebrows, international teacher-speak for 'you-have-my-attention-for-30-seconds-and-30-seconds-only'. She spreads out her hands. 'A song, Miss! What do you think? We could make a music video.' And my scheme of work for that term goes straight out the window.

The thing you need to know is that I don't, at this early point in my career, have a 'normal' relationship with this class. I have, by timetabling fluke, taught them English for the past three years running, and they have quickly figured out two points of weakness in me. First, I am slightly crazy about my subject; and secondly, I will bend over backwards to make them happy. These guys are Set 1, Key Stage 3, and they are an absolute joy. This is the class I went totally off-piste with before Christmas and – National Curriculum be damned – introduced to Chaucer, purely because I knew they'd love the fart jokes. These are the kids (inner-city London kids, from every background and ethnicity under the sun) who were so gripped by a short extract from Jane Austen's *Emma* that we ended up just sitting and reading for, like, several weeks – the entire novel. Then, because it was a hot June and they had worked so darned hard on superb *Emma* essays over May half-term, we dug in and watched *Clueless* over a couple of lessons, with one member of the class always keeping an eye out for senior management on 'walkabout'. No joke. Because nothing about what I do with this class hits any official 'learning objective' from the Assessment Criterion. It's all about hooking their interest and shoving a load of material their way, then waiting to see how they process it. Which is why Marissa knows she is on safe territory pitching me a wild idea like this.

And so we find ourselves, a few weeks into September, running around Wimbledon Common with video cameras from the Drama Department, taking footage for their *Macbeth*-inspired music video, '99 Problems but a Witch Ain't One'. It's a total riot, in a good way. And I sort of can't believe we've pulled it off. The class, loving Marissa's idea, immediately spent a double period penning Shakespearean lyrics to capture the plot of the play we'd been studying and – career suicide at the time – watching tons of music videos in order to plan a storyboard for the film footage.

Somehow, I had managed to secure the school bus and an extra member of staff (long-suffering Mr P) to make this 'educational project' happen. We had sent letters home and, being Set 1, they bounced straight back. The level of organisation, imagination and positive collaboration required to pull off something like this, with a class of 30 in a London academy, is not for the faint hearted. Think: planning, groups, travel, editing and, of course, popcorn for the official screening. Now, standing with our backs against the wind as we wait for the bus to pick us up, Mr P examines me seriously over his takeaway coffee. 'I hope you've had your fun', he says to me, not unkindly. 'Because this isn't happening again.'

And he's right. For the rest of the academic year, I have to pull my socks up massively to demonstrate that I am capable of more than delivering comedy character voices and juicy gossip about the writer's personal life. I can teach assonance and compound nouns, too; the things that matter. And I'm never given that class again. Which is funny, because when I think back to nearly a decade of teaching at that school, this is one of the few memories that stands out, clear as a storyboard in my mind. I wonder if those kids – now in their twenties – feel the same, and whether, after all, I taught them to love Shakespeare. The only problem being, there isn't a learning objective for that.

concern about the old lady next door who doesn't have anyone to look after her, and they will worry about it that night in bed. When children start school, though, it's like flipping a switch; almost any parent will tell you that. On a daily basis, this same child now directs their energy towards maintaining their social position in the group, pleasing their teachers and thinking relentlessly about work and homework. Of course, the class will cover topics to do with the world and also the local community as part of their syllabus, but the engagement is no longer spontaneous. They are being *told* to care.

More specifically, school children are being made to care for the purposes of completing a unit of work, such as a poster or letter to their MP, which will be graded. Activities of this nature – and they occur frequently across all subjects – are redundant for two reasons:

1. At best, *shallow research* is devoted to the topic itself, leaving children perhaps understanding the terms 'pollution' or 'plastic recycling', but not much in the way of real content. This is because we assess and 'grade' children in the UK based on cognitive skill sets (reasoning, organisation, written expression) rather than on the information itself. Nobody gets a high score on a test paper by simply *knowing* a lot.

2. The task itself is also primarily an exercise in *low expectations* and produces poor results. Showing students what a poster looks like, and then asking them to produce their own posters, tends to create lots and lots of similar posters. Nobody is stretched or challenged, and what the group has been presented with is a 'dummy run' – a bogus task masquerading as something meaningful – and the kids aren't fooled.

Home-educated children differ from this, largely because their schedules are a lot more relaxed, enabling them to slow down and be present. It is very grounding knowing there is nowhere you *have* to be that day. It allows for exploration. A homeschooled teenager, for example, might hear a news story over breakfast which engages them. What should they do next? Maybe they grab their iPad and start researching the story, for a while looking at various articles and video clips. Then a name comes up that they don't recognise. You tell them to check the encyclopaedia and they discover that this is a famous chemist. What's the link? Perhaps it would be worth organising a visit, or seeing if they can get hold of an email address to pose some questions. Is there a movie? You're definitely going to have to check that out at some point. Importantly, these lines of enquiry might not all take place in the same day, or even the same week. Our brains are constantly forming connections and processing the information we gather, which is why learning isn't linear. It's more like a scatter graph.

By choosing to home-educate, you are opting as a family to rethink your value system. You are making the decision to participate in the world rather than taking what you feel you are 'owed'. And you are sending a strong message to your children: you are a part of this, too.

Creating Space for Childhood

When we were in London, I did some tutoring for a family with three boys, all under the age of ten. The parents were looking for someone to prepare their eldest, Joe, to sit the entrance exam for the local grammar school. Joe was an active, 'outdoorsy' boy who wore over-sized football shirts and seemed to be permanently carrying a bat or ball under his arm. I saw him every Monday evening for about a year, in the kitchen of his home in Clapham. The cupboards were covered in post-it notes and calendar reminders, such as 'Pick Charlie up from chess club', or 'Wash football kit for Sunday'; and I remember tentatively asking Joe's mum about this one evening as I left. 'Oh that', she said, gesturing to the rich foliage of memos adorning the fridge. 'It's my brain dump. Our schedule with the boys is just so hectic, I need to visualise it to make it happen.' And she must have a point, I thought. It did look very hectic, although Joe's family were by no means unusual within their social circle.

A problem with the ever-increasing pressures within the school system is the false assumptions we now hold about the very nature of childhood: 'Children need to read widely.' 'Children need extra-curricular activities.' 'Children need to see their friends at the weekend.' I mean, do they?.... Because some of the happiest, most absorbed children I've observed of any age are those squatting with a bucket and spade next to a rock pool, watching for signs of life. Childhood should, after all, be a bubble in which time slows down and we can learn about who we are and the world around us. There is plenty of time to grow up and form a schedule.

In order for childhood to be properly educative, therefore, it should be based around the following concepts:

- A slow pace
- A sense of security
- Lots of free play
- A rich learning environment

Home is the natural place for this to happen, but there is a distinct progression here. Childhood does not last for ever, and there are clear stages of development from infancy through to becoming a young adult, where a shift in focus naturally occurs. A 16-year old may well have a more packed schedule than a five-year old – and, I would hope, it is a schedule that they have designed to meet *their* needs and interests. Let's have a look at how this works.

The three stages of a home-educated childhood:

- **The Bubble (0–7):** Children of this age primarily need a secure, caring home environment, and learning during this time-frame happens at a slow pace. Young children might benefit from a variety of interesting books, games and resources to explore. They also need plenty of fresh air, free play, affection, healthy food, and some close friends and family who widen their social orbit and provide occasional playmates.

- **Developing Skills and Interests (7–12):** These are the years when children begin to noticeably change, becoming taller, stronger, and ready to take on more academic and physical challenges, depending on their predisposition. If clear friendships are emerging by this point, it is time for a bit more of this contact, as well as extending the weekly schedule to include more clubs and sports, where your child expresses interest.

- **Entering Adulthood (12–18):** Now this young person might be looking to the future and considering what role he or she would like to play in the adult world. If it looks like some form of qualification would be a useful pathway, you might expect to see some significant increase in the amount of self-directed study. Increasingly, this young adult is spending more time outside the home and travels independently to visit friends, go to the cinema, or pick up groceries.

Becoming a homeschooling parent is more than just choosing a different way of educating. It is, undeniably, a step out of the mainstream, which puts you and your children into closer contact. You are now a parent *and* a guide in their learning journey; what I will call a *Parent Practitioner*. This is an important notion to bear in mind. Without stamping out what is natural about who you are and your relationship with your children, you now need to be more aware of the way that you speak to your children, and especially how you deal with boundaries and discipline. A good approach will cement mutual respect and nurture your child's development.

Ten Questions to ask Yourself Daily

There are four types of teacher that I have observed:

- **The Friend:** This teacher tries too hard to be 'mates' with the kids and lacks firm boundaries. Children don't thrive in an environment where they feel there is no one in charge.

- **The Disciplinarian:** By contrast, this teacher is too rigid in their approach. Although Disciplinarians often have fewer conflicts with children, this is likely because the children feel powerless against such brutal authority.

- **The Magic Happens Here:** There is always a teacher whose enthusiasm is irrepressible. Sometimes, however, an overly dynamic teacher can sap the energy from the children they are trying to inspire.

- **The Quiet One:** Here is the teacher we all forget about; the one who wasn't exciting or particularly stimulating but, somehow, left to your own devices, you got a lot out of the subject that year. We need to consider how this happens. As a home educator, you are not standing in the role of a teacher, of course. But these 'teacher types' are useful to bear in mind to ensure that you maintain a balanced approach, and aren't, for example, too strict with your children. I strongly suggest you make a note somewhere of the questions I am listing below, and revisit them often during your time as a home educator. *Reflective practice* is the key.

1. What can we learn from this activity or experience? (Be in the moment, and try to imagine it from your child's perspective.)

2. What is my child thinking or feeling right now? Can I pause and put myself in their shoes for a moment?

3. If I am familiar with this topic, would it be best to explain it, or should I let my children find out for themselves? (There is no right answer here; it's about judging the moment.)

4. Should I be clearing up again, or would it be respectful and appropriate for me to ask my child to help put the toys away?

5. Does my tone of voice need to be this aggressive/frustrated/disappointed, and how many times have I addressed my children like this today? Is there another way?

6. How do I speak about homeschooling to other people when my child is present? Do I sound confident, or am I making jokes and excuses? (It's a strong decision to take, so best do it with conviction!)

7. Is physical intervention really necessary? (If it is not a matter of safety, I would recommend finding another strategy.)

8. Is it important for us to cover Geography/Maths/Art this week, or am I just feeling the echo of my own schooling telling me that we must follow the set curriculum?

9. Does it matter right now whether they eat their greens/put their clothes on backwards/refuse to wear a sunhat? I don't want to be arguing all day, so which battles am I going to pick?

10. How am I taking care of myself right now? What are my needs, and how can they be met so that I have the energy to give back to my family?

You will notice that, as childhood transitions into adulthood, the elements of a busy and comprehensive schedule would be naturally incorporated into the self-directed schedule of most young people who have been given the room to develop in this way. It is not universally the case that people seek social contact or participation in group activities, but it is common enough that we can take this as a rough guide that would fit the profile of many young people. The message here is not to rush childhood. It is an incredibly valuable window of time which can, if managed correctly, provide your child with firm foundations which will set them up for life. Rushing children to adhere to an adult-led schedule before they even know who they really are has the opposite effect.

Embracing Autonomy

Growing up as an autonomous person is about more than figuring out your intellectual strengths and future career path. It is about embracing the very essence of what it is to be human. Have your children ever been skinny dipping in a local pond or river? Do they lie on their backs and watch the clouds pass by? Do you allow them to go out wearing whatever they like, whether that's a Pokémon t-shirt and leggings, or fancy dress? These are questions that it is helpful to keep in mind when we talk about raising young people to be autonomous.

I was lucky to have a relatively free early childhood. Thirty years ago, children ran around the local area in groups a lot more than they do now, and there was generally less screen-time, with no mobile phones or online gaming; this meant that we would often have older brothers or sisters joining the group, adding another level to the game. I was also a school refuser, and for a couple of years this worked out well for me. The village school was relaxed in those days before strict Ofsted (the Office for Standards in Education) scrutiny, and initially they allowed me to do half-days, as well as a lot of 'time off' when my parents just couldn't bear the battle, and instead I would spend the day inventing stories and playing on my own. This time taught me a lot about myself, which has served me well in life. I know, for example, that I am happiest in my own company and make no apology for this. Nobody forced me to invite the entire class to my birthday party because it's 'what you do'; something which – shamefully – I did once to my own daughter. I also discovered the world of my own imagination and, for a time, was able to dive into that and more or less do my own thing, rather than having to follow direction from a teacher. Eventually, my parents were pressured to bring me back into full-time education and, rather tearfully, I went. I had friends, and did very well academically. But I suspect the most significant period of my education was those early years spent alone lying in the long grass, watching the clouds and making up stories in my head. I am grateful, at least, for that.

If mental-health issues such as depression and anxiety are linked to feelings of powerlessness, of not being in control of your own life, then the connection to make with education is palpable. Young people in England – over-tested, under-stimulated and subjected to legally enforced schooling – are among the most negative in the world, in terms of self-image and outlook for the future. Why are our students, in spite of (or, probably, because of) generally improving test scores, so overwhelmingly consumed by feelings of hopelessness and apathy?

For anyone who hasn't been into a mainstream secondary school in the past decade, let me give you a hint of the problem we are facing. There are plenty of incredible young people of all ability levels who attend school, but a significant proportion display alarming stress levels and related health problems: insomnia, poor concentration, irritability and depression. Still more are disengaged entirely from what is happening to them – a response that I would now consider to be a subconscious self-defence mechanism; and some classrooms positively drip with disdain, barely concealed scathing, and a toxic sense of entitlement. Whilst it is unpleasant teaching in this environment, these behaviours are all self-destructive, and the only victims, of course, are the children themselves. Who knows what the world could be like if future generations were *not* subjected to this damaging regime, and instead were given more autonomy, more value and more responsibility for their own lives?

Human existence has to be about more than qualifications and job applications.

It really must, because it is this intangible element, this very sense of self – of your own spirit – which carries you through the twists and turns of life. I would like you to consider for a moment how the potential autonomy of being home-educated might manifest itself in your child. Constructing a strong sense of your own identity and values in the peaceful space that exists outside the noise and coercion of the playground is a gift, not a risk.

Becoming Trustworthy

What does it mean to 'become trustworthy', and why is this topic included in a book about home education? It seems like a rather conservative concept, I know. And yet, if we look back at this chapter, we can see that 'becoming trustworthy' is in fact the organic culmination of a successful education. A trustworthy adult is someone who is strong-minded but even-tempered, managing life and the emotions that go with it well. A trustworthy adult is also one who takes care of their environment – within the home and way beyond – as well as exhibiting creativity and resilience when faced with challenges. They have firm foundations – and it shows.

So, what exactly would the concerns be if a child has *not* successfully transitioned from childhood to adulthood, by becoming 'trustworthy'? This question touches upon the very fabric of our society, and the rips that break it. Think, for a moment, of a person who harms either themselves or others. That person is not trustworthy. Now how about a person who is unable to manage their stress levels properly at work and falls into hyper-anxiety or depression? Such a person is not reliably taking care of their own self-interest and well-being. Many of us, in fact, feel we don't know what we are good at and spend a lifetime feeling – legitimately – that we're 'missing out'. Education, arguably, has failed us all somewhere along the line.

Trustworthiness becomes especially significant when our children enter their teenage years. This period of time is a real test for parents and children alike, as they struggle to form a new way of engaging with each other, allowing the adolescent room to grow into autonomous adulthood whilst keeping parental anxiety at bay. In fact, the 'teen stage' of development often goes badly for at least one of the parties involved in the process. Some young people react strongly against parental authority at this point, challenging their opinions and taking risks with their own safety more frequently than is wise or necessary. Others remain under the wing of their parents throughout these years and into their 20s, often building up resentment and blaming their parents for creating dependency by smothering them.

The advantage when you are homeschooling your child is that you are actually building trust and confidence in *each other* every single day, right from the very beginning. Your children spend more time with you, observing the judgements you make concerning the running of the household, finances, facing problems, and managing the safety and well-being of siblings. Their trust in your opinion becomes stronger and is founded in experience. Similarly, parents are in closer contact with their children and are able to better understand their character, learning in the 'early years' when to back off, how their child thinks and – most often – that their child is actually able to make smart decisions for themselves. They become more trusting of their own child and, by the teenage years, will be in a better position to understand their decision-making and have faith in their judgement. Homeschooling, therefore, can mean *more* independence and *less* butting of heads during this time, as well as a better atmosphere in homes where there is less conflict and more trust.

When examining the question of 'trust', we may well ask ourselves, 'In whom should we entrust our children's education?'. It's a good question. When we delegate responsibility for our children's education to the school we are, presumably, making the assumption that this is a trustworthy establishment. Now I don't want to write a book about politics – nor do I wish to enter the twilight zone of addressing *who* sits on the Board of Governors and the average profile of staff who make the Senior Leadership Team; but I cannot go further without making it clear that schools are *political* institutions, and – especially within the state sector – they are closely controlled by the whims of government policy. Teachers are not autonomous, and schools are not self-directed. The young people whose exam sessions were destroyed by Michael Gove's 'hit and run' EBacc nonsense almost a decade ago were victims of the same outrageous manipulation and lack of accountability that we see today, in the gross under-reporting of COVID-19 deaths during the height of the pandemic (Booth & Duncan, 2020).

I realise that we could blow smoke at almost any political party, but the point is not headline figures and protest marches; it's about *what happens in the classroom*, and who has our children's best interests at heart. Trust, absolutely, should be foremost in our minds when we think about education.

The world needs more trustworthy adults, and in order to secure this, we must ensure that our children receive a solid education. It is most important not to rush them through the essential stages of childhood in an attempt to meet predetermined, adult-driven 'milestones' of success. No, young people must find their own way. And to help them to get there, they need less worksheets and more mystery, less circle time and more tree-climbing. For too many generations, we have shown dogged loyalty to an institution born out of a very dark chapter in human history; the industrial revolution. Well, now our eyes are wide open. On to Chapter 2.

In a Nutshell

- Children are born with a natural instinct to learn, which is tampered with from the moment they start formal schooling.

- Education is about preparing the 'whole person' for spiritual – as well as, potentially, material – success and happiness in adult life.

- Academic learning is one aspect of a holistic education which also includes emotional well-being, building basic life skills and allowing space for the natural stages of childhood.

- The measure of a successful education is a young adult who has become 'trustworthy'; responsible for themselves, the planet and the people in their life.

In this chapter, we have looked at how a proper education impacts the individual – your child. However, as we move through the book, you will increasingly notice how changing your approach to educating your son or daughter changes the entire ethos of your family unit. This is what I call the *Whole Family Benefit* of home education, and it is something that you will learn for yourself, day by day, if you choose to take this route with your family.

CHAPTER 2

How Children Learn

There is nothing about a caterpillar that tells you it's going to be a butterfly.

R. Buckminster Fuller

The system of state education that exists in the UK today began to take shape in the second half of the nineteenth century. This was the height of the industrial revolution, a time defined by extreme inequality, appalling working conditions and child labour. The gradual shift toward compulsory state education was designed to serve the following purposes:

1. To contain large numbers of children to allow their parents to continue to work long hours in (mostly) factory jobs. Prior to the industrial revolution, this way of working and living simply didn't exist.

2. To promote literacy among working-class children to ensure that they would continue to be useful members of the workforce, as the evolving demands of industrialisation began to take shape.

3. To instil British values in the populace, teaching discipline and respect for authority through the hierarchical structure of the 'public' school, where mostly male teachers were supported by female 'assistants' and corporal punishment was regularly practised on children (Gray, 2013).

In fact, it is only in more recent years that the governing ideology of schooling has moved from keeping people 'in their place' to attempting to act as a vehicle for social mobility: this was certainly never the original purpose. Over a century ago, in 1912, Edmond Holmes published a damning report on his research into state schooling entitled *What Is and What Might Be*; and – quite incredibly – his findings almost exactly mirror our present-day criticisms of the education system. In Part I of his book *The Path of Mechanical Obedience*, Homes notes 'the prevalent tendency to pay undue regard to outward and visible "results" and to neglect what is inward and vital', and argues against the rigid format of school which – neglecting the fundamental bodily requirements of the 'growing organism' – insists on 'lay[ing] thin veneers of information on the surface of [our] mind' (Holmes, 1911).

Schools today face the same challenges as they did over 100 years ago. We have gone absolutely nowhere in our bid to improve state schooling (or any schooling system). In fact, with the 'recent' emergence of super-strict academies and the madness of semi-compulsory A-level study – 'exams conceived for ten per cent of the country… now funded to be taught to seventy per cent' (Clanchy, 2019) – we have actually gone backwards. What is the problem with school, then? Is it a lack of funding, poor recruitment, weak leadership? I think it is none of these things. And I will say again what has been said so many times before; the problem is *school itself*. It is simply not a natural environment, and it cannot support the way human beings actually learn.

This chapter will explore how *real* learning happens.

Learning through Wonder

Children love 'big ideas', and they are never too young to be exposed to the awe of the world. This is the basis of what inspires us to learn. True wonder is something that cannot be experienced second-hand, on a computer screen or PowerPoint projector; it must be witnessed in real life, most often through contact with nature, but also through museum visits, art galleries, theatre trips and cathedrals. Children's brains work best when they are flooded with enriching experiences, rather than sitting in ability groups engaged in mindless 'busywork' (Gray, 2013). Children also like to be outside running around, taking risks and feeling the warm flood of endorphins when they land safely after a big jump, or discover a real birds' nest in the river bank.

Most teachers understand these principles, and schools do try – sometimes quite admirably – to take such educational psychology into account when planning the academic calendar; but it's an uphill battle. Here is why:

- **The limited National Curriculum:** As we touched on earlier, learning in schools is governed by the National Curriculum all the way through primary school, and into around Year 9 of secondary school, after which the prescribed content of each exam board dictates what topics will be studied. More than this, they also dictate *the way* that learning will happen and should be manifested. These are both tremendous impediments to learning through wonder. Not only are school children compelled to follow a strict schedule of topics regardless of personal interest, but they are also blatantly told *how* to respond to the information they're presented with through the language of assessment, such as 'compare', 'understand' and 'identify'. Being forced to jump through a series of hoops which for many children – quite rightly – appear meaningless and arbitrary has the effect of strangling independent thought and switching a worrying number of children 'off'. This is the very opposite of learning through wonder.

- **The logistics of large numbers:** England's primary schools are currently operating with the largest class sizes in the developed world. Secondary schools, too, have class sizes sometimes as high as 35 students in one classroom. Nor were these classrooms built for the kind of numbers we are dealing with today. I remember training in schools where students were so tightly packed that there was no room for acting out a scene from *Romeo and Juliet* or allowing group presentations; there was barely space for me to cross the room. But large class sizes bring other logistical and social problems, too. Visits require additional members of staff and must be less ambitious; the pace of learning slows dramatically; and disruptions are frequent. The children who actually *want* to learn practically jostle each other to be sat on the front row at the start of term, in the hope that they might learn something, in spite of the circus going on behind them. There is nothing wonderful about that.

- **The focus on testing:** The extreme focus on testing, levelling and report-writing annihilates anything good that could possibly come out of a childhood spent in school. Testing is not by any means a true measure of learning. Instead, it turns the pursuit of knowledge into a hollow game in which points are scored, not by developing understanding but by committing to memory the 'correct' information and submitting a formulaic response, in line with the assessment criteria. Secondary teachers, for example – myself included – routinely find themselves in the awkward position of doing a disservice to our most able students. 'That's great thinking, Leah, but it's not going to be on the exam paper.' Or, 'Be careful not to spend too much time looking for connections on this piece, Jack, because there's only ten points you can pick up for that'. And in primary schools, the emphasis is the same, with children as young as four and five mapped out on NC spreadsheets, and their 'ability level' constantly flagged up to anxious parents. The new trend in teaching, in fact, is for all children to know their current 'working level' and the skills they need in order to progress to the next sub-level on the assessment chart. This is supposed to provide a sense of autonomy in directing their own learning, but the very idea is laughable. Children have about as much autonomy as does a horse between the shafts; there is just nowhere to go. Regardless of school efforts to bring wonder to the classroom, when the focus is so persistently drawn to measuring the very value of our thinking, it's a no-go from the start.

The environment of school, therefore, is not conducive to promoting learning through wonder – although children certainly will gain some comparative relief from a 'fun' lesson or 'down-time' activity such as watching an interesting documentary, which allows them to briefly unplug from the incredibly high stress-levels of the school day. Perhaps we can all remember the tight feeling in the pit of our stomach on a Sunday evening when we knew we were about to begin another school week; indeed, we may still today feel the echo of that stress in our working lives, or on behalf of our own children. But the toxic effect of school stress actually goes beyond this familiar 'sinking feeling'. Neurobiology shows that levels of cortisol – the stress hormone – in children are typically highest during the school day, dipping after school and going right down at the weekend and during holidays (Gray, 2013).

Now you may have heard it said that a certain degree of stress actually 'sharpens' you up, but research proves this theory to be wrong. When the brain is flooded with cortisol, it actually inhibits neuro-connectivity and restricts the growth of certain areas of the brain (Schore, 2017). This is especially problematic for children under the age of ten, whose brains are developing most rapidly. School stress literally slows learning down and, in extreme cases, has the effect of stunting natural brain development in a growing child. It is simply a wonder that we have allowed this to happen.

Learning through wonder happens every day in home education – from standing in the middle of a crop field listening to the hiss of the wind, to taking a mid-week cinema trip with homeschool friends to watch the latest super-hero movie. Homeschooling allows more time for 'big questions' to be answered, and experienced home-educating parents will be sure to keep a notepad, or a list on their phone, where they keep track of emerging interests and areas to explore.

We took our own children to the Tutankhamun exhibition at the Saatchi gallery last year, for example, as a surprise for my daughter who has now read every book on Ancient Egypt that the local library has to offer. But you can think way beyond this familiar territory, if you want to. Homeschooling also allows time for holidays, which often mark special memories in childhood. No longer constrained by the structure – and price-tag – of school holidays, families are free to travel whenever it is most convenient and least expensive during the year. This is a real plus for worldschooling, which we will cover later in the book.

Observation

Children learn most effectively and naturally from observing others, and in hunter-gatherer societies, younger children will often stand back to observe older children engaging in a task like tree-climbing or making a fire pit, before attempting it themselves. In fact, one of the issues with the schooling model, where children are separated into age-limited groups and taught that it is bad to copy, is that this stamps out the natural instinct to learn through observation and imitation (Gray, 2013).

But school learning is not, of course, limited to what happens in the classroom, and plenty of social and emotional learning takes place in the playground, where observation occurs more readily. This undoubtedly has some beneficial effects, and you may witness in almost any playground in the world a younger girl watching older girls play a complicated clapping game, or a group of Year 1 boys crowding round to admire the football skills of an older player. It is a shame that such natural observational learning cannot translate to the classroom, and that children rely instead on having lessons 'drummed into them' via the exhaustive efforts of their teacher to harness a false learning environment.

There is some concern regarding school-based observational learning, however. Due to the competitive nature of the school setting and the fact that free play is so enormously under-staffed and lacks the presence of significantly older children – say, secondary or college age – to balance the interactions, there can be a tendency towards unpleasant, anti-social and bullying behaviour. It only takes a few dominant individuals to change the general behaviour of the entire playground, as each child learns rapidly through observation that it is not safe to be vulnerable in this environment, and that they must therefore 'toughen up' in order to survive. We will discuss bullying and the damaging effect of expecting children to 'toughen up' in Chapter 3; however, it is important to acknowledge at this point that this is one of the major obstacles to enabling the benefits of observational learning to flourish in schools.

Not long ago, I was visiting a local family to discuss the idea of their daughter coming to our house one afternoon per week for immersive French speaking. They are a 'nice' family who, like us, immediately saw the 'issues' in our village school, and so chose to send their twins to a private school in town. During my visit, the twins' mother Alison spent considerable time trying to convince me of the benefits of their expensive educational decision. I smiled and nodded, perfectly interested to hear her opinion. Presently, two boys – her own son and a school friend – came tearing down the stairs and raced out into the garden, where there was an almost immediate crisis with the sister – the girl I was there to visit – who had been playing on the swing. Both boys began shoving the swing in an attempt to get her off, and there were a few tears and raised voices, before they were all brought into the kitchen for a sharp word. It turned out that the two boys were always 'rough' together, and tended to 'wind up' siblings, whichever house they played at. During the hour that I spent with the family, this same behaviour pattern was repeated several times, with the girl eventually withdrawing to sit with us at the table in order to avoid the constant torment. She was still a little tearful when I left, and I felt sure that she would be pushed or teased again before the end of the day – and that, quite naturally, speaking French with my children couldn't have been further from her mind. She, too, was trying to survive, and was a victim of the unhealthy observational learning that can occur within the caged environment of schools, however much money you throw at it.

Having witnessed scenes just like this throughout my teaching career and, most worryingly, in my personal and professional interactions with other families, I cannot help but wonder how we have allowed this *permissive culture* to evolve. Of course, not *all* school children behave in this way, but it is common enough to merit a general remark. It is understandable that tensions run high at the end of the long school day, and it's certainly exhausting for parents trying to placate fractious, frazzled children in the hours between the school pick-up and bedtime. It can sometimes be easier to 'switch them off' by giving them a dose of screen-time when they walk through the door, but that doesn't make the problem go away. Time and time again, I see teachers and parents opt out by shrugging their shoulders, rolling their eyes, and advising me that this is 'just what kids are like'. The trouble is, it really shouldn't be. And I expect it is only when we stop outsourcing our responsibility for raising the next generation that we might actually engage with what's going on, and the impact this has on interactions in the adult world, too.

Within a happy homeschooling family, the majority of daily observation and learning will happen between siblings. This is a significant deviance from the school model, whereby siblings are instantly separated by the experience of school, and often bring hostility and competitiveness home with them, causing frequent disputes and tensions. I have spoken with a number of parents who all claim that their children need at least a week of the summer holiday to pass by – filled with squabbling and rivalry – before they eventually 'mellow' and begin treating each other with respect again and, amazingly, having a good time. We will look more closely at the damaging effect of schooling on family bonds and, especially, the parent–child relationship; however, this widely accepted 'norm' of bickering siblings is really something that the modern education system can be held responsible for.

Left to their own devices, siblings are each other's best source of information and practice regarding the important information to learn, and they achieve this through observation and imitation, as well as deliberate modelling on the part of older siblings for the benefit of their younger brother or sister. This is a *mutually beneficial* exchange, allowing the younger child to observe a wide range of ambitious possibilities within a safe setting, whilst the older child hones and cultivates a deeper understanding of the skills they have acquired. The patience and creativity of an older sibling as a 'teacher' is more powerful than an 'Outstanding' lesson plan, any day of the week. And similarly, younger siblings will 'drink in' the information provided by their older brothers and sisters whilst simply sprawling on beanbags, in a way that no classroom situation can mimic. Yet over time, the effect of schooling can erode sibling bonds to the point where there is little common ground, and certainly no room for learning and growth. The post-lockdown drive to get children 'back to school' is based on a philosophy that there is little to be gained from spending time at home with your siblings, and it is, I believe, a tragic misrepresentation.

Experience and Apprenticeship

It is a seductive idea that going to school creates independence. If this were true, it would be most convenient, as it would work for both parties – children universally blossoming at school, with parents free to go to work and have some time away from the challenge of parenting. But this notion is a fallacy, and it has no more truth in it than the idea – popular at the time – that Victorian factory workers were 'happy' in their roles, and wouldn't have wanted more freedom if it had been offered to them. It is an untruth that works for those in power, because it removes much of the guilt associated with oppressing a group of people. When we tell ourselves that school is 'good for them' – in the same way that a nasty dose of medicine or a cold shower 'does you good' – then we are in denial about the reality of the schooling system, and the way that children are actually programmed to learn.

From birth, children learn from observing the real world. They see their parents and older siblings walking, talking, eating food and reading books – and they think, 'I want to try that!'. As children begin to grow up, they will have a wider range of influences to examine and 'borrow' from, including more refined skills such as humour, timing, taste and interests. As children begin to establish their sense of identity, real curiosities will develop, and here is where children will seek to learn in more detail, in the role of an apprentice. A boy who loves bike riding might start spending time in the garage changing a tyre with his dad, taking note of how this is done and the different tools used. A girl who enjoys swimming might start going to the pool more regularly, observing how other swimmers perform strokes and the equipment they use to train their bodies. This is the organic way in which we are all programmed to learn at a basic level, and from this starting point, further research and reading may come in time. For home-educated children, this way of learning represents the majority of their time; whereas for children whose lives are governed by the demands of school, there are far less opportunities to learn naturally through experience.

Saying that children cannot learn freely now because 'they will never cope' in the adult world is as absurd as saying that a one-year old will never walk if they don't do it *right now*. In Chapter 1, we looked at the *stages of childhood*, and saw how children naturally grow into increasing independence and career-mindedness, when given the space to develop at their own pace and enjoying childhood. The introduction of compulsory schooling, in the latter part of the nineteenth century, has created a paradox here. Because, as parents, we desperately want our children to be successful and independent, we have bought into the idea that school is the correct place, in fact the *only* place, for this to happen. Tears on a Monday morning 'toughens them up'. Piles of homework 'teaches the work ethic'. And anyway, they would 'much rather be with their friends' than hanging out at home – right? As I will discuss later, the extreme importance we place upon school friendships is actually sometimes an indicator of the extent to which family bonds have been damaged through the distress of forced schooling, causing children to invest their need for attachment elsewhere. Moreover, these industrial concepts of 'toughening up' and 'hard work' are all disastrous to a small child's emerging sense of self and personal direction. In order to eclipse our guilt, we think that we are 'helping' our children out in the long run by physically and emotionally coercing them to spend five days a week in this toxic setting. We have bought into the *false independence of school*.

Children do not learn to be independent by entering an environment in which they have no choice. The children who survive school with relative ease are often those who adapt the fastest, learning to sit down when told to, put their hand up if they have a question, never be rude to the teacher, avoid bullies, and curb their own personality and interests to fit these new requirements for survival. We forget that this was never how children were raised for the vast majority of human history. We have lost touch with the way education happened before mass agriculture – and then the industrial revolution – changed the landscape of parenting entirely. Because for children to learn naturally, through real life, the requirements are actually very straightforward.

- **Babies and toddlers need...** constant love and reassurance, praise, plenty of activity and language to observe and imitate; a stable home.

- **Young children through to teenage years need...** a wider range of stimulus, including more exercise, wider reading and learning resources, emerging friendships and interests.

- **Teenagers growing into young adults need...** continued reassurance and support from home, along with increasing opportunities to learn from peers and older mentors the skills and behaviour they feel they want to imitate in adult life.

The demands of the modern world mean that we have complicated our thinking about what children *need* in order to learn and thrive. We have forgotten the elements that form a strong, happy childhood, and have been swept away by the language of league tables and ability levels – stuff which simply didn't exist a century ago. Our children learn best when they are observing desirable skills and behaviours in the real world and processing this information independently, using their own brains; the organic process of experience and apprenticeship.

In his ground-breaking book *Free to Learn*, Peter Gray examines why unleashing the instinct to play makes children happier, more self-reliant and have better standards for life. Here is a summary of the  argument he sets out about where school fails, and the vital role of play in a child's learning journey.

Our Schooling Crisis

- The most enduring lesson of school is that learning is work, to be avoided when possible.

- We have developed a damaging attitude that learning and progress must be directed by adults, and that children's own activities are a waste of time.

- Research shows that anxiety and depression correlate strongly with people's sense of control, or lack of control, over their own lives.

- A study of children conducted in a wealthy suburban neighbourhood in the United States revealed that children who felt most pressurised by their parents to achieve in school, and who were most frequently shuttled from one extra-curricular activity to another, were the most likely to feel anxious or depressed.

(Gray, 2013)

Play: The Natural Educator

- In early hunter-gatherer societies, children were free to play nearly all the time; no one expected children to do serious work until they were in their late teens.

- Anthropologists report that hunter-gatherers do not distinguish work from play, as we do. When we turn learning into work, we undermine our intrinsic motivation to learn.

- A playful state of mind is the way we learn best. Anything that causes anxiety, or which restricts our freedom to be creative, brings real learning to a halt.

- This natural and playful way of living was broken by the onset of the agricultural revolution and, then, the industrial revolution, which required children to work long hours for the benefit of the family. This paved the way for public schooling.

- Hunter-gatherer societies are playful, with their skills requiring continuous creative adaptation, as opposed to the values of obedience and discipline indoctrinated by post-industrial cultures.

(Gray, 2013)

Gray concludes that we have lost sight of the natural way to raise children. I would agree with this, and wish to add that we are all victims of this – so busy in the 'survival mode' of our own existence that we fail to look up and consider how we got here, and why things are the way they are.

Free Play

Play, according to Peter Gray and a number of prominent researchers, is the essential state of mind required to engage in true learning and activate key instincts – such as curiosity, risk-taking and communication – without which we are not really *learning* at all. Children who are allowed to continue playing freely, past compulsory school age through into their teens and beyond, tend to make quite astonishing academic progress, without formal instruction. This is because they have maintained a 'playful' state of mind, and have not separated the experimental process of learning to read or calculate numbers, for example, from the 'play mindset' of climbing a tree or pretending to be a pirate. Significantly, children who are *not* given the message that school is 'work', and play is quite separate, use their natural intelligence to seek learning opportunities in the world around them, rather than trying to figure out creative ways to *avoid* work by resisting adult-imposed learning and getting rid of homework tasks as quickly as possible.

Do you remember how your children as babies learned to walk and talk? You didn't 'make them do it' or sit them down for a lesson, did you? Instead, gradually, these little people just became fascinated by something you could do, which they identified as an important skill to master. Babies and small children are uniquely placed to be highly efficient in sensing the key skills required for survival and adaptation, in a way that we are not, with our adult 'baggage' and expectations which (generally handed down to us as they were from our own parents) are most often outdated.

A baby will therefore observe you talking and, one day, start paying close attention to your mouth and the way it moves to form sounds, imitating the same movements and testing the noises they make. At this point, nobody is giving the child structured 'lessons' on sound groups and collections of vocabulary: instead, they are using their brains like a super-computer to absorb and organise huge amounts of random information and create connections to make 'sense' for themselves. This is, of course, why babies need so much sleep! Because then, one day, you will find them standing of their own accord, using their muscles, smiling at their own accomplishment, and saying '*up*' or '*look*' quite accurately. We are full of pride. And yet, just a few years later we will be with the very same child sitting at the kitchen table, pouring over the list of prescribed spelling words, testing them on the arbitrary information that has been deemed important by the adult world that week. We most likely feel some tension here. Play has been taken out of the equation, and the natural, explorative learning opportunity has been snatched away because adults think they know best how to deliver what children 'need to know'.

This is problematic for many reasons. Most significantly, of course, we are robbing children of the chance to learn for themselves, through play. By bringing a structured, linear mindset to the organic, stimulating process of learning, we suck out the fun and deliver the message that children are not to be trusted, and must be 'told what to do'. Many of our children take this message firmly on board. However, the fact that we put a time-limit on play as meaningful (Reception is typically more free range, but formal lessons really 'crank up a notch' in Year 1) also shifts cultural expectations of how children – and adults – should 'be'.

Warning children still in primary school against 'messing around', and advising them that they need to 'get some work done' on a Sunday afternoon, has the long-term effect of knocking essential life skills out of growing children. I believe this is a contributing factor to the global mental-health crisis that faces us today. As a counter-example, when attending our local homeschool group I have seen youngsters aged between 12 and 15 engage in a fierce and totally immersive wizarding battle, entertaining everyone with their dramatic sound effects, at an age when we normally expect monosyllabic grunts. They are not immature, nor naive; they are playful. And one day, they will make good people to settle down and build a family with. They are fun and free. They are everything that we, as adults, wish we could still be – wish we could still *do* with our own children – but we lost it somewhere along the way.

Thus, play is not a waste of time; far from it. Playfulness forms the basis for mental resilience, creative thinking and adaptability; and by almost universally losing the dimension of real play as we enter adulthood, we put ourselves risk.

Conversational Learning

Most days, especially during lockdown, we take a walk or go for a bike ride. My kids love their bikes, and we can easily cover up to ten kilometres, winding our way through the woods at the back of our house and then down on to the river track which runs all the way through into the next county. Bike riding is therapeutic and a great opportunity for chit-chatting. My son always starts like this: 'Mum, what's your favourite *Star Wars* movie?' Then, 'Who would you be in *Star Wars*? It can be anyone apart from Darth Vader, because I'm Darth Vader.' And then, 'Mummy, what are clouds made of?' Good questions, all of them.

Children learn an incredible amount through such conversational learning, and this is something that is almost entirely shut down in schools, mostly for the practical considerations of behaviour management and noise levels. In school, children are expected to work a lot in silence and to listen for long spells throughout the day, without interrupting or commenting – even when they have an interesting observation to make. More than once, I have found the brightest and most engaging student in the room to be a hindrance to managing the lesson 'as a whole', because it is a mixed-ability group, we are covering a difficult topic, and frankly I know that this child's radical contribution to the lesson will disrupt the 'concentration' that I have worked so hard to establish. School children mostly haven't been given the tools to understand how to manage free debate in a group setting, and even with smaller sixth-form classes, any unstructured attempt often descends into chaos. It can be easier just to crack on.

Without conversational learning, though, two important things happen which interfere with the way children naturally learn:

1. Questioning and discussion are dramatically reduced, to the point where some children will get through an entire lesson without once speaking or being spoken to. Several might ask practical questions such as 'Is that the title, Miss?' and 'Can I go to the loo?', whilst still fewer will put their hand up to participate with an appropriate response to the teacher's line of questioning. Interestingly, experience tells me that those who participate most actively in this game of pleasing the teacher are generally the middle-ability children. Those at the bottom end either don't understand what's going on, are busy disrupting the lesson, or are too afraid of being mocked for being 'thick' to dare participate. For different reasons, children at the top end academically are similarly disaffected and tend not to bother, knowing that their questions are way beyond the scope of the lesson and understanding that the 'game' is simply to grasp the Learning Objective, which they could do three years ago. Nobody is really learning in this environment; it is just about processing the content.

2. With real conversational learning a very limited option in most classrooms, then, teachers are reduced to other ways of evidencing learning. If I am tutoring a student after school one evening and I make a passing comment that relates to a period in history, I can quickly sound out whether the child feels confident, or not, with the broad impact of this time. It takes a momentary rally of conversation, a few shrugs or nods and, if a nudge is needed, I might chat for a couple of minutes with that child about what they do know, and how we could apply it to the text we are studying. In a school setting, though, this would

mean almost a quarter of the lesson being dedicated to a single child, without any concept of whether the rest are following. This is why we inflict so much 'busywork' on school children, from colouring, to worksheets, to word searches and comprehension questions. As if these were, in themselves, useful life skills. They are not, but still we use them as a poor substitute for the enrichment and clarification that conversational learning affords.

I expect that you most likely already do plenty of conversational learning with your children, without even realising it. If you are new to the *idea* of conversational learning, though, it might be helpful to bear a few things in mind, such as the importance of making eye contact (if your child is comfortable with this) and helping them to formulate the question, if they're struggling to express their ideas. You should also remember that the world is filled with more information than anyone could possibly acquire in a lifetime; and for the purpose of passing examinations, the 'correct' information required to jump through the hoops can be picked up in a relatively short amount of time, assuming your child wishes to take that route. Therefore, your job is not to 'know the answers' to every question under the sun. As literacy skills and academic independence develop, your child will naturally gravitate towards the topics they find engaging, and can conduct their own detailed research at this stage by visiting the library, through online learning, and by questioning experts in their field of interest. Try to consider your role in conversational learning to be that of *a guide*, helping your child to frame their questions, offering answers where your knowledge provides useful information or examples, and suggesting where they might find further information.

Conversational learning is not just chit-chat; it's the beginning of something much, much bigger. Understanding the value of conversational learning, and our role as parents to provide room for this to almost constantly occur, reveals a different 'mode' of interaction for families who school and homeschool alike. In her ground-breaking book *Toxic Childhood*, Sue Palmer observes the increasing processing difficulties experienced by children where there is a 'lack of conversation at home' (Palmer, 2006), and we must all be careful here. As the screen-world of tweets, hashtags and status updates increasingly takes over our lives and absorbs our attention, we must as parents focus our minds on our duty to educate our children; to be present, to look them in the eye, to think carefully about the questions they have. Put your phone away in a drawer, switch it off, or at least remove distracting apps and notifications. Being available for real conversational learning with your children enriches your own life, too, and can re-align your thinking to put social media and toxic newsfeeds in the bin where they belong.

Natural Curiosity

Happy children are into *everything*, and as time goes on you might notice certain key interests emerging. Curiosity is the spark that switches us 'on' to learning, and it is something that the best teachers do, with some success, in the artificial environment of the school classroom. I say 'artificial' because, after all, I didn't hear Mr H's Year 10 class exactly *gagging* for a lesson on *Macbeth* when they lined up outside his classroom. Nevertheless, Mr H understands the power of curiosity to harness the attention of the class and he does a great job, covering the whiteboard in fake blood and propping an old mannequin from the Drama department at the back of the room as a makeshift Banquo. The scene is set, and it's going to be a murder mystery. Great lesson plan, Mr H! Honestly, if he can manage to maintain a semblance of order in the room, this is the kind of lesson bored schoolkids dream of.

But it's no replacement for the rush of natural curiosity a child feels when, independent of adult intervention, they make a discovery on their own. The swish of a tale disappearing beneath the seaweed in a rock pool, the first time you take them to see a West End musical, the feeling of falling into another world when you open the pages of your favourite book. This is the stuff of natural curiosity, and children need it in bucket-loads. All children are capable of being curious and explorative in their learning, but it is true that many – though not all – children who are subjected to the daily routine of school find precious little time to develop this important skill, and for some it fades altogether somewhere around the age of nine or ten. When this happens, it is a shame for the child, but also a shame for society as a whole. We need as many curious people, as many explorers and discoverers, as possible in today's changing world.

What school also appears to neglect entirely (and as parents, we buy into this) is the importance of what I call *deep-end learning* for nurturing curious minds. All children are curious – this is certainly not about intellectual elitism. As an example, our eldest recently taught herself to play the first half of Beethoven's *Moonlight Sonata* on the piano – an achievement gained from about a week of curious observation and plenty of 'tinkering' on the keys. I was very sceptical to begin with. She has never shown an interest in the piano before, cannot read sheet music, and point-blank refuses to engage with scales, finger placement, or any of the 'beginner' stuff. So I swallowed my total disbelief and watched her figure it out, bar by bar; if you close your eyes and ignore the 'issues' with technique, it sounds spot-on. This taught me a lot about the power of curiosity and the importance of deep-end learning in harnessing the mind.

Eleven months after the birth of our first child, I go back to working part-time at the academy I had sworn I wouldn't set foot in again. Requesting part-time in a school like mine means either getting shafted with the nastiest timetable imaginable, or having the pure grit to fight hard and insist on complete classes and nothing less than 0.8 spread across four days. When it comes to dealing with management, though, I am less 'grit' and more something that rhymes with it – and so I end up with the nasty timetable. So nasty, in fact, that it includes GCSE French.

It's not a total shocker. Everyone knows we speak French at home, having heard me on the phone at 6 a.m., cursing like a pirate because – again – I've been dumped with all the marking for a split class. Which is how Mr B, Head of Modern Languages, came to approach me in the staff room early one morning when I was making microwave porridge and mid-way through the daily phone rant to my long-suffering husband. 'Excuse me', he said, in his crisp, Parisian accent. 'I've heard you're not enjoying your English timetable this year – correct? I have a suggestion for you.' And I took it. Three full French classes, including one exam group, in exchange for the scrappy clean-up operation I'd been given in English. Plus my usual sixth-form classes. Was I game? Sure.

So now I am standing in front of the class with a glove puppet who, I've been told, asks the group to 'echo back' the lesson on the board. The kids love it, apparently. Perhaps I am doing it wrong. *Je vais, tu vas, il va, nous allons, vous allez, ils vont.* I can't quite believe that, 25 years after my own experience of French at school, this is still the way languages are taught; and, more concerningly, that these guys have been doing French since Year 6 and we are still stuck on the present-tense conjugation of 'aller'. And this is the exam class! They simply aren't going to survive the summer papers. Mr B is already on to this, and has a language assistant intervening with the weakest ones, as well as a strategic plan to magically erase some of the hopeless cases (the kids who just don't come to school any more; it happens all the time in Year 11) from the register, so the departmental average doesn't actually implode. Off-rolling. Clever.

I put the rabbit down and smile weakly at the class. Someone at the back giggles nervously and on the middle row, Coby – my lesson plan kryptonite – stretches his arms behind his head and plays mutinously with his tongue piercing, watching my reaction as if to say, 'What's your plan *now*, lady?'. (This is bottom set, by the way.) And I'm under strict instructions to keep it simple, giving them the absolute basics they need to scrape a C Grade if they're lucky. The Foundation Paper is capped, in any case, and these guys can't even count to ten. I try a new tack. For the rest of the lesson, I speak only in French. Not GCSE French for the Foundation Paper, but fast, fluent and expressive, with a hint of the twangy southern accent I've picked up from my husband over the years. They don't know what to make of it. First they laugh, then they sit up and seem vaguely interested and, by the end of the lesson, we have a list of new vocabulary on the board and a homework task to watch a load of their favourite stuff on YouTube *en français*. Immersion theory.

And this is how I teach them through to the end of the year, when we celebrate the start of study leave with a little party, rather than revision sheets of irregular verbs. They are still a weak group, and there is little to be achieved at this late stage by cramming content for the exam. I'll just be pleased if they bother to show up. But what has changed dramatically is the atmosphere. I am still talking to them all the time in French and, increasingly, they seem to understand enough about tone, facial expression and wild gesticulation, to be able to follow and even enjoy this unorthodox approach. At least half the class speak another language at home – Arabic, Portuguese, Urdu, Yoruba – and are comfortable swimming between languages, occupying a twilight zone where the languages are not necessarily distinct or accurate, but you generally 'get the idea'. I doubt their parents ever sat them down and asked them to conjugate verbs; they just picked it up.

And perhaps, I think to myself, if this was how we taught languages in school from the start, I wouldn't be sitting here now, sharing a box of brownies with quite a nice group of multilingual kids who, ironically, are about to bomb their language exam next Tuesday.

For regardless of any affront to musical sensibilities here, *all* children are capable of learning in this way, and most would prefer it. Not necessarily piano, but anything they are 'into'. Adults believe otherwise, though, and this presents a problem. In school – and in many contexts, outside of school – all learning is broken down into a series of adult-prescribed steps, which the child must follow to gain 'competency'; a method which in no way engages curiosity, nor shows recognition of the neurological benefits of presenting children with considerable challenge. If school children generally display disinterest in the learning that takes place (or placate parents and teachers with false enthusiasm), it could be because what's happening there is so eye-wateringly dull.

Thus, school fails to recognise the true scope of a child's potential. And when we buy into the notion that all learning is gained in school, we are also assuming that it is the teacher alone who magically holds the cards and is the source of all knowledge – what we might call 'The Fallacy of

The Expert'. I have been put in this position myself many times by well-intentioned parents, and it left me feeling highly uncomfortable. I am, after all, only a person, and I never came into teaching with much more than a love of reading and a vague idea that kids might be fun to work with (*ha-ha*). This is a polite way of saying that teachers come from all walks of life, and by no means necessarily represent the gold standard for your child in terms of subject knowledge. The remark from an American colleague of mine, when I discussed this chapter with her, was in fact that 'anyone who can fog a mirror can be a teacher' – which, dry humour though it is, doesn't seem funny if there's a shred of truth in the statement.

Whether you are home-educating, therefore, or simply aiming properly to enrich your child's learning beyond the scope of school, you would be well-advised to encourage them to pursue their own interests and lines of natural curiosity. Practise some caution when you observe your child 'time wasting' or 'mucking about', and consider for a moment whether what they are doing actually has some value and is, essentially, pursuing an interest. My toddler, for example, has been driving me nuts recently taking his shoes off every time we try to get out of the door. I put them on; he takes them off. Round and round we go and, with the older two in tow moaning about having to wear sun cream or singing 'Sunflower' at the top of their lungs… – it can feel quite stressful. In a bid to stop him wrestling them off for the hundredth time the other day, I knelt down face-to-face and asked him, with a quiver of desperation, '*Why*, baby? Why are you doing this to mummy? Can we please go now?' He smiled at me. This was what he'd wanted all along. 'Toes!', he said, pointing. 'Peepo!'

Kinaesthetic Learning

I feel like I keep coming back to bike rides; it's not something I can edit out. Bikes, bike rides, fixing bikes, and ogling 'bike tech' is a big deal with my kids. Why do they love their bikes so much, though? *All* kids do. When you ride a bike, your breathing changes and you think differently, engaging your mind and body together; blowing away the cobwebs. That must be why my children find them such a fertile setting for rich conversational learning. It's the same when anyone sings in the shower. It invigorates the spirit and seems to open up our minds, making us resonate like a tuning fork. It literally 'switches us on'.

Kinaesthetic learners know this instinctively, and will seek opportunities for active learning as often as possible. Indeed, many children in a classroom setting find it excruciatingly difficult to sit still for most of the day, which makes sense when we look at the adult population. Some people work at desk jobs such as accounting, some work at active jobs such as carpentry, and still others work at jobs which require a high level of physical fitness and activity, like a body coach or dancer. Today, our school children are largely expected to be sedentary – a state which is unnatural for *any* child; but for people whose natural predisposition is towards kinaesthetic learning, it is an actual barrier – it shuts them down.

The number of children diagnosed with Attention Deficit Hyperactivity Disorder (ADHD) is on the rise every year, and although a small number of children will seriously suffer from the relatively rare ADHD, many more are being wrongly diagnosed and, in some cases, are placed on powerful medication to enable them to simply sit still in class. Some of these children are, I suspect, kinaesthetic learners. And it is a suspicion that haunts me today. What are we doing drugging children so that they can 'take' the mind-numbing rigour of schooling, when we would happily pay a local handyman £200 to put up shelves and marvel that he is so active, so efficient, so good at his job? We have lost sight not just of how children naturally learn, but of the natural *diversity* of the population. We don't all learn the same way; this is why home education is a lifeline if your child is a kinaesthetic learner.

I think my middle son might be. Unlike my daughter, who has always and without coercion enjoyed activities like rhyme time, colouring, reading and watching TV, my son does none of these things. He is mostly moving around the house; on his feet, his balance bike, his skateboard, or his sister's roller skates. He is an 'active' boy. More than that, he finds any situation in which he is forced to sit still and listen quite excruciating. We tried rhyme time at the local library, because his little brother is the right age for that, and my middle son would literally squirm on the carpet, twisting himself into funny shapes and slapping his face with all the hallmarks of a child who, had I sent him to school, would be singled out as a 'problem' and, down the line, could well be branded with the ADHD label and everything that goes with it. I have indeed felt a pinch of worry a few times with him. I am not a kinaesthetic learner myself, and I don't always understand how he processes things, constantly on the go as he is. I have even tried sitting down with him to do a puzzle or look at a book, but he quickly wriggles away and is dancing around the room, kicking a football, or standing on his head. Then, just before Christmas, he started butting into the learning that was taking place with his older sister. I would be reading with her and he would slow down as he swept by on his bike, peering at my finger on the page and saying, quite astonishingly: 'D-R-A-G-O-N. Dragon. Bye!' I frowned at him. 'You can read!', I said, gobsmacked. 'Yeah, I know. Bye!', came the response. He was, at the time, only just four years old.

A year on, and he is still as active as ever, but is a competent reader, emerging with writing, a keen musician, and superb mathematically – handling big numbers going up and down ('What's one thousand and twenty take away ten?' or 'What's fifty plus zero?'). He is entirely self-taught, almost never sits down, and values doing tricks on his bike above any book or school-type activity. I am very proud of him, as I am of my bookworm daughter and the shoe-slinging baby. They are very different learners, and each of them can be supported and nurtured within the flexible environment of homeschooling.

If your child is a kinaesthetic learner, or simply benefits from physical activity, you may want to consider the following when planning your homeschool routine:

- Learning can happen on the go. See my earlier discussion on conversational learning (pp. 38–40) for more on this.

- Try to connect learning with physical experiences, such as gardening, cooking, painting, litter picking or building a den.

- Think about structuring your family routine around opportunities for fresh air and serious physical exercise. You will never get calm time for learning with your other children if you don't help your kinaesthetic learner to settle their body.

- Try not to criticise or comment on their discomfort, if you find yourself in situations that don't suit your kinaesthetic learner. A big smile and a warm hug are often all they need to settle their need for movement long enough for you to find an opportunity to make a polite exit. Perhaps piano concertos aren't for you right now!

Recognition

What children seek, above all else, is recognition of their achievements. This simple truth is the rocket fuel that will take your child almost anywhere, and will in adult life form the basis of their sense of self-worth and personal motivation. I have lost track of the evenings I have spent sitting on the garden swing watching the boys play ball. They crave recognition more openly than my daughter, who tends to curl herself, cat-like, into a corner of the sofa and wait for me to come and find her reading some breeze block of a book, like *The Hobbit*. 'Look at me!', they keep saying, over and over. 'Mummy, look! *Look!* Watch this! Look at me!' And I keep nodding and pulling various expressions of awe and incredulity. They love it. And they are both getting better every day.

It is simply not the case that demanding children turn into unpleasant adults. I am sure this can occur, but it is not by any means the default connection. In my experience, the most demanding and emotionally needy children I have encountered are in fact those who are emotionally *neglected* at home. Divorce or separation, the emotional or physical absence of a parent, nobody to help with homework, too much screen-time, and many other factors can cause a child to experience emotional neglect. When a child lacks the simple recognition of their existence and their achievements, however small, this emptiness becomes a void that they might spend their entire lives trying to fill.

Importantly, impactful recognition does not involve any material reward, and this is where the link with school can be made. All too often, parents resort to meaningless attempts to mould their child's behaviour or school performance by the use of sticker charts, reward schemes and even cash payment. Rather than motivating a child to learn and develop freely for the pleasure of having done their best, this teaches children to apply minimal effort in exchange for scraps of 'recognition'. It sets up a cycle of thinking that can last a lifetime. What children *really* need is the simple acknowledgement of their effort, and the reassurance that they are loved and special, no matter how big or small that achievement. Sadly, it is sometimes difficult for parents to do this. Certainly, it is impossible for a teacher in charge of a class of 30 to devote this sort of attention to any one student; and so in exchange for genuine recognition, students are compensated with ticks and stickers, house points and name charts. And so at school, too, children are emotionally neglected.

Let's be clear about what we mean by 'recognition' here.

Recognition is... stopping the task that you were doing, making eye contact and giving the child your full attention. Observing enthusiastically but without overly interrupting or interfering. Waiting for the child to be 'done', and showing them with your face and your eyes how proud you are, as well as telling them what a big achievement this is.

Recognition is not... talking over your shoulder to the child whilst busily engaged in another activity. Providing an appraisal in the form of feedback or questions. Putting the child down with a sarcastic comment if their achievement doesn't seem worthy of praise to you. Offering an arbitrary 'reward' such as a sticker, a packet of sweets or money.

A child who is raised in the sunlight of consistent recognition and warm praise for their efforts develops a robust sense of their own abilities, pushes boundaries, and takes pride in their own daily achievements. A supportive home-educating family is a good place for this to happen. By contrast, a child who lacks the human connection of genuine recognition and, in a poor exchange, is given progress ladders and 'well done' stickers doubts himself and learns to chase after small material gains. It's a no-brainer. Simple recognition opens a child up to learning; any system of assessment and reward shuts learning down.

Play-fighting releases a chemical called BDNF (brain-derived neurotrophic factor), which stimulates neuron growth within the cortex and hippocampus regions of the brain – areas responsible for memory, learning, language and logic. You want smart, happy kids? Start with a pillow fight. Here are some basic safety guidelines.

Safe Rules for Serious Play-fights

1. **Hands up, loose wrists:** The key is to adopt a gentle defensive position at all times, and mostly just let them maul you and tumble about. Protect your face and keep your wrists loose so that, if you are playfully slapping their head or shoulders, they are receiving just light strokes with minimal force.

2. **Beware the rebound:** Kids love wrestling, as well as being caught, grabbed, scooped off their feet and so forth. Just be aware that if there is a lot of energy in the game, you should watch when you release them that there isn't a wall or unexpected step directly in front to cause an accident, as they are likely to launch forward.

3. **A note on chasing:** Again, this is to do with speed and watching where they're going. If you can see that your child isn't paying attention to their surroundings, be sure to use your normal voice clearly to remind them to slow down and watch for the edge of the counter; then you can get back to the 'I'm coming to get you!...' thing.

4. **Preventing dislocation:** This is really important, as children are growing, so their joints are more relaxed and easier to dislocate. My advice, if you are lifting, spinning or throwing, is to take a hold on the actual joint (such as the wrist or ankle, rather than the hand or foot) and, if possible, support as well under the arm or knee, so that you don't put joints under any strain.

5. **Cushions:** Obviously cushions and pillows are brilliant for play-fighting, but beware that a heavy cushion can knock a child off their feet; so judge it carefully, and if they want the game to be rough, make sure there is a soft landing. Very safe and one of my kids' favourites is when you take two cushions and bring them together with a 'clap' on their head. A fun sensation, but it doesn't hurt at all.

6. **Know your own body weight:** I think this is especially important for dads, because a typical adult male body-weight is significantly heavier than that of a woman or child. What I always tell my husband to watch out for, if he's rolling around on the floor being pummelled by our three, is to ensure nobody gets a limb trapped under his back.

7. **Watch for tiredness:** Play-fighting is as exhausting as it is exhilarating, and when tiredness kicks in, this is how accidents can happen. Watch for signs that your child is getting worn out, and try to slow the game down and move on to another activity, so that it ends well. In fact, Steve Biddulph notes that winding down is 'the crucial thing... [which] teaches a child, through play, the mastery of his energy and angers' (Biddulph, 2018).

8. **Checking in:** If your children are fierce and really want you to 'go for it' with the rough-housing, then 'up' the game a bit, so long as everyone feels safe and happy. Because you are the adult, the essential thing is to check in regularly, and make sure that they're still enjoying the game, and aren't feeling overwhelmed.

9. **Supporting neck and spine:** Regardless of the age of your children (our baby likes being tumbled about as much as the older ones), it's paramount that you watch how they land if you are throwing. Throwing them? Yes, of course! On to mattresses, piled up duvets and so forth. Check the landing, support the neck and back with your arms, and ensure that they don't land flat; not with a jerk.

10. Of course, never retaliate: It goes without saying that if you engage in play-fights, you could end up with a black eye. My daughter is getting quite big now, and an accidental knee to the nose really flippin' hurts. It's natural to want to shove them away if this happens, but obviously you can't. Instead, just calmly stand up and make it clear that – for you – the game is over for now.

Play-fighting doesn't come naturally to everyone, and I think it's worth pointing out that not all children universally love it. Use your judgement to consider what's right for your family; but for the vast majority of parents, I would suggest that safe, energetic play-fighting is a key ingredient in maintaining mental well-being in children, as well as regulating their mood, balancing energy levels and improving concentration. Enjoy!...

Mixed-age Play

Children are built to learn best from mixed-age play. Historically, children would have played in small groups with ages ranging from teenagers right down to babies, and this is how human beings have evolved for most of our history through to relatively recently – when the economic and social changes discussed earlier gave birth to compulsory mass schooling. Identifying the benefits of mixed-age play is not in itself ground-breaking; other researchers have covered this topic in more detail than I can cover here, and I would urge you to consult the Further Reading section for relevant titles. I will, however, introduce you to two terms in this section which help to capture the basic significance of mixed-age interactions at an educational level. When children engage in mixed-age play, they enjoy optimal conditions for learning and this is due – among other things – to *critical cross-pollination* and *organic levelling*.

Critical Cross-Pollination refers to the way in which learning for children in mixed age groups is not defined by subject, topic or learning stage. An older child with an interest in the solar system might be looking at a book on space, when a younger child comes to sit in their lap. 'Ball!', the child will say, if they are very young. And the older child, with their scientific brain, is now encouraged to consider the shape and appeal of the planets to a small child, pretending to make them bounce, or sounding out other simple words for the child to copy, like 'moon' and 'rocket'. A slightly older child might want to look at the book with the older child and be interested in hearing them read for a while, but then this child might want to make a spaceship out of cardboard, or talk about an imaginary trip to a far-away planet. 'Where would we travel?' 'What would we take on our trip?' 'Can you fart in a space suit?' The younger child's thinking has been enhanced by exposure to the older child's interest in the solar system, and the older child has been encouraged to be flexible in their thinking, moving between scientific interest, baby phonics and fantasy play. Their brain is stimulated to form connections, and move between platforms of thinking in way that *predisposes* them to think in a more free, independent way in the future.

Organic Levelling can only happen in mixed age groups. This is because when children are all the same age and stage, they struggle to establish their own identities within the group, and resort to competitive, sometimes bullying behaviour in order to establish a hierarchy and carve out their place in the group. Through mixed-age play (especially in small groups of up to ten children), this simply doesn't happen. Because of the natural diversity of different ages, stages and genders, all of the children involved in the game feel their 'place' within the group to be clearly defined. They also each have an equal value within the group, which helps them feel accepted.

As an example, the eldest child may nurture the younger ones and feel respected because of this position, but a rather wild girl or boy who's a little younger might serve an important function as the group's 'comic relief', making the babies laugh with slapstick tumbles and uniting the group with their goofiness. In a large group of same-age children, however, neither of these roles work out in the long run. The older child may be criticised for being 'boring' by their peers, because nobody of exactly the same age actually wants or needs nurturing in this way; and the funny younger child could well be mocked for being a 'clown', especially if another child is jealous and wants to hold this position within the group themselves.

The important point with mixed-age play is that each child's position is secure but also 'fluid', meaning that in a few years' time, the goofy one with the comedy falls may well simply 'outgrow' this phase, and naturally rise to adopt the more senior and responsible role within the group. Nobody is 'pigeon-holed' or 'blacklisted' in such groups; there is permission to grow and evolve.

This is learning as nature intended, and it is how most of us enjoy a more settled and less hostile environment in our working life as adults, compared to the more stressful dynamics at school. It is common practice in the workplace to seek out advice from a more senior colleague, and for everyone to be comfortable in the mutually beneficial exchange that this provides. The older, or more experienced, colleague makes time for the new recruit, knowing that it is essential to pass on skills and knowledge and, in so doing, feeling the strength and wisdom of their position. The younger colleague feels enthusiastic to learn, and has no problem listening to the advice of the older colleague; they accept their position in the group and know that, by definition of their youth and inexperience, they will likely make mistakes along the way, but might also bring fresh new ideas, which makes them valuable too.

Notice how, if the advice were being given by a same-age colleague in a postgraduate mass recruitment scheme, for example, the exchange of skills would likely break down. Without the *critical cross-pollination* and *organic levelling* that happens so naturally in mixed groups, both colleagues may well feel in competition with one another. The one giving advice may feel that the other is 'foolish' because their understanding differs, whilst the one who needed advice in the first place may be irritated by her same-age colleague taking a 'superior' position which he has not earned by age and experience. And thus does the natural diversity and acceptance of the mixed age group break down, and in its place, rivalry occurs. This is, of course, what happens every day in school.

Mixed-age play is therefore essential for learning. It is, however, not just difficult to achieve, but actively *discouraged* by schools in the following ways:

1. **Year groups:** Probably the most divisive aspect of most schools is the segregation of children into year groups. This means that school children spend most of their time learning with – and trying to make friends with – children with whom they are not only in direct competition, but also have little to learn or gain from. The mistake here is the assumption that by grouping children in this way, they will all be of a similar stage, and so it will be easier for the teacher to deliver the lesson. But this approach is disastrous for two reasons: first, it wrongly assumes that all valuable learning comes from the teacher; and secondly, it makes the false assumption that children born within twelve months of each other will share the same interests and be at roughly the same academic level. This is not the case, and the only reason average attainment statistics might make it *appear* the case is because school makes it so.

2. **Competition and ranking:** School children are constantly tested and encouraged to 'know' their academic level and, these days, what their targets are on the assessment chart in order to get to the next level. The problem with this – quite apart from the toxic stress that it generates – is that these targets are not in fact the child's targets at all, but an adult-

imposed wish-list, the language of which children are forced to learn and place value upon. Without the normalisation of diversity that occurs when children pursue their natural curiosities and set their own targets (which, for the average five-year-old should surely be something like, 'Make a submarine out of mashed potato', rather than 'Get to Level 4 in my reading'), true diversity becomes an unfamiliar concept, and children jostle for position within the narrow confines of the group using the only currency that they all understand – the pecking order. This is why you might hear a very small child calling their classmate 'dumb' if they're struggling to read, or a child in the lunch queue being labelled a 'weirdo' if they haven't heard of Spiderman. School children have been robbed of the natural diversity of the mixed age group and are operating under conditions where assessment – and so, implicitly, judgement – rules. No child can learn effectively in this environment.

3. **Playtime segregation:** Even outside the classroom, children are mostly corralled in year groups for most of their recreation time. This is especially so at primary school and, as a consequence, when more free-flow between age groups occurs at secondary school, many children struggle with this and do not have the skills to manage positive interactions with students older or younger than themselves. Even in some secondary schools, though, children remain channelled into age-segregated groups for break-time, extra-curricular clubs, lunch bells and occasional outings. And the unhealthy effect that this has on the 'whole school' mentality of the school is further amplified by the highly charged atmosphere of events like Sports Day, and the structure of age-related privileges (commonplace within all schools) such as prefect badges, the mentor system and areas of the school which are accessible only once you enter a certain academic year. Because children do not routinely mix across the ages in a positive and supportive way, these kinds of initiatives often ignite aggressive hostilities and 'marking of territory' for children on either side of the invisible boundary.

We began attending Forest School just a few weeks after deciding to homeschool. This is a weekly group in our area for home educators and their families to meet in the woods and drink hot chocolate by the firepit, while our children roam within a certain radius of the adult 'hub', making dens, climbing trees, playing chase, and shooting homemade bows and arrows. Lots of families attend, and the children mix in a group of around 30, with ages ranging from 18 year-olds and about to start university, who've come to help out with the fire and supervising dangerous equipment, down to babies on their mothers' hip or, more frequently, sat in the lap of an older child who wants some 'down-time' and has come to sit near the adults and play games with the little ones.

What I observe every time we go to this group is quite magical. Boys as old as 15 or 16 will be running at full speed between the trees, leaping and rolling impressively to fend off imaginary attackers, followed by a pack of younger boys (my middle son included) wielding sticks and copying their combat moves. The older boys are mostly doing this for the entertainment of the younger children. They have understood the importance of their position as role models, and they are entering the game with good spirit. But they are also, I think, enjoying the benefits that this brings to them, too: realising the strength and speed of their own bodies, and unleashing their more mature imagination to create a war game that is like fertiliser for the minds of their young followers.

The girls are no different, and although they do often play in same-sex groups – like in school – the divisions are far more porous. My daughter will be sitting frighteningly high up on a tree branch with two girlfriends and her new 'bestie' – a slightly younger boy called Aston, who isn't keen on rough play. Aston is incredibly capable for his age, and knows how to whittle wood to make a spear using the pen knife that his parents have taught him how to use safely, and trust him with. He is showing the girls how to do it, and although he is over a year younger than them, they are all admiring his handiwork and asking him to carve other items out of wood. Everyone feels good in this setting. It is the ideal environment for learning, love and laughter to flourish. And they all do.

As I was writing this section, I came across the Roots of Empathy project, again in Peter Gray's writings. This is a growing, worldwide movement which aims to reduce aggression and improve caring and mental well-being, in school and beyond. The project began in Canada, initially as an intervention aimed at preventing the cycle of abuse. Children from violent or neglectful backgrounds are more likely to go on to be violent or neglectful with their own children, and the question is what to do about it. By bringing a parent and their baby into a classroom once a month for an entire school year, the project aimed to cultivate curiosity in childhood and promote some appreciation of the world from a small child's perspective.

The results were incredible. Schools participating in the project noticed an immediate reduction in bullying and an increase in the children's positive interactions during class time – a change that would last for the entire month, through to the next visit. Roots of Empathy now exists in the UK but, typically, is not as high profile as it should be, because kindness and well-being are not measured on assessment grids and carry no league-table points. It does confirm the incredible value of mixed-age interaction, though. Give a teenager ten minutes of 'peekaboo' with a one-year old and their mood will shift, concentration improves, and that essay on gravity might just get finished before lunch.

Since quitting teaching, I find myself writing mostly in the early morning when my husband and children are still fast asleep. I like this time  of day, watching the grey light steal through the blinds and paint ghostly lines on the opposite wall; the silence. Around 7 a.m., they tend to wake up and we have breakfast together before getting started on the day. At first, I was cautious not to allow my new working life to impact on the kids at all, but as time has gone on, I realise that they actually love it when I tell them that I need half an hour or so to edit an article; it gives them time together.

This morning, it is a warm start to the day and I am re-reading a chapter from the book I'm referencing under the shade of the washing-line. We are fortunate to have quite a big garden, and I can see the three children at the end of it, passing a football between them and chattering animatedly. My daughter, the eldest, has organised her brothers into a triangle and is encouraging them to pass the ball round. She feels mature and confident, with the younger children listening to her direction. But my eldest boy, the middle child, is good with a football and, without challenging his sister's authority, demonstrates a few tricks every time he receives the ball, which his sister admires, being old enough to know that it is kind to praise. They both feel good in their roles. Even the baby, now nearly two years old, is learning heaps from running around with his older siblings, and can already dribble the ball and play catch. He too has a role in the group, and enjoys pretending to fall over, which makes everybody laugh.

They are constantly learning from each other, and with secure roles and identities based on age and gender within the group, there is little competition or rivalry. This is also how they play nowadays when we meet up with other home-educating families, disappearing upstairs or into the garden for hours on end to play elaborate games without fuss or argument, often running in a mixed age group which might range from 14 or 15 down to toddlers. And I notice, sadly, that this isn't always the case when children go to school and select their friends from a narrow range of same-age peers. There is more of a point to prove, and less natural regulation of social dynamics in this environment.

It has been, I think to myself, a long time since I heard the expression, 'You're not my friend any more'. I'm not sure what my children would even make of that statement now.

Time to Digest

Effective learning requires one ingredient that school is simply unable to provide, and that is time to slow down, digest and 'process' the learning. This time is essential for children's brains to make sense of the information they've received that day, as well as enabling pathways for further enquiry to open up; the organic beginnings of independent investigation and discovery. Children do this 'processing' in a variety of ways:

- Quiet, unrelated play which allows their mind to relax and roam
- Topic-related role-play and games
- Reading or watching the TV
- Plenty of quality sleep
- Interrogative conversation, not directed or probed by an adult
- Drawing pictures and creating visual representation
- Repeating the activity or learning moment again and again

Allowing children time to digest the learning that has taken place is, in some ways, the most fundamental element of natural learning that children are robbed of when they start school. Not only does school (or nursery school, for many children) spell the start of a constant state of tension and underlying pressure to perform socially and academically, but it is also the first major blow to the child's natural 'body clock'. The impact of this is underestimated throughout the school system. and of course by parents, who are – often unwittingly – complicit in destroying their child's natural rhythm.

We all have a body clock which, if we're lucky, we live by more and more as we get older. Some of us are 'morning people' – like me – and wake up before dawn to work, take a run or finish household chores. Others are 'night owls' and enjoy being wide awake while others are asleep. These people operate best at this time, and feel 'switched on and alert' through to the early hours of the morning, often sleeping in a bit later as a result. Babies also have a body clock, and a natural rhythm of naps and activity which allows your baby – and toddler – to grow and learn, with plenty of rest to process the vast amounts of information they're absorbing. Some children will nap frequently and for short bursts during the day; others will go down for a long nap somewhere around the middle of the day. I am always astonished when I hear another homeschooling parent tell me that their children sometimes sleep in until nine or ten in the morning, because mine are all up and full speed by 7 at the latest.

Schools – almost universally – start at 8.30 or 9 a.m., and this means an early start (incredibly early for some) in order to make it on time. It's called the 'school run' for a reason – right? Somehow, every morning, it feels like we are all *just* on time. From my memories of the year that my daughter spent in school, I recall children still eating toast on their way down the pavement, parents frantically brushing ponytails outside the car, book-bags being rifled through on the playground bench, and many sleepy-looking little ones leaning against parents' legs looking, for want of a better phrase, fairly 'pi**ed off'. I get them. That's how I felt too, as a parent, and also during the years that I was teaching, although the difference is I was there by choice and was being paid for it.

No child, unless their home life is truly terrible, is at school at 9 a.m. by choice. Almost all children have made it there thanks to a supreme effort from their parents to wake them, get them in the shower, sort breakfast, check book-bags and notices, hustle them to the car and, in some cases, emotionally counsel them and dry their tears, in order to get them through the school gates. Once in school, this assault continues, as every moment of the school day is taken up with activities, assembly, bells and change-overs, enforced social time, and more.

There is literally no space to relax and process – something children so desperately need. And guess what? At the end of the school day, this hectic schedule continues for many children, in the form of after-school clubs, enrichment activities, homework and 'family time', which must be shoe-horned into the end of the day. As I am writing this, I'm feeling ashamed that I ever put my kids through such a performance in the first place. But of course, we all do.

The lack of time to digest immeasurably damages our school children's ability to learn and process; but more than that, it has a wider impact on the whole family, as well as the future behaviour patterns of our children. Here's how.

Whole-family impact: The school run involves everyone in the family, from mums and dads tag-teaming to take turns being late to work, to new-born babies in snowsuits being passed around while their sister's long hair is plaited, or while their brother's unsigned reading-log is located. It impacts on the well-being of the entire family unit, therefore, and means that time spent as a family from Monday to Friday is mostly wrapped up in travel time, rushing to organise clothes and equipment, or the daily battle of homework. Importantly, Lawrence J. Cohen explains how human life is 'all about connection' (Cohen, 2013), noting that 'many disconnections arise when children have to join our world and our schedule'. I find this to be the case with school.

Forming harmful behaviour patterns: The reason most of us drag our children to school each morning is because we were once dragged to school ourselves. This goes back and back. We have no collective memory of a time before compulsory schooling. However, by teaching children that they 'must' wake early in the morning, brush their teeth and work long hours regardless of whether or not they enjoy their work, this provides a clear blueprint for the rest of their lives. More than this, because we as parents have to organise almost everything in order to make the school run logistically possible, we are allowing our children no space whatsoever to develop the essential life skills discussed in Chapter 1. They are passive recipients of a routine imposed upon them, which they can either struggle against, or give in to.

Human beings have body clocks for a reason; we are all different, and we process information at different times and in various ways. By home-educating your child, you allow them to respect their body clock, and to 'tune into' the healthy routine that is natural to all of us, rather than learn to fight against it and set low expectations for well-being in their future lives and careers. The idea of shaping learning to fit better with children's diverse body clocks and allowing time to digest *could* and *should* be given more consideration in the education system. This would make a big difference, and we will be looking more closely at a school that does this later in the book.

In a Nutshell

- Children learn best from pursuing their own natural curiosity.

- Children learn from observation, and we should pay attention to the influences they are receiving.

- Children learn effectively from informal conversation, and from observing children of different ages during free play.

- What Peter Gray refers to as 'mindless busywork' and constant assessment in schools are distractions from real learning.

- Children require time to digest and process learning, in line with their natural body clocks.

Before we move on to the Chapter 3, I will briefly clarify what I mean by 'learning moments'. It is important to state that true learning must be self-directed, must not be interrupted, and impacts the 'whole child'. The nature of brain inter-connectivity means that half an hour figuring out a piece of music on the piano, or building a bridge out of lolly sticks, can activate your child's mathematical mind far more powerfully than 20 minutes of actual algebra. We might think of this as the benefits of *non-direct learning*, and we should be mindful of this when home-educating. Looking through a magazine, listening to music, speaking in another language, and learning how to skateboard – all are activities which activate the brain in ways which improve the ability to learn more globally.

As you read the next and final chapter of Part I and move into the personal stories in Part II, try to detach yourself from the notion of education being about 'covering content', and think rather about the significance of wiring children's brains to *want* to learn. Home education is about laying the foundations for a mind that is open and curious; willing and able to learn to the best of the individual's ability. In this context, it is irrelevant whether a child knows the dates of World War I or not. What we're looking for in these stories – and in our own children – are *learning moments*, where the penny drops, the world is seen in a new light, and the sparks of curiosity ignite neurological pathways that, over time, predispose a person to enjoy and seek the benefits of learning throughout their lifetime.

CHAPTER 3

The Benefits of Home Education

I'm so glad I didn't go to school, because if I had, I would never have the life I have now.

Billie Eilish

When I was training back in 2008, I met Simon, who was a total hoot. We bonded over our tricky tutor groups and his then-girlfriend, Alice, was a former thespian like me, and still took part in amateur theatre productions alongside finishing her medical training. I used to drag my partner along to these shows in our pre-parenting days, slipping in at the last minute with a stash of sixth-form marking in a carrier bag, just in case the play turned out to be a real stinker. They were generally pretty good, though, and afterwards we would go for a drink together, and howl with laughter over the missed lines and wardrobe malfunctions that seemed – funnily enough – to actually enhance the experience. Simon and Alice got married and had two children, and we had all moved away from London by the time we reached our 30s. My husband still sends the occasional text to Simon, whilst I exchange long emails with Alice, the most recent of which, as I write, I'll share with you now.

16.5.2020

Hi Anna; me again.

What is it with the bloody phone? I can never say what I want and the girls are constantly nagging for attention. Actually, that's what I wanted to talk to you about (the girls), but I never get a moment to be private without one of them listening in. So, here goes…

Me and Si have finished reading your manuscript and yeah, we like it. I mean, it's a fairly tough read, you know? We love you and we love what you guys are doing, but this had us talking all weekend about our kids and the future we see for them. You know we've been really happy with the school we chose since Lilly started, and even Heidi seems to have settled well; no crying. So, what am I saying here? I don't know what I'm worrying about, really.

I guess, maybe, it's the fact that we've all spent so much time together recently and I can see how much the girls are enjoying it. They barely get to see Si during the week when he's actually 'at' work, so this lockdown is a big treat for them. They've been building a treehouse at the bottom of the garden with him and, to be honest, we've more or less dropped the flow of schoolwork that the teachers keep sending. It seemed like a pointless battle and, since then, they seem to play better together and be more interested in things.

Anyway, it's looking increasingly like schools will start to reopen sometime soon, so we are thinking of gradually bringing back a bit of structure, and encouraging Lilly especially to catch up on some of the topics, so she's not behind. There have been a few tears. Basically, she doesn't want to. And Heidi is having anxiety – I think – about Si going back to work and having to settle back at school.

I feel like the bad cop, all the time, but I suppose that's just what life's like, right? I mean, that's kind of the point of your book, in a way, right? To follow the best path for your family. You make your choices and I guess this is just part of the deal with school. I think it's normal, but every once in a while, I do have doubts.

Love and hugs to you and your lot. Alice x

This chapter looks at the *multiple benefits of home education*, for the child and also for the *whole family*. Because no, I don't think Alice's story is normal, or rather I disagree that this experience should be 'normalised'. Here's how to work towards a healthier 'norm' for *your* family.

Tried and Tested

Home-educating is wonderfully reassuring for families who want to see their children succeed to the best of their ability. We only need to glance back at the thousands of years of human history prior to compulsory state education to acknowledge that where we are today is founded on generations of successful learning without school. Importantly, there are two advantages to learning through life – the 'homeschool way' – which history shows to be true.

1. **Learning embedded in real experience sticks in our memory:** This is why we never forget how to ride a bike, why we all remember the first book we fell in love with, and why the only science lessons we actually recall involved Bunsen burners and heart dissection. This is also how key things got passed down over thousands of years to the people living today – like language, story-telling and scientific discoveries.

2. **Learning acquired by pursuing our needs and interests tends to be highly skilled:** Prior to mass public schooling, most children were educated by their families and learnt the skills required for adult life from parents, as well as from other children and adults in the local community. The skills required for a trade or to be a successful hunter-gatherer tend to be complex, involving multiple specialisms and 'real-life' knowledge. This is something that has been eroded by the uniformity of school.

When I first started home-educating my children, although my faith in the school system was at a low point, I was by no means convinced that homeschooling would be a magic wand to undo the mediocrity of mainstream education. I mean, kids are kids. They love TV and hate doing their homework, right? But I was astonished by what I saw. In large part home-educated children learn extremely well when left to their own devices. One of our homeschooling friends, age seven, has launched a successful art business and produces incredible paintings which people pay to have printed on canvas for their homes. Another friend's child is so fascinated by science that they have memorised all the elements of the periodic table, as well as their properties, just because they're interested. My own daughter has gone from rumbling reluctantly through her assigned Level 4 reading book to fluently reading any book from the shelf at bedtime for her brothers. Last night it was *Harry Potter and the Prisoner of Azkaban*. I'm not entirely sure what the baby made of it, but still. She's six.

There are bright and motivated children who go to school, of course, and over the years I have had the pleasure of working with some of them. However, what I have observed during the time-frame in which a 'stand-out' child joins secondary school in Year 7, and leaves at the end of sixth form, is a palpable shift of focus, from personal interests and hobbies to – mostly – achieving high marks on examination papers and concentrating on building their resumé for university. A boy who enters my English classroom age eleven and is quite clearly a poet (and there are less and less of these children coming through, due to the mounting pressures at primary level) will find no space for that in the secondary school classroom. He might impress me with some unexpected poetic homework submissions in the first few months, and because I like him, I might tweak the lesson plan occasionally to incorporate expressive writing in the form of a poem or creative prose (something which is given no value in the curriculum). But as the boy starts to grow older, he quickly realises that poetry has no currency here and, because he is smart, he drops this essential part of his soul and starts turning out damned-good essays instead. He will get top marks, for sure. But will he remember that there is a poet, or song writer, inside of him when he goes out into the world? Or will he have learnt to ignore it and press on with 'what really matters'?

When you choose to homeschool, you are entering a way of living and learning that has always existed. You would therefore do well to stand back a bit and just observe your children, to see what they're capable of. It might be worth exploring autonomous learning with them, and there will be more on this in Part III. Most of all, try to remain calm and positive. You are not playing with fire here; nor are you failing your children by doing something 'alternative'. There is nothing alternative about home-educating. On the contrary, you are rejecting a relatively recent social experiment – mass public schooling – in favour of a tried-and-tested method of educating your children within the family and local community. It works. And it allows your children the freedom to grow into the person they were born to be.

Living Better

Earlier this year, a former colleague of mine retired. We spent nearly five years working together in the sixth-form office, and became good friends during this time. Her text message back in January went like this: 'Anna! How's tricks?

That's it; I'm done. No more Mondays for me. Champagne for breakfast? Kay x.' This made me laugh and I wrote back something like: 'Congrats! It's always Champagne for breakfast here... so glad you could join us!' Which isn't strictly the truth, but Kay knows what I mean. She homeschooled her daughter through to secondary school and was, in fact, the first person within the context of mainstream education who gave me a strong, academic rationale for homeschooling. Back then I thought that she was a bit crazy. I liked her a lot.

Homeschooling has the general impact of improving your quality of life in several ways. Sleep improves, families seem to 'get on' better, exercise and eating habits are healthier, and most parents will see their children surpass expectations socially, emotionally and academically, with less effort and more leisure time. When done correctly, one is replacing mass public schooling with a tried-and-tested method of educating your children within the family and local community. It works. And it allows your children the freedom to grow a better way to live. In the aftermath of the COVID-19 pandemic, again and again we are hearing the call for working from home to become the new 'norm'; cutting travel time, reducing emissions, and vastly improving quality of life for millions of people in industries where this is a real possibility. This is what Aaron Eden @Edunautics refers to as 'rehumanising work and education' (Eden, 2020); and conscious of the toxic impact of our modern lifestyles, we all seem to want this change for ourselves. We should want it for our children, too.

Consider, for a moment, how family life is transformed when we simply reclaim Sunday. Let me explain. A few years ago, American research psychologists looked into happiness and unhappiness in public school students. Their findings were that 'average happiness increased on the weekend but then plummeted from late Sunday afternoon through the evening, in anticipation of the coming school week' (Gray, 2013). Anyone holding this book will most likely identify with this feeling. Most of us went to school, and we learnt that the 'Sunday blues' is just a part of life; and we expect no less as adults. That's why we see car stickers, rucksack badges and Twitter GIFs all saying the same thing: 'Monday sucks!' But what if it didn't *have* to be like this? What if, through careful career planning and mindful educating of our children, we could all reclaim these 'lost' 24 hours and raise our kids to embrace every morning with excitement and intention for the day to come? At the very least, that gives us Sunday back, and that's 14 per cent of our entire lifetime.

Living better is about more than just emotional well-being, though. Our mental health is also governed by the physical environment, and for many families, unhealthy habits start at school. I will begin by acknowledging that undoubtedly, there are some families for whom school provides stability, stimulation and hot meals which are not available at home. However, this does not represent the majority of families, and such benefits for disadvantaged children really fall under the bracket of social welfare rather than education. For most of us, then, school spells the start of negative lifestyle choices for our children, including junk food, constant snacking, screen addiction and lack of exercise. Many of these bad decisions are the simple result of playground peer pressure, driving parents and children alike to 'conform' by agreeing to unhealthy branded treats and video games in bedrooms, in a bid to avoid the social alienation that goes with being 'different'.

More than this, though, impoverished well-being is a direct consequence of the poor-quality environment of school itself. The size of classrooms and the sedentary schedule of the school day mean that children spend the majority of their time sitting down, or with very limited movement. Notwithstanding Jamie Oliver's healthy schools campaign, school dinners still serve fruit juice boxes, chips and sugary puddings almost every day of the week; and moreover, in the rush to meet the demands of the weekly schedule, parents are often pushed to resort to snack-bar breakfasts 'on the go', and convenience food at dinner time. It is also easy to lose sight of the fact that our tired children come home at the end of a long day of 'screen learning' (almost every lesson will make use of videos and screen presentations) to be consoled by their parents with – you guessed it – *more* screen-time in order to 'unwind'. This toxic lifestyle cocktail simply doesn't exist for most families prior to entering the school system, and it's a cycle that doesn't (need to) happen with homeschooling.

What home-educating also provides in bucket-loads is the time and inclination to embrace nature on a more regular basis. Regardless of our preferences for leisure time, it is undeniable that there is a lot of learning to be done in the natural world – by which I mean a trip to the park, a woodland walk, exploring the local quarry, building site, river, or – if you are very lucky – the beach. Being immersed in nature provides 'teacherless lessons' in everything under the sun, from insect life to agriculture, and from art to creative writing. Factoring in regular time during the week to experience nature is a fundamental part of *living better* and, importantly, has a direct impact on our well-being and concentration.

Rather than spending time cooped up at a desk under the glare of artificial strip-lights and tinted windows, your child is using their body in the fresh air, absorbing endorphin-boosting Vitamin D and learning an empowering way of living which will carry them through the challenges of life. It *is* within your reach to give this to your children – and to yourself – but it does require some fundamental changes, especially concerning your working life. I will be talking more about how to do this in Part III.

Nostalgia is, by definition, a sentimental reflection on times gone by. It is not rational, nor does it bear the scrutiny of interrogation. In this way, many of us look back on our own school days with something like fond affection. The PE teacher who once reduced you  to tears in front of the whole class is now a comic caricature from your childhood, with whom you might exchange jokes and memories about old school friends, if you're still in touch. Similarly, the workload – especially around examinations – is now a distant memory, and what is left is just a flavour of the past; the squeak of your school shoes as you crossed the hall to sit that last Biology paper. The scent of pencil shavings. Is it school you remember so fondly? Is it the friendships you made there? Or is it just a romantic longing for your youth which, perhaps like all of us, you didn't fully appreciate at the time?

Most of us send our children to school not because we enjoy the idea of incarcerating them against their will, but because we have the vague sense that it will 'do them good' in the long run, and get them where they need to be. It is worth pointing out here that we went to school in a rather different era of education, compared to the current high-pressure environment. In the eighties and nineties, school was still school, but it was arguably a 'better time' in education. Primary schools still enjoyed long lunchtimes and half hour breaks for play in both the morning and afternoon. School attendance was more relaxed, with many children doing only half-days throughout Key Stage 1, and family holidays frequently booked during the school term without fuss. Academic pressure was also a notch lower and – get this – the *value* of grades was higher. An A* (now Level 9 – sort of) was actually pretty impressive, whereas today, in spite of (or rather due to) excruciating pressure exerted on schools from Ofsted, league tables, parents and governors, student results at both GCSE and A-Level are increasingly rendered a nonsense. Almost *everybody* passes, most do fairly well, and the percentage of students achieving top marks goes up with every cohort. It is a *false economy*: a mushroom of highly stressed, over-tested, yet uniformly 'samey' students emerging from a damaged system that needs, all in all, a total revamp.

Because it does. Far from acting as a vehicle for social mobility, the top-down structure and assessment-driven ethos of the school system is actually a solid preserver of class boundaries and economic division. Year on year, children from underprivileged backgrounds achieve poor exam results and are pushed on to Diploma schemes, or else crash out of A-Levels, while their more affluent classmates sail through with top results which, in the world of mainstream education, is nothing more than currency for the next stop on the conveyor belt. If we abandoned testing altogether and young people made job or university applications based on their own unique resumé – a summary of their learning journey, experience and personal interests – the world might be a better, fairer and far more interesting place.

Let's drop the school nostalgia right now, and think about what we really want from an education.

Finding Your Comfort Zone

My husband and I took our children to a birthday party just before lockdown happened in the UK. It was held at a giant soft play which, if you are lucky enough to have never stepped foot into one of these places, is essentially a warehouse packed with padded gym equipment for kids. Think: slides, tunnels, ball pit, spider's web. They love it, and they all go a bit mad of course. But this time I felt relaxed, and the reason is because we now homeschool; a decision which has allowed us to step outside the 'rule book' and find our own rhythm. I am no longer concerned that I might jeopardise my child's social life if an activity does not feel appropriate; nor do I feel that I have to apologise for my child's behaviour, or make arrangements with families about whom we don't feel totally sure. And so on this occasion, when my eldest was asked whether she would like to go with some children to the cinema after the party, our answer was 'thank you, but "no"'. Simple as that.

It's not always been as clear as that for us and, in fact, later that afternoon as we helped to clear up the party table, one of the mums sat down next to me and had a good cry. It was about the cinema thing. You see, school contains a mix of very different families with different 'norms' and values, all trying to function as one. Most parents are keen to see their child liked and accepted at school, because they know in their hearts that the consequences for the child if that's *not* the case can be very hard indeed. So the start of school means, for many families, putting aside a lot of their basic principles and expectations which, in fact, are part of what makes your family *who you are*. They might be religious values, social values, codes of conduct, or healthy principles about eating and TV time. Of course, it's all a balance, and there is definitely a solid argument for exposing your child to different ways of doing things – yes. But not in this case. Not for Jayne who, head in hands, had just allowed her six-year old to take the bus into town in the company of some older kids and an 'accompanying adult' she didn't know too well.

What is your *comfort zone*, then? It might help if you consider this to be the orbit of experience that feels right for your children at any given point in their journey, through childhood and into the autonomous freedom of adulthood. Importantly, we must respect that this is a joint process, not just what *you* feel ready for. Children are naturally eager to absorb new experiences and challenges. We want to support and encourage them in this; but we must also act as the voice of reason that keeps a check on where the dangers lie, and what is appropriate according to our child's age or – more importantly – *stage* of development. The complexities of modern life mean that, unfortunately, we cannot always allow our children to 'learn for themselves' because the repercussions of a wrong decision are sometimes too serious to play with. Therefore, whilst it is not possible or wise to afford our children the exact same liberties that children – for the most part – enjoyed throughout the mid-part of last century, we can, especially as home educators, shape an experience for our children that allows them to taste freedom and independence in ways that remain fundamentally safe and 'within limits'.

When we send our children to school, though, our comfort zone is tested on a daily basis, and our perception of how best to offer our children the autonomy they crave can become blurred. The sudden leap from spending plenty of quality time with your child to suddenly 'losing' your four-year old for most of the week can bereave loving parents to the point where we are chasing our tails in the effort to demonstrate our affection and please our children, often in the wrong ways. Here are some examples of the ways in which parents taken out of their comfort zone by the influences of school can make bad choices regarding their children.

- Over-planning and *micro-managing* our child's free time outside of school, in an attempt to make the limited time we spend with them always feel 'special'.

- *Molly-coddling* our children by allowing them to treat their home like a hotel; never asking them to clear up or participate, because we worry they are tired after school and we don't want to 'push them away'.

- Allowing far *too much screen-time*, because it's 'what all the other kids do' and we don't want our child to be left out.

- Spoiling our children with *material goods* such as toys or sweets when we collect them from school, because we know the real luxury – our time and attention – is lacking.

- Agreeing to *big things* such as sleep-overs before we – or our children – are ready, because we fear our child being excluded from the group if we don't.

- Permitting our children to *speak rudely* to us or their siblings, because we rationalise that they are exhausted from school and need to 'let off steam' at home.

- Accepting that our children seem to value fleeting friendships at school above family connections and *being in denial* that there is something wrong here.

Looking at this list, it is important to remind ourselves that we are not 'rubbish parents' who willingly indulge our children in all the wrong ways. These negative behaviours that we have 'normalised' as part and parcel of going to school are the combined result of our strong nurturing instinct and confused parental compass. As we'll explore in more detail later in this chapter, the very act of leaving our young children in the hands of 'professionals' on their first day of Reception is, by definition, a contradiction to the ingrained parenting instincts that we have held for thousands of years. We hand our child over to school because it has become the new 'norm', and for many parents, the next 15 years are marked by an ongoing tug-of-war between our natural parenting values and the pressure to 'fit in' with what everyone else is doing, or going along with.

A good example of this is computer and phone access, which Sue Palmer, in her book *Toxic Childhood*, refers to as 'electric speed'. Palmer emphasises the importance of 'unplugging', and allowing our children to develop in 'slow time', the way all 'highly intelligent primates have needed [to] through the ages' (Palmer, 2006). Homeschooling resolves these sorts of problems; ending the internal battle for parents and dissolving the *illusion of autonomy* from which many school children suffer. Free to make their own choices and enjoying a small and familiar friendship group, your homeschooled child will know what is good for them and when they are ready for the next stage. And so will you.

In the end, it was okay for Jayne and her son, Toby, who emerged safe and sound from an afternoon screening of *Sonic the Hedgehog*. For Jayne, though, it had been an afternoon of blind panic. Toby was, in reality, far too young to be taking this trip without a familiar adult or, at the very least, responsible teenagers who were family members or long-standing friends. I know, because I followed up on the story, that Jayne spent several hours outside the cinema, in tears, praying that he was inside watching the movie and hating herself for the snap decision she had made, faced with the pressure of wanting her beloved son to 'fit in'. She had gone way outside of her comfort zone and, in truth, most likely her son's as well. There is plenty of time for Toby to grow up at a steady pace.

Avoiding Tribalism

School children spend their formative years in an educational institution. By 'formative years', I mean the years most crucial to the formation and shaping of whom they are to become. And by 'institution', I mean a large organisation founded for a specific purpose. The trouble with this is that these very important years are spent not observing the variety in the world and the wide range of interesting individuals who make it up, but rather, turned inward and focused on the extremely narrow influences of their 'peer group'. Human children are not really *designed* to grow up this way, but it has become the 'norm', and they do the best they can.

Take a child who comes to school with a lot of anger, for example. There is very little effective pastoral support in schools these days, and the school counsellor with her cosy 'beanbag corner' is practically a relic of the past. So what does this child do? Within the natural dynamics of a mixed-age group, an older child or adult with time to spare might pick up on this anger and take the child to one side, checking in with what's going on and informally counselling them as to how to manage their feelings. Equally, if very small children are present, the child feeling angry might choose to settle themselves by spending half an hour playing ball with a toddler, thereby curbing their emotion and finding a way 'back in' to the day. We see this pattern of behaviour happen all the time within family groups, and it is highly effective.

Trapped in a constant public setting with peers of the same age and maturity, however, is not constructive here. An angry child is easily provoked to react in class, and many children who are 'switched off' from education make it their daily sport to encourage the 'hot-headed' kids to blow up in class, thereby stopping the lesson. An angry child might also transfer that feeling to another child by physically or verbally lashing out during the day. The child is volatile from the start of the school day through to the end, and it is possible that none of the teachers properly pick up on this, unless a major incident comes to light. A lot of this volatility is regulated – or gets 'thrashed out' – amongst the students themselves.

This is the basis of how groups initially form in school. Because so much of what happens during the school day passes under the radar of the adults in charge, there is a need to form loyalties which go beyond shared interests and a sense of friendship. There is also a need to survive and to have protection within this hostile environment. The trouble is that group loyalty subsequently goes too far and, in itself, becomes a source of renewed tension. What you wear, who you hang out with, and the kind of music you listen to can all be controlled by the group you're in. For some children, the group's influence can even affect their behaviour in class, and relationships with their parents and siblings at home. This is what I mean by 'tribalism' – people who are overly loyal to the 'group', and have lost track of whom they are themselves.

Very few adults go around in gangs; those who do must feel extremely unsafe in their daily lives. It is simply not a natural state in which to operate. When we look at life as recently as a few centuries ago, we see generally smaller communities of people living and working together, with children helping out around the home and going off to play in small mixed age groups. Because of the different ages of the children and their various engagements in the wider life of the community, each group in this context is fluid, and may only remain a 'group' for as long as the game lasts, before shifting again or dissolving altogether. This is the natural way that children play and human beings interact with each other.

By socialising in this way, homeschooling families see very little evidence of a 'pack mentality'. Children mix freely between groups and are not expected to permanently socialise; they can have 'down-time', too. Playing on your own is usually respected and valued within the homeschooling community, with no social repercussions. If this kind of dynamic could be cultivated in schools, then I would be lobbying for less teaching time, longer recreation and free access to a wide range of free play and learning resources. There is a school model emerging which has precisely this kind of structure and I will tell you more about it later; but for now, for the majority of schools, break-times have actually been *reduced* with a clear agenda in mind: to keep children safe and maintain the focus on 'teaching and learning'.

A note is appropriate at this juncture on radicalisation and religious extremism. Acts of terror begin at school; make no mistake about it. I haven't sat through the Met Police staff briefing every September not to get this message loud and clear. When I began writing this section, I wrote an email to Naziha, a friend and former colleague, and a Muslim mother. We agreed on what needs to be said here together, so the rest of this paragraph is from 'us'; from Naz and me. No parent wants their child to be radicalised. No parent wants their child to die.

Radicalisation takes many forms – White Supremacist, Islamic, Gang Affiliation – and it begins in the classroom, during the bus ride home and, of course, online. Tribalism reaches out for disaffected young people and can end their lives, and the lives of others. It is not in the name of any god or coherent belief system that our children are radicalised. It happens because of a gaping problem in the way our society functions, with school at the centre.

Kamal is incredibly bright, but he would never tell you that. Tall and regal, with high cheekbones and a permanent expression of mild disdain, he stands with his back against the wall – first to arrive, but slouching nonetheless. He smiles lazily and takes his seat at the back of the class. The year is 2009 and this is my first teaching post; I am nervous as hell.

Kamal, Eliot and the Trap of Tribalism

But Kamal isn't here to cause trouble. More than that, he's a calming influence on Quinn, Jacob and Eliot, who sit next to him. The bottom set is always full of boys. Eliot, wild-eyed and constantly twitching, is the most disruptive because he seeks to shoot down anyone who contributes even a scrap of effort to the lesson. 'Gay man!' 'That's dead!' 'Effing brown-noser!' Which is why most of the class don't bother until, most days, Eliot is escorted from the room by the deputy head.

I wonder what Kamal is doing here, with his long hands and elegant prose. How did he end up in Set 4? His school record tells me that he lives with his grandparents nowadays, and that neither mum nor dad are in the picture. I quiz Kamal's form tutor about this one morning on the way to briefing, but she is hazy on the details. Apparently this is above my pay grade, but I guess something pretty bad went on. Bad enough to make a very able student sleepwalk through Key Stage 2 and wind up in Set 4 at the start of Year 7.

Half an hour in, and Eliot is still muttering insults like an incantation from behind his school-bag which remains resolutely on the table in front of him. I busy myself with the middle row; two Muslim girls bowing their heads diligently over a single copy of *Animal Farm*, whispering in German, and Abby Brock, who managed to receive a detention on day one of secondary school by throwing a bottle of deodorant at the Head of Year. Enough said. It's not a 'warm' group. And so far I have been careful with Kamal. Careful, above all, not to single him out as being overly bright (which he is), or sensitive (which is he, too). Because that would be suicide in this class.

But one day, I let my guard down just a fraction. I am touring the class, confiscating phones and mumbling about the 'top-button rule', when I stop at the back row and notice Kamal's homework assignment on the desk in front of him. Set 4 don't do homework, nor do they attend the subsequent detentions, so I am curious now. I cast my eyes over the page, pausing once or twice to hush Quinn, who is sprawled on the floor complaining about 'growing pains'. I can feel Kamal's gaze on me, trying to judge my reaction. I shake my head a few times, chewing my lip, then lower the page and look him in the eye. He has no idea just how good this is, does he? So I tell him. 'This is breathtaking. This is astonishing. This is really, really good stuff.'

And I notice immediately the shift in atmosphere. Eliot has clocked my praise of his backrow buddy, and he's having none of it. He lays into Kamal – and me – with such aggression that even I am taken aback. And he called me a c*nt last week. But the casualty isn't me at all, because next lesson Kamal comes into the classroom with a different walk; a different attitude. And he hasn't done his homework, either. This goes on for most of Year 7, and I barely see a hint of the elegant writing that I know he's capable of. By Year 8, he is still languishing in Set 4. By Year 9, he is banned from school trips. He and Eliot are the ring-leaders of a 'challenging' group of boys who are all at risk of exclusion which, in this part of London, is one step away from being recruited into a gang.

Tribalism has teeth and it bites hard into the best kids, too, changing lives for ever. In the end, Kamal left school at 16 with a handful of worthless GCSEs and, quite incredibly, a 'C' grade in English. He was, after all, a great writer.

Freedom from Bullying

Bullying is a separate thing from the 'tribe-like' behaviour children display in most school environments. The two are connected, but can also play out differently.

When my daughter attended the Reception class of our local school, I would stand in the playground with her and wait for the bell to ring. Plenty of parents did the same, and we would stand there with babies on hips and toddlers round ankles, watching the kids play tag until it was time to go in. The Year 1 class, who formed a line next to Reception, seemed to have frequent trouble with this. There were daily behaviour problems – shouting, tears and pushing. I could see through the half-drawn blind of the classroom that their teacher was busy prepping the first lesson of the day and, almost invariably, the classroom assistant was engaged in conversation with one parent at the top of the queue. In short, nobody really had a clue what was going on between the children, and this is, I venture, quite standard operating procedure for a school. Think about it: how can you, honestly, have your eye on *all* of them *all* the time? You can't. So, back to the story.

One morning, I noticed there was a particularly vicious outburst from the back of the Year 1 line. Three girls had formed a semi-circle around another, much smaller girl, and they were all shouting at once. As usual, nobody wanted to get involved. Most likely, they were all 'troublemakers' and deserved each other, right? Well, that's not how I operate, so I waded in, barked at the girls to break it up and demanded to know what was going on. It wasn't difficult to figure out. The small child was blotchy with tears, while the three larger girls glared up at me defiantly, clearly not used to adult intervention. Their expressions read, 'We do what we want; back off'. I waited for the class to go in, then held their teacher back to explain the situation. I told her that, at the very least, there were four children in her class who were not in a positive state of mind to engage with much in the way of learning straight away. The teacher rolled her eyes comically and gave an exasperated expression, as if these girls were always causing her a headache with their bickering. As if the situation were equal (which it wasn't) and a case of typical 'girl dynamics' (which it was not, again). It was bullying, and it was quite obviously going to continue. This was a major episode for my husband and me in forming our eventual decision to homeschool, although at this point, none of our own children were involved. But I'd got the idea.

One in five school children report being bullied in the past year. I think the statistic is much higher, and from my years of secondary school teaching, I would be fairly confident in saying that many children don't report bullying because they know it won't be properly dealt with and the situation will, ultimately, be worse for them if they 'tell'. They are absolutely right. I can recall parents of children in my tutor group asking me candidly over the phone: 'Please tell us the truth; if we make our child come to you with the issue she is facing, will it be dealt with?' And my heart would skip a beat. Because of course I can make damned sure that doesn't happen in *my* classroom again. But what about the walk to the next lesson? The playground? The bus-ride home? Prison rules don't even come close to it, because the staff ratio is higher, and discipline is firmer.

But I can see you might not believe me, so I'll tell you another story. In the first week of my new job as an NQT (Newly Qualified Teacher) there was an incident in my form group. A Year 7 boy had told a girl sitting next to him that he was going to smash her teeth with a bottle and make her suck his penis. The girl was brave enough to come forward the next day, accompanied by her mother, who said she'd been crying non-stop and felt too terrified to come to school. By the time I began my second year at the same school, I wouldn't even blink at a story like this; they were so frequent and, sometimes, rather worse. I understand and respect parents who simply don't want their children exposed to this stuff.

Choosing to home-educate in order to avoid bullying or side-step the negative influences of school is not running away from reality. School is a far cry from reality, and the idea that children of any age should be 'toughened up' to bullying ignores two glaring problems with this theory.

1. Human children develop slowly and accumulate skills to 'deal with life' over the course of many years. A young person of 18, naïve or not, is of an appropriate age to know when a person is unkind or a comment is unpleasant and, hopefully, to consider the appropriate course of action. A child of five is still building their motor skills and basic understanding of the world, so making the threat of hostile bullying far more confusing and complex to deal with. Exposing children of this age to repeated harassment is, in fact, *delaying* their development rather than igniting some 'self-defence mechanism', because in fact, research shows us that children faced with a threatening situation freeze: their personal growth literally stops, and any chance of learning is of course out the window (Biddulph, 2013).

2. When we say that we are aiming to 'toughen up' our children, the implication is that we are expecting them to be bullied in adult life. This is a self-fulfilling prophecy. By exposing children to bullying (so often not picked up, or not properly addressed by the school) we are sending them a clear message: this is what happens, and you can't do anything about it. There is nowhere to escape in school, either. A child who receives this message often enough will eventually take the message on board and, in their adult life, might fail to remove themselves from a situation where bullying occurs, whether in the work-place or in a domestic relationship. They have become a victim, and they have lost the measure of what is acceptable.

It is important to remind ourselves here of the human impact that bullying and rivalry have on a developing child. Nobody who takes the time to witness and empathise with the experience of bullying can deny that this affects learning, and where it goes unchecked over months and years, it can destroy the mindset and life chances of an otherwise perfectly able child. The research is clear: any form of threat or harassment kills learning, as does the pressure of competition and assessment. We only need to refer to Maslow's Hierarchy of Needs (see Figure 1) to understand that a child operating under highly stressful or threatening circumstances is incapable of evolving to higher thinking and processing; their outlook literally stops at 'safety'. For children in this position, the mindset becomes

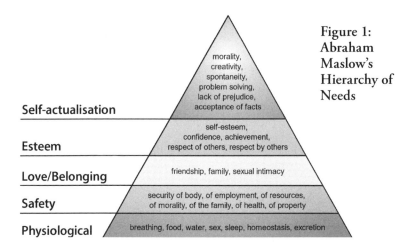

Figure 1: Abraham Maslow's Hierarchy of Needs

primal and target-driven, in the way that anybody *would* when trying to survive. They fail to reach out for genuine creativity and pleasure in the process.

I would place the recent Black Lives Matter movement and the backlash of violent police repression within this context. Bullying begins in schools, taking on new shapes and forms in the adult world. I haven't witnessed a two-year-old insult another child because of the colour of their skin. Yet many adults emerge from school carrying 'baggage' from the underlying racial conflicts which thrive in an institutionalised setting, where bullying is prevalent and the environment itself is divisive. Racism – by which here I mean specifically conscious or subconscious prejudice – is a form of bullying, and thrives wherever people feel oppressed, fearful and without true freedom. School is precisely this place and thus, far from 'bringing people together', it is a breeding ground for the development of 'them and us' polarity and the growth of extreme mindsets. And this is not just a 'playground problem', because schools themselves – through their curriculum, their lack of scrutiny, their exclusion statistics and their universal reluctance to use the word 'discrimination' when addressing internal disputes – clearly exhibit institutional racism. It is an issue that repeatedly fails to be addressed when seeking solutions to systemic racism. Of course we cannot tackle it 'through the system'; the system itself is a major contributor to the problem, and it always has been.

Ultimately, there are many reasons for home-educating, and bullying is just one of them; but I get it, one hundred per cent. Allowing your child to grow up free from bullying will almost always create a strong, fair-minded individual. Someone whose thought process has not been impacted by suffering, and who views other people as equals, not enemies. I have met a couple of children like this through teaching, but I have met many, many more within the homeschooling community. These kids simply don't pick on each other. They have closer adult supervision during the early, formative years when they are learning how to be social and respect each other; and significantly, they play openly in mixed age groups, free from competition and comparison. They have not been poisoned by the 'school' effect, and they would not tolerate a bully. It is reason enough to homeschool.

Finding Focus

By allowing your children to enjoy more freedom in their learning, you will quickly see their personal goals and interests shift. Many school children – and I would certainly have put our family in this category, so there's no judgement here – appear to be on a conveyor belt of adult-established targets and expectations which extend way beyond the classroom. Take a typical eight-year-old girl. Her entire day is governed by school, from the things she has to get ready first thing in the morning to the adult-directed structure of her academic day, and the homework she must complete in the evening. More than this, she might also have extra-curricular activities, such as gymnastics, which her parents (with the best of intentions) began taking her to when she was only five years old, and to which she now devotes two hours a week training. If she really stepped back and considered it, she might not know for sure whether she even enjoys gymnastics or not. But it makes her parents happy, and she has learnt that fulfilling adult expectations is the goal.

You know, the first thing my daughter dropped when we began home-educating was ballet. I was initially surprised and disappointed; she is, without hesitation, the best in her class, and I felt like this added a nice physical discipline to the week. But she was adamant: 'I don't like it.' So we quit. And quitting felt tough for *me*, not her, because I was brought up 'not to quit', and to stick at things and see them through, regardless of whether I was particularly interested, or considered an activity to have purpose in my adult life. This is just some of the baggage that I bring with me when I home-educate my children, and it is important that I leave it at the metaphorical door. Because that's not what homeschooling is about, at all. My kids, at least, know that.

Let's all agree that people mostly have a broad range of general skills, but are actually *good* at – even *passionate* about – just a few things in life. For most of us, and for the majority of children today, our talents and interests are something we might begin to discover in our early teenage years. We might devote some time outside of school working on these areas, but the majority of our time is planned for us and spread fairly evenly across a wide spectrum of skills and subjects. If you are a boy who likes football, that's great; you might be able to play for half an hour at lunchtime and then again on a Saturday morning. The problem here is that, although the idea of a 'broad education' seems admirable, it does not actually align with the way we operate as human beings, or as a collective society. Put simply, people are all good at different things. The sooner we figure this out for ourselves and begin cultivating our skills and interests, the more experts and transformative thinkers we will have – not to mention increased emotional well-being, productivity and job satisfaction. Turning out identically programmed people should never be what education is about. The state-led ideology of forming 'well-rounded' individuals is perhaps seductive, but it loses sight of the unique mindset of human beings, as well as the diverse and highly specialised nature of modern employment. The 'factory model' for schooling, by failing to evolve, creates a whole host of problems down the line, because the world 'out there' doesn't at all match what's happening in school.

In Part III, you will find a list of the key terms and concepts within the world of home education (p. 144). One of the approaches you'll read about is the Charlotte Mason method of exposing children to a 'rich diet' of the 'best ideas'; an educational approach still popular nearly 100 years on. When considering this particular philosophy within the context of enabling our children to 'find focus', I would encourage you to allow your children free rein to cultivate competencies relevant to the world we live in *today*; what we might call *Modern Mason*. The breath-taking speed of technological progress, global change, scientific developments, and the evolving landscape of employment opportunities – all mean that we would be short-sighted indeed to value, for example, letter-writing skills above editing software proficiency. Film, music and gaming are not just pastimes; they're a big business. And caring about the planet lacks context without relevant engagement with the platforms where projects are shared. In seeking to detox our children from the chaos of the school system, we must not look backwards to a 'golden time' of education. Young people are best placed to gauge their personal interests and seek reference points in the real world. Our job as home educators is to assist them in that process.

Being a homeschooling parent is a tough call, requiring more than just a strong coffee and a dose of good humour to get you through. In collaboration with a group of home educators whom I surveyed for this section, I have collated the following list of important tips for staying happy and healthy as a home educator.

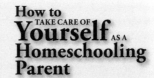

How to TAKE CARE OF Yourself AS A Homeschooling Parent

- Sleeping and waking: You are going to need sleep for this job! Bags of patience and buckets of energy don't just come out of thin air. Aim to be in bed not too late during the week, if possible. Many homeschooling parents do set an early alarm, though. This allows time to take a shower, get dressed, have a coffee and generally get 'ahead of the day'. It's up to you, but remember this isn't the same as the school run; the kids aren't going to just disappear for eight hours so you can do your tax return.

- Diet and exercise: Flexible homeschooling can be extremely demanding, so try to eat well if you can. Think: wholegrain, plenty of fresh fruit and vegetables, beans, fish and pulses. A good way to ensure you are all eating well is to encourage the kids to help out regularly with cooking healthy meals. Equally with exercise – try to just build it into your day. If you have younger children, you might be able to put your trainers on and take a run alongside their scooters, or with teenagers in tow you could choose to hit the gym or swimming pool together.

- Mobile phones and social media: A huge distraction and time zap for any parent is the time we spend on our mobile phones, especially when it comes to managing social media. This is especially important when you are homeschooling, though, as you are more than ever responsible for cultivating positive habits in your children. Try switching your phone off during the day, or placing it in a cupboard or drawer. 'Out of sight, out of mind' works for a lot of people.

- Bedtimes: Whatever the age and stage of our children, we all need some 'off duty' time to be able to unwind in preparation for another busy day. If your children are under the age of ten, be firm about the bedtime curfew, at least during the week. Older children might want to read with the light on for a while, but they should still be getting plenty of sleep at this stage. Teenagers' body clocks often change, and many will choose to go to bed late; but be clear that it's not okay to leave the house in a total mess for when everyone else wakes up.

- Backing off: Home-educating is most effective and enjoyable when learning is at least to some extent child-led, so try to back off and resist the urge to dictate the learning process. Many unschooling parents (we will define exactly what this means in the next chapter) never plan or schedule learning, but rather keep a retrospective journal of the learning that takes place each day. Relaxing into home education, and allowing your children genuine autonomy in their own learning, constitute a key step towards thriving in this educational setting, and so discovering what your children are really capable of.

- The world of work: It is certainly a challenge to figure out your working life and how this will fit alongside home-educating. It is, however, a testament to the powerful impact of homeschooling on people's lives that many families change their careers and entire lifestyles around making this work. I know we have. Working flexible hours from home, or tag-teaming part-time, or shift-based jobs with your partner – these are going to be the way forward here.

- Know your triggers: Stress affects learning, and you want as little of it as possible when you're home-educating. We cannot control what life throws at us, but one thing we can work on as parents is identifying our stress 'triggers', and finding ways to pre-empt and manage these scenarios. Walking away from a situation, counting to ten, and deep breathing are all really effective stress-management tools, but only when you know what pushes your buttons in the first place. This can be your homework – one to figure out!

- Get involved: To fully embrace homeschooling, you need to understand that you are learning, too. This can be incredibly liberating, and often changes your entire family dynamic, as 'mum' and 'dad' become more complete and interesting individuals for children to engage with. You might discover a new skill, hobby or topic you're interested in, listen to more music, be more respectful of your own needs and desires, and start setting ambitious goals for your own life. What makes you a fantastic homeschooling parent is the fact that you're showing your children how to live well and fully, every day.

Whole-family Benefit

We have this beautiful upright piano in our house. My husband picked it up for free on eBay and surprised me with it, after we relocated from London. I haven't played the piano in years but still, it's nice to know he's still inspired to do daft things on my behalf. It stood in the hallway of our house, with some occasional plonking, for about a year. Then we started homeschooling. I was hopeful that the kids might want to incorporate music into their education, as this was not offered until Year 4 at the local school, and I had always considered it a great loss. I wondered how to capture their interest without literally sitting down to 'teach' them, and I decided – surprise, surprise – to take up playing again. Home education does this to you; it has everyone going that extra mile.

But what is the *opposite* of homeschooling? It is school itself. And what is the opposite of willingly going the 'extra mile'? It is going somewhere you don't really want to. Let me explain. Almost every parent I have spoken to within a personal or professional context has described to me what I believe is an almost *universal experience* for the modern parent: the sinking feeling when your child turns three. There are few parents out there who won't identify with this. In the UK, three is the age that most children are eligible to begin preschool and, for parents, it is the year when they must make choices regarding their child's primary-school education. This can be a daunting process, not least because schools seem incredibly big, impersonal institutions where we struggle to imagine our very young children coping. But they all do, eventually. Children are resilient, and can adapt to some exceptionally challenging situations – although naturally, there is sometimes a heavy price to pay. And we are right to worry; four is far too young to be starting school. The rationale is purely economic, and the counter-argument that children who *aren't* forced to do this are somehow disadvantaged has absolutely no substance.

In fact, when we send our children to school in distress, or force them to complete homework tasks against their will, we break family bonds, and distance ourselves from the natural responsibility we feel for our own children. It is not difficult to see how trust can break down irreparably in situations where children feel powerless in an adult-dominated world, and one in which, significantly, their own parents are complicit in the coercion. Typically, the effect of this can be the familiar scenario where a child becomes rapidly independent and 'distant' from their parents, wrapped up in their own world and glued to the screen of their mobile phone or computer game, where a virtual life is going on. In more extreme cases, though, this disintegration of the family unit and sense of powerlessness for young people can lead to various control-based manifestations of distress, including eating disorders, substance abuse, self-harm, and *parent phobia*. We will often hear the parents of children whose lives have unravelled in this way comment sadly that he or she was 'always such an affectionate child', and I think that's the way it goes. The closer the bond, the harder the fall.

It is extremely common, after some initial distress during the 'settling' phase at the start of school, for children to become highly invested in this institution which they never *voluntarily* sought to attend. Many children become obsessed with their classroom teacher, idolising them and seeking their approval at every opportunity. Others form strong 'friendship' groups, and parents quickly adapt to the apparent insignificance of their opinion compared to what 'so-and-so' says, or what 'so-and-so's mum lets them do at the weekend. This is to be expected. When we break attachments that were formed in the womb, and coerce our children physically and mentally into a hard regime that they're far too young to understand, we must expect that attachments will form elsewhere. It is, as always, part of our children's *survival programming*. We drive our children into forming desperate connections during their early school years, and then wonder why they are so powerfully influenced by their peer group at age 15. It is a predictable enough backlash, and one which, it seems, could be avoided if school were non-compulsory and began at an older age.

No healthy four-year old seeks independence from the family unit, and indeed, forcing a child to do so generally creates a fragile constitution and a tendency to forge dependency elsewhere. Left to their own devices and allowed to learn at their own pace at home, children will naturally seek steps towards independence and separation from their parents over a period of several years, with no need for coercion.

Homeschool flips the school model on its head because, fundamentally, home-educating parents don't believe the fallacy that putting children through such trauma is somehow beneficial. Ask any homeschooling family why they're doing it and you will get largely the same response. It boils down to two things:

1. We do not believe that school is a healthy environment for our children to grow and learn.

2. We believe that we are responsible for, and capable of delivering, effective education at home.

They are simple enough principles, but they change everything. Without school as a source of stress, many of the conflicts that exist between parents and children dissolve almost instantly, and family harmony is restored. Without parents having to enforce school values, they are free to be more 'themselves' and feel more relaxed with their children. The relationship is no longer a battle of wills, but a co-existing of equals. You can learn as much from your children as they can learn from you, and we are never 'done' with learning. This understanding is the key to experiencing the *whole-family benefits* of home-educating.

Was there, for example, a hobby or sport that you enjoyed as a child but have since let go of? Or somewhere you have always wanted to travel, but things got in the way? My guess is that within a year or two of homeschooling, you'll have ticked all these boxes, and more. Because, funnily enough, the longer you homeschool, the more you realise that it is not about being a 'teacher' to your children, but rather a good role model. If you want your children to read, the best thing you can do is sit down with a cup of tea and a book. If you want them to be curious about the world, you must model that behaviour yourself. This has a revitalising effect on families, and breathes new life into parenting, sibling dynamics and even your couple.

We might also refer to this shift in dynamic as *being present*, compared to the *waiting game* of school- and office-based life. Our lives can often feel like they are passing us by, measured out in alarm clocks and breaktimes, weekends and half-terms. We spend all our time gravitating towards the next 'thing': seeing our friends on Monday, getting to the end of a boring double period, looking forward to the next Bank Holiday, or making it home on Friday night. There is a madness in this frantic culture – with its non-stop cycle of anticipation and anti-climax – that only reveals itself when we take a step back. Home education enables us to see the world, and our place within it, from a different perspective. It teaches us to slow down and honour our parental responsibility, as well as contemplating how we might like to work on our own personal development. Families begin home-educating for any number of reasons, but they stick with it because of the *whole-family benefits* that it brings.

Here are just a few ways in which you as a person might change through home education:

- More time and inclination to read books and listen to interesting radio shows.
- Genuine interest in your children's questions and ideas.
- Better understanding of 'what matters', and hence less battles.
- Much less shouting.
- Learning to trust your children.
- Feeling less like 'mum' or 'dad' and more yourself; a person, with dreams and ideas.
- Embracing the importance of your position as a role model.
- Less housework and more tree-climbing.
- Better eating, more exercise and more fresh air.

- Developing a connection with 'world issues', and finding ways to show support.

- Less hostility towards others; more love and empathy.

- Reflecting on your own education, career choices and what you want from life.

- Laughing and playing with ease, both with your children and partner.

Home education isn't just about children; it reshapes the entire family. And by shifting the focus from the child as a 'project' at the centre of an adult world, to the whole family learning and developing as equals, there is a more natural place for the child to understand personal growth in context, and seek the benefits for themselves.

Learning without Boundaries

We have looked in some detail so far at the various boundaries of the school system, including timetabling, age segregation, teacher-led learning, the focus on assessment and the limited scope of the National Curriculum and Exam Boards. So how, exactly, does home education liberate your child from these constraints? Just a few of the ways are listed below.

- An individually tailored curriculum (or no curriculum) allows your child to pursue their actual interests.

- Home-based flexibility enables children to range between activities and learning, becoming experts in key areas of interest.

- Child-led learning is a recipe for blue-sky thinking, liberating the individual from the lifelong trap of 'pleasing the teacher' and instead, focusing on their own goals.

- Without constant assessment, children's minds are more relaxed to learn, and the focus is on education, not on passing exams.

- A daily structure guided by your child's body clock and your *whole family rhythm* enables more complex learning to happen during peak times within the day.

- By allowing children to learn through play in mixed age groups, the atmosphere for learning is better, and children develop their collective knowledge by sharing.

For a couple of years, I found myself marking GCSE exam papers for two of the UK Exam Boards. My initial decision to change Exam Board was because I didn't think I was a good fit with the first company – but I quickly discovered that they're all the same. Examiners are encouraged to 'mark positively', the result being that almost everyone passes and there is a glut of mediocre grades around the middle band. At the top end, though, examiners become extremely picky, and there is – especially in English – a good deal of dispute over exactly who the top marks are awarded to. This is for two reasons:

1. Examiners mark scripts using highly prescriptive and long-winded Assessment Criteria, which blur the instinct of professional judgement.

2. The Mark Scheme simply doesn't go high enough to award the really exceptional students, and this affects the integrity of assessment for *all* students.

Why am I telling you this? Because I want to make it clear to you that the exam system – and thus the school system itself – really is limiting. Whether your child is struggling to cope at school or whether they are an academic 'high flyer', the very nature and structure of the organisation runs contrary to how we instinctively learn and develop as individuals; and it fails spectacularly at the final hurdle – examinations. I want my children to be free to learn without such boundaries, and I hope that there will be more people out there who've been raised this way when they grow up.

I find there is a lot of talk about our 'broken society' and the problems we face, but time and time again we fail to identify the real culprit. We perceive public education as a perfect system, untouchable and unquestionable; a collection of formidable authority figures and consummate professionals working tirelessly for the benefit of your child. This vision is false. Teachers are people, and policy-makers are politicians. And I am not judging you for being fooled by this; it is a great charade. What is more, after a decade of working in various areas of education myself, I fell for it, too. I should have known better, but I was scared of stepping out of line. School rules take a lifetime to unlearn.

In a Nutshell

- Home education is an historically proven and effective way of learning.

- Homeschooling removes children from the destructive impact of school-based tribalism and bullying.

- Families who choose this path enjoy a better quality of life and can find their natural rhythm – part of the Whole Family Benefits of home-educating.

- Children who are homeschooled can find their 'niche', and are not limited by arbitrary constraints on their learning.

In Part III, I will answer some questions that you may still have about home education and how it works practically, legally and logistically. For more information on the ideology of home education and child psychology, check the 'Further Reading and Resources' section for titles at the end of the book.

PART II

The Stories of Home-Educating

'My favourite home-education book is called This Is Not a Maths Book *because I like the exciting stuff in it, like drawing cardioids with a compass. My favourite story is 'Dragon Masters' and my favourite class is street dance. I don't want to go to school because you have to go there every day and there are too many children. I would miss out on doing fun stuff at home and I wouldn't be able to properly play with my friends. When I grow up, I would like to be a deep-sea diver, drive a motor boat and be an underwater archaeologist. Being home-educated is really nice because you get to do lots of fun stuff like snap circuits, and going for a walk in the middle of the day.'*

Gabriel, age 6

STORY 1

Welcome to Homeschooling

by **Emilie Bailey**

• deschooling • finding your feet • healing trauma

We started homeschooling on 13 January 2020. The kids had only been back to school for three days after Christmas when we decided to pull them out. It felt wild at the time; dramatic and more than slightly frightening. Only two weeks prior to making this decision with my husband Ben, I'd had a conversation with a close friend who knew of someone home-educating her two children. My friend was incredulous that anyone would do it – *could* do it. For instance, what if the children grew up wanting to be doctors – what then? I'd shrugged her question off, not knowing the answer. In fact, I didn't know anything about home education back then. All I could say was that I didn't know, but I suspected that actually, my eldest son in particular would probably *love* to be homeschooled.

The one thing at that point that I did know was that our child had become miserable: stressed, sick and hating going to school. Honestly, we were facing continual illness, low energy, memory loss, heart palpitations, extreme picky eating, daily soiling and wetting, low self-esteem and massive rages (often in the mornings prior to school), and usually at some point in the afternoon. During that first week back after the Christmas holiday, the rages had cranked up several notches, and couldn't even wait for the safety of home as they had done before. Now they had begun on the journey home, which wasn't at all long – the school is only a stone's throw across the road. All this at the tender age of six, just a little over a term into Year 1. What had happened to our once joyful, confident boy? I mean, a year ago he had even been asked to walk other children into the classroom at the start of Reception because he was one of the only new children not crying at the gate, so eager was he to start school and 'be brave'. He was popular, too. Very quickly he had friends who in the morning shouted greetings his way and, in the afternoon, would wave goodbye until we disappeared down the road and around the corner.

It's a lovely, small community where we live, and both my husband and I work within it mostly from home; and the school is welcoming, too. At least, compared with the others. We liked how gentle and nurturing it felt; the

Deputy Head had undergone 'emotions coaching' and was teaching this to the rest of the staff and to the children. She also held 'positive parenting' classes which seemed in alignment with our gentle-parenting ethos. How lucky we felt to have such a school on our doorstep for our sons! But unfortunately, it still wasn't enough. It had gotten to the point where every night, my eldest was anxious about going in the next day, and the mornings were distressing from the word 'go', with him upset and then refusing to get ready for school – culminating in us practically having to drag him across the road sullen-faced, almost crying, to force him through the school gate. It had become unbearable.

At the time, it was difficult to lay a finger on what exactly was happening to make him feel this way. When asked, he would say he hated being away from home for six hours a day, and that he didn't like being 'forced' to do things; for example, sitting down and being made to read and write. I would now add: too much structure, too much constraint, and the chopping and changing between subjects and activities, even if he hadn't quite finished the previous task. He's a child that likes to take his time. And he's also quite a proud, private person. Having to ask to go to the loo – often not getting there in time – and having to use the smelly wet toilets; all this was torture to him. Also getting changed for PE in front of everyone; he hated having to show his underwear for fear of being teased.

He'd keep quiet about interactions with friends in the playground that he found hard to deal with because he'd learnt that telling a teacher didn't change much, and in the classroom, work that he found too hard made him feel stupid; whilst work that he found boring he struggled to keep a focus on, and it made him angry inside that he still had to do it. Lunchtimes were particularly hard, especially dealing with food that he was coerced to eat. He was a 'good boy' at school, very compliant, so the staff couldn't tell there was anything wrong until towards the end of his time there. He was keeping it all in and, at home, we were on the receiving end.

The evening of 5 January, my husband had been out to dinner with a friend, who happened to be a teacher. Ben asked him about his thoughts on homeschooling. The conversation that ensued completely convinced my husband that this had to be the way forward for our eldest. He was so excited at the prospect that he messaged me about it whilst on the train home, then we stayed up talking about it and researching online until we both fell asleep at almost 3 a.m. We woke up convinced that this was a very possible solution, but I needed to know more. Anna and I had become friends years ago, both living in West London, but we'd lost touch for a little while after she'd moved away; both of us having had second children and Anna expecting her third. We were busy! But at Christmas we'd been back in touch, and she had told me that she was homeschooling her children. *Wow!* I remember thinking, *what a super woman she must be!* Then for a few weeks over the festivities, I didn't think of it any more, until that Monday night when I messaged Anna, desperately seeking some advice on our home-ed idea. She basically told us to 'go for it'.

After an evening on the phone together, I ordered the book *Free Range Education* (Dowty, 2000), and devoured it in just a few nights. I read a lot online, too, and exchanged regular conversations with Anna, as it felt like such a huge, life-changing decision to be making. It was nice to share our thinking and experiences. Quite quickly, I also discovered Ross Mountney's blog and books, *Learning without School* and *A Home Education Notebook*. I couldn't believe the connection I was feeling towards these homeschooling families that I was reading about, and how incredibly rapidly home education seemed to be becoming the right way for us. I couldn't believe the similarities between our children and theirs, their fundamental beliefs on life and ours; beliefs I hadn't registered even having, until reading about them now. *How* had I not ever entertained the idea of home education before?

Ben and I also consulted our parents. We have ex-teachers on both sides, so we were curious what they would say. Everyone was supportive – much more so than we'd expected. But then everyone who knew us well, knew of the struggles we'd been having, and especially those of our eldest, who'd so suddenly become a shadow of his former self.

By Thursday 9 January we had made our decision that we were going to start homeschooling, if that was what the kids wanted. Our plan was to sit them down on the Saturday to explain all about it and gauge their reaction. We hadn't been sure what to do about our three-year old, as he wasn't despising going into preschool; but then again he often wasn't too thrilled about it, either. Besides, we already felt pretty converted to the possible joys of homeschooling, and we felt that if we offered this to one child, it had to be offered to both. So that is what we did.

I will never forget our eldest's reaction when we told him the news; that if he didn't want to, he need never go to school again. He literally couldn't wait for us to finish speaking to say 'yes!' *Yes, yes, yes!...* So quick was his answer that I spent the rest of the weekend revisiting the same conversation with him to make sure he understood what this really entailed, should we send a letter to the school on Monday requesting his de-registration. Yet it was a resounding 'yes' all weekend. And our youngest, too. '*Yes, yes, yes, yes, yes!*' We celebrated by going out as a family to one of the local National Trust parks that sunny Sunday, and we became members for the year, thinking that we were now going to need new places to visit whilst other people were in school. It was a mixture of thrill and excitement, of nerves and boldness. I felt a massive sense of freedom and relief; mostly for my eldest child, but actually for all of us.

It took a few days to receive a reply from the school which I found quite nerve-wracking; but when it did come through, it was kind, supportive and informative. It told us we might expect a visit from the council at some point; and, sure enough, within three weeks we received a letter from an inclusion officer saying they'd heard we intended to home-educate our children, and could they visit us at home to talk it through and offer any support we might need. I had read that we were not obliged to accept any visits from the council, and that often these visits for others had not been positive. But the letter seemed quite warm in nature, and we felt we had nothing to hide; so we accepted. and I'm pleased to say it was a positive experience for us.

The inclusion officer was also a mother, had been a primary school teacher and clearly understood we were doing this for the well-being of our children. We actually enjoyed it! She explained a few things that I had already read up about, like not having to follow the National Curriculum for example, but it was reassuring to hear it from someone 'official'. That first week of no school was glorious; and our eldest was euphoric. It was like a huge weight had been lifted from his small shoulders. Colour came back to his cheeks; he was joyous, he suddenly played beautifully with his younger brother, and he was inquisitive again, eagerly asking question after question – which I felt slightly pressured by at first! Mornings were no longer a rush-filled nightmare, and nights no longer anxious.

Because we had started home-educating rather unexpectedly, both Ben and I had quite a full diary for a few weeks, which meant that to begin with it would be a bit of a juggle. Before embarking on our new way of life, we had decided that we would share the responsibility of home-educating, as we both work for ourselves, and wanted to continue this way if possible. Ben would be in charge two days a week and I would take over three days a week, meaning we could both squeeze in some work around being with the kids.

It was manic at first! Despite having read a bit about unschooling and thinking how wonderful it sounded, I still couldn't quite let go of the notion that we ought to be teaching them particular subjects in a scheduled way. I also couldn't help but feel some pressure from well-meaning friends and family who didn't understand what we were doing. Looking back now, it was actually very helpful that we were so busy with work those first few weeks, as it meant we couldn't dedicate much time to setting up a schedule or drawing up a curriculum. We had some literacy and numeracy workbooks – still mostly unused – from the summer before, which we brought out on to the kitchen table most days, and we did a lot of arts and crafts, which we naturally do a lot at home anyway. But mostly the kids played and made up their own games, and we went out a lot so as to escape the workbooks which stared at us from the kitchen table, still untouched. We don't even bother with that now.

Advice from those 'in the know' had been to join a local group ASAP, as it can take time to find where you might fit in, and because it helps to have that support, especially in the early days. The first group we went to was very welcoming and everyone was lovely, but it just didn't feel quite right. This may have been due to it only being 'week 2'; we were still so new to it all, and I was feeling a bit flustered at the best of times. I also hadn't been prepared for the sense of loss I was feeling at no longer being part of the school. I kept asking the kids if they were okay, if they were missing school or their friends but they gave a resounding 'nope' every time. We did keep up with playdates, so I suppose that was enough for them. Ben felt no loss either; it was just me!

Then about a week later, one of the school mums I knew was homeschooling her eldest contacted me, congratulating us on pulling the kids out of school; she'd heard from one of the neighbours. She belonged to a home-ed group very near us which sounded wonderful and right up our street, so we tried it and loved it. It was great to have someone there we knew, who could show us around and introduce us to other families there. We started attending every week through the rest of January, February and into early March, signed the kids up to a mini-athletics class there, and were about to start the Drama workshop, trampolining and climbing, when the Coronavirus took hold; and so for now, understandably, everything is closed.

So, where are we? I am writing this in mid-April, almost a month into COVID-19 lockdown, and I feel grateful for many things, including the fact that we started home-educating when we did, and that we did it voluntarily. I really feel for the many parents who have been forced into it and who are struggling right now. It seems like many families feel they have to re-create 'school at home', as well as also working remotely, of course. How unbelievably stressful! I am grateful to have discovered unschooling, as this seems to be the way we naturally do things. I doubt we are 100 per cent there with it yet, but it is still early days and we are learning all the time.

I am still pulling late nights, reading fanatically about home education and unschooling online and in books, and now writing this! There are some wonderful blogs out there giving guidance, ideas and encouragement to home-ed parents, and even to non-home-ed parents, with plenty of suggestions to help families function better during the lockdown. I do know a few friends with children in school who started off quite structured – trying to complete all the school work thrown at them – who are now much more relaxed; and I even know of one parent who is currently unschooling after reading a home-ed writer on Facebook and becoming inspired.

I could never have thought our lives would change so much for the better in four short months. That's not to say it's all plain sailing; is it *ever*? And wouldn't that be boring; what lessons would we learn? But right now, we are feeling healthy, mostly unstressed, excited at the prospect of our children's future, and of our future, too. Already we are planning what we would like to do after lockdown eases. My eldest's dream is to exhibit his art work, and one day sell it. Yesterday, after declining my youngest's school place for September (he is still adamant he does not want to go to school but we had applied back in December prior to homeschooling), I took photographs of my eldest's paintings and set him up with an online gallery on Instagram, which I now manage for him. One of our old school's organisers who has seen his gallery has already offered him an exhibition at either the Summer or Christmas fair, and he has some prospective buyers too, plus lots of words of encouragement from other artists online.

My youngest, meanwhile, is *Star Wars*-mad and has some impressive light-sabering moves; it's all he wants to do right now. We're thinking along the lines of potentially discovering some form of martial arts with him, or perhaps drama and dance; we'll see. A family trip at some point would be nice too, especially now we are not constrained by school term times.

We feel lucky. And I can see on their faces that the boys feel it, too.

Emilie is a photographer and tweets as @emiliebailey

STORY 2

Buckle Up, Buttercup

by **Anna Dusseau**

• a homeschool morning • then and now • addressing change

It is just after 7 o'clock, and the pale light coming through the curtains tells me it will be another chilly morning. This is February, before the world went into isolation, and I am rubbing my sore neck after a rough night with the baby. Teething sucks. Beyond the blinds, I can hear the rumble of tyres on gravel and the thud of doors slamming, as the neighbours bundle into their cars and begin the journey to work and school. We aren't rushing anywhere, though.

I get up, pull on a jumper and make my way to the kitchen, leaving the baby and his big brother sleeping in bed a little longer. They need it. They are both growing like sunflowers – their appetite voracious, and their mood grouchy when woken too early. And we have, after all, done our fair share of school runs. I push the button on the coffee machine and close my eyes, listening to the clunk of the boiler kicking in, the splutter of an engine starting across the road. It is Tuesday morning. We have been homeschooling for six months.

My daughter is always the first to rise after me. I'm sipping my coffee and flicking through the paper when she comes padding in, 'den hair' alarmingly high this morning and eyes shining as she slaps Tom Fletcher's *The Creakers* down on the counter and slides in beside me. She is one of those children who goes around with their nose in a book, to the point that you have to actively remind her that there is a road coming up, or that the food is hot, or that she's looking a bit green in the back of the car and let's put it down for the last part of the journey, shall we?

It's funny how things have changed. She never used to be a bookworm, and in fact was rather resistant to reading when we had the post-school spellings and phonics book showdown. 'I've read it before', she would complain. 'Why do I have to read it again?' I could never really answer that one. Nor could I find a fun way to engage her with the weekly spelling test. But we don't bother with any of that now. She is six years old and can breeze through a chapter of Phillip Pullman; I'm pretty sure she can spell okay. Or that she will do, when she's ready. Down the hallway, the boys are waking up.

Since we started homeschooling, breakfast has become a leisurely affair, and today is no exception. We eat healthily because we have the time to, and I suppose we make food preparation and nutrition an integral part of home education. This morning it's dippy eggs and soldiers which my four-year-old son has buttered and cut himself, so they are slightly wonky. 'What do you call this?', I tease him, and he looks up from his comic book. 'Half a rectangle? A demi-fangle?' I laugh at my own joke. He frowns disapprovingly and goes back to his comic. 'It's still a quadrangle', he murmurs, shoving two pieces into his mouth at once and chewing slowly.

Maths is his thing; a fact I have only discovered since homeschooling began. And he's gone from a rather shy boy who cried and clung to me every morning, hating the school run and hating his nursery school, to this little guy who is so gripped by *The Life of Fred* maths series that his mental arithmetic is actually faster than his sister and, at our home-ed forest school group, will muck in with climbing trees and playing chase without so much as a backward glance. Nobody can believe how confident and articulate he has become, seemingly overnight. I guess he is in the right environment now and I wish I had figured this out a lot sooner. Swallowing my guilt, I pull a face at the baby and hand him another spoonful of peanut butter. Whatever the size of your family, the youngest is always the wild card, right? This one lives on peanut butter and pickles.

No two days are the same in homeschooling, and although today is looking busy – music, choir, library and friends for dinner – this particular Tuesday ends up, predictably, crafting its own course. It is the day that begins with the tale of the Golden Fleece and ends up with popcorn and pyjamas. And all the moments in between, from my older two pouring over the mythology chapter of our much-loved and battered *Cartoon History of the Universe*, to the Argonauts puppet show behind the sofa for which my husband receives a handmade ticket when he wakes from his night shift. Then there's the look of surprise on the librarian's face when my four-year old asks what books they have on the hydra. And finally, the sight of them piled on the sofa with their friends that evening, eating pizza and popcorn, having spent the afternoon making monster traps in the woods at the back of our house – now mesmerised by the 1963 film of *Jason and the Argonauts*. The point is that this kind of immersive, child-led learning journey is the dream of any teacher worth their salt. It's just so *hard* to pull it off in the school classroom. In the world of homeschooling, though, this is the extraordinary everyday.

It's difficult to write a book about home education without implicit criticism of the school system. The very fact that we are choosing to reorganise our lives around committing to homeschooling indicates a problem. Why do so many families like us prefer to see their taxes pay for schools which their own children do not benefit from, rather than participate in that world? The issues are complex and, overwhelmingly, what I want is to give you something positive to take away. I was, after all, doing the school run myself only a year ago; I get it.

And so, after bathtime and bed on this chilly day in February, I find myself sat cross-legged in front of the laptop, chewing my sleeve, not knowing how to begin a book about home education. The living room is still littered with cardboard puppets, six-headed sock hydras, and the smell of buttered popcorn. At least I don't have to get everyone up and dressed at the crack of dawn any more, bundling book-bags and the baby over one shoulder while fumbling with frozen fingers for the car keys. Okay then, shall we start there? No more alarms, people. Switch off and plug in.

Anna tweets as @NotTheSchoolRun and blogs at www.homeschoolguru.org.

Story 3

It Takes a Village

by **Ciaran Sneddon**

• homeschool memoir • rural childhood • exams and employment

There is a moment directly after you've told someone you're home-educated where you can see their face flicker between confusion, concern, surprise and a mental weigh-up as to whether or not they should ask the question that just popped into their heads. This second of hesitation reveals what that next question would be. If they seem confused, they'll splutter something like, 'Oh wow! I'd never have guessed – you seem quite normal!' and then instantly backtrack on the notion that being taught at home is abnormal. If their initial reaction is one of concern, they might adopt a gentle tone and condole with, 'But you have friends now!' A surprised response often leads to the most pleasant of follow-up comments, praising the fact that I've turned out alright after all that. However, by far the most common reaction is, 'Why on earth did your parents *do* that?'.

It is, I think, a fair question. The answer is naturally quite complicated, with many factors influencing mum and dad's decision. I grew up in a very

small village nestled in the east coast of Scotland, bordered along one side by woodland and by fields on another. It was as stereotypical as you could imagine a 'wee' Scottish village to be. There was even a supposedly haunted, half-ruined castle within ten minutes' walk, occupied by a rather peculiar family with a penchant for kilts. The village itself was one of the main causes of my homeschooled childhood; the local primary school had just two teachers to cover seven year-groups, which created a challenging dynamic, as we would soon discover.

My parents got the first flavour of home education when I was around the age of three. My elder sister's September birthday meant that my parents could legally choose to keep her out of school for one more year, as she had not turned five before the term started. During the year that followed, my parents discovered the joy of home education – both were social workers, with no history of 'teaching' – and one of our closest friends was also still at home, having similarly deferred entry.

The next summer came, and after a few months of seeing my sister off at the school gates and enjoying the sole attention of my parents, I realised things were changing back once again, and my sister would be learning at home. There were many reasons for this decision. The teachers were distracted by running several classes at once, making for a restricted learning experience; my sister had not gelled with her classmates; and my parents missed the joys of homeschooling.

By the time I was due to start school the following year, there was really no question that I would be entering formal education. Our family unit had become accustomed to learning together, and I was happy to work away on materials aimed at my older sister. Heading into the first year of primary school would have felt like a step backwards, I suppose, and so I sort of accidentally became home-educated, too. I wouldn't set foot in a school until I was an adult visiting for work.

Of course, in those early years it didn't feel particularly unusual to be taught at home. Many of my childhood friends were in the same boat as me, and we would regularly meet up with groups of fellow home educators. One of the things I *do* remember is having a very inter-generational friendship group. I think this was intentional on my parents' part, and I suspect partially in response to the many 'your children will be lonely...' or 'they'll turn out antisocial...' comments. For a big portion of my pre-teen years, and even beyond, the 'taxi service of mum and dad' would run my sister and me between a packed programme of extra-curricular activities every single night. These included youth choirs and football teams, natural history groups of pensioners, and a French night class at our local college.

I often reflect that I was very fortunate to enjoy a Famous Five-like existence as a youngster, which I don't think too many of my generation were afforded. Without the restrictions of a classroom, I was free to spend my days in all sorts of ways: clambering across the countryside to count butterflies, zipping across the loch in a sailboat to the island where we had built a team shelter, enjoying a cookery class on the beach, where we produced salt from sea water like hunter-gatherers, writing poetry and sketching in the middle of a millennia-old stone circle.

These freewheeling days often blur into one, but there are quirks of my parents' teaching styles that stick out from the hazy memories. My dad – a man with an unhealthy obsession for any TV programmes that involve antiques being sold at auction – would get us to watch *Bargain Hunt* with him under the pretence of it being a maths lesson. 'Figure out the percentage loss', he'd say, as Tim Wonnacott frowned at a Clarice Cliff failing to meet its pre-sale estimation. Mum's approach was more eclectic. There were the 'French stir fries' that we would sizzle up on the beach, allowed to communicate only in French until we'd finished our plates (or should that be *assiettes*?), and the creative-writing prompts that required us to create elaborate set-ups with our Playmobil toys, with accompanying illustrations or free writing.

She experimented with different teaching techniques too. In the early days, it was very hands-on and practical. I remember her often saying something like, 'Why would you just sit and read about the Romans? Why wouldn't you go and see an *actual* Roman fort?' That explained the weekend trip to Hadrian's Wall, where we decided we deserved an 'I walked the length of Hadrian's Wall' t-shirt, even though we had only traipsed along a relatively short section. I dread to think how many Historic Scotland and National Trust worksheets we got through during our field trips to various attractions during those years. Whenever we did a good bit of work at home, we would 'earn points' that would add up to being able to go to another event or historic building. The idea of a class going on just one field trip a year always felt a bit galling; and I remember a feeling of *schadenfreude* as my school-going friends had to leave after just one talk at the Edinburgh Book Festival, as I swanned around with a weekend's worth of tickets to different talks.

As we got older, things naturally became more study-focused. Each week, my sister and I would receive a list of tasks for that week, and as soon as we had completed them our time was our own. As a big fan of having time to do what I wanted, this approach worked well, and I credit it as being the reason why I have a good level of self-motivation today.

Of course, as the years rolled on by the questions changed. It was no longer, 'Do you have any friends?', but rather, 'How are you going to do your exams?'.

This has always been the part of my home-education journey about which I have found the hardest to be ardently and unbudgingly positive, because in truth my experience was a neat combination of luck and rule-easing. I was always comfortable with learning; and as long as you don't ask me to take on a particularly complicated algebra problem, I'm pretty happy with most academic subjects. Of course, if you're an employer or university curriculum leader, you might not believe me until I present some sort of qualification to you.

In Scotland, doing exams if you're home-educated is made all the more challenging because our qualifications aren't handed out after one big test. Instead, your grades are given out on the basis of a year or two's coursework. This is hard to replicate outside the classroom environment, and so it was essentially a non-starter for me to match my peers' qualifications. I don't think this is the case in England, where homeschooled kids can sit national qualifications in the gymnasium of their local school, along with everyone else.

Thankfully, though, I never felt the calling to be a doctor or a lawyer (and if I had, I might have hopped into school for the last few years of my education). Instead, my interests always lay with writing and story-telling; and by the time I was having to seriously think about life after home education, I had built up a wealthy portfolio of work experience at local newspapers and radio stations. I had made short films with friends, both documentary and drama, and had a working knowledge of editing softwares. This combination was enough to secure me an interview, and subsequently a place, on a media course at my local further education college, despite not officially meeting the entry criteria. At that point I was aged just 15, and several years younger than my classmates. That course got me an interview for a two-year journalism course at the same college, which in turn allowed me to jump into the final year of a BA (Hons) at an English university. By the age of 18 I had already graduated with a first-class degree.

In the year before I graduated from university, my family threw a party in our local village hall. It was inspired by the expression 'It takes a village to raise a child', and all of the invited guests were people who had been part of that 'village' for my sister and me. Looking around, there were all the parents who had sat with mum and dad over countless cups of tea, while their homeschooled children joined me for my self-hosted book club. I spent the evening with my choir leaders, pensioners from the natural history groups, my college French teacher, and of course friends from school and home ed.

In retrospect, I didn't really grow up in that tiny village in Scotland. I grew up in a village founded by my parents, with the best interests of my sister and me flowing right through it.

Ciaran is a writer for The Week Junior *and tweets as @ciaransneddon.*

Story 4

How Did We End Up Here?

by **Nana-Adwoa Mbeutcha**

- doing it differently • our big family • growth mindset

If I look back, I've never really been one to follow the trend. When everyone got a Nokia 3310, I opted for a Panasonic XXX. When all my friends were going on boozy party-hard summer holidays, I was on a Christian retreat. And when soon-to-be brides dieted in the lead-up to their Big Day, I decided to eat *more* in the lead-up to mine! So it doesn't really come as a big surprise that when most people are sending their kids to school, I've chosen not to. It's a curious story, though; and in a way, I've actually surprised myself here, because educating my children myself at home was not something that initially sparked my interest at all!

When my daughter, who is my eldest, was born in 2014, I just assumed she would do all the normal things, like poop, cry and attend school. However, one 'fateful day' when she was still very young, my husband floated the idea of home education by me. I practically laughed in his face. In fact, I dismissed it

so much that I don't even remember much about the conversation other than a resounding 'No!'. I mean, people train really hard to be teachers; they surely know what they're doing – and quite frankly, I *don't!* Now we jokingly refer to this occasion as the 'fateful day' because, even though I outright dismissed the notion of keeping my child (and soon to be 'children') with me every day, little did I know that the seed had been planted.

Over the course of the next few years, I kept encountering people who either home-educated their children, or were home-educated themselves. And these were all very 'normal' people. In fact, they were extremely *interesting* people, who all spoke with tremendous love for home education and their children. Before I could stop myself, I was now actually considering this alternative way of education myself. However, I was – and still am – a very busy person, with a hectic career and 'fingers in many pies', so how could I possibly make this work? Plus, by the time my eldest was ready to start school, I now had three children, and was pregnant with my fourth. I mean, talk about busy!...

As home education pretty much found me (it certainly wasn't the other way around), I really had no idea initially what I wanted it to look like for us. Was my intention to create child geniuses, to expose them to the wonders of the world, to filter out the increasingly secular ideas that were creeping into the Catholic schools where I'd have sent my kids, or to allow them time to nurture their talents? Whilst all of these seemed like reasonable reasons to home-educate, I quickly realised that none of them were my driving force. My primary motivation was to give my children the space to learn and explore at their own pace, learning the things that interest them, and growing in family life as we all muck in and do this together. The more I thought about it, the more I thought, '*Why* should I hand over my child to the state, for them to decide what my child learns and how they spend their day?'.

Despite all this, I still applied for my eldest to go into Reception – ha! I just needed it as a back-up because even though the idea of home-ed had really grown on me, there was still a voice telling me I must be crazy because, like I said, I had a four-year old, a three-year old, a 19-month old, and I was pregnant... – oh, and we were also in the process of relocating! School was 'up my sleeve' in case it all fell apart, but it was absolutely not our Plan A.

So September 2018 came and home education started, though in a very loose sense. We were doing simple workbook exercises at home, but mostly just playing and exploring. But two weeks into that month, a tragedy struck our family. My second daughter, whom I was pregnant with, died in the womb. This obviously affected us all as a family, but what I was really grateful for was that my children were not at school during this time. Some parents may feel that during challenging times, they just need space and the children need the 'normality' of school. However, for me this highlighted and cemented the beauty of our homeschooling life. We grieved together, we laughed together, we 'escaped' together, and we learnt together. We did 'life' together!

And life is full of the good, the bad and the ugly. But that's okay. Every single instance that occurs is one that we can learn from, and should learn from. Whilst children can be taught a lot in school, they can also miss out on and be sheltered from some of the essential normalities of life. Attending midwife appointments and really learning about a baby's development; having juice and a biscuit with local people who feel marginalised because of ill-health or disabilities; mixing with children of all ages; helping the younger ones and learning from the older kids; following their mum to work at times and witnessing the juggle of life; having time to immerse themselves in a topic that they love with little interruption; fully understanding the core values of their family and therefore having a strong sense of who they are. My list could go on.

For me, home education isn't about raising highly intellectual kids; it's about allowing my children to learn in the most natural way, at the most natural pace, with the support of their family. What brings me joy is not that my children can read or do their sums (well, that does bring a bit of delight), but that they are *happy* children, who have been given the chance to continue playing, to learn about all aspects of life under the guidance of those who love them the most, and who have been given the opportunity to develop who they are – the real 'them' – and not whom their teacher, their friends or the government say they are.

Nana-Adwoa forms one-fifth of the Dope Black Mums podcast, and can be found on Instagram @nanaadwoambeutcha.

Facts
AND
Statistics

(if you like that kind of thing...)

In the UK:

- Establishing the number of home educators is difficult, as the Department for Education does not maintain records of families known to LEAs in England and Wales. The estimation is that the number of children being homeschooled has risen by about 40 per cent over three years, with the 2018 figure standing at around 48,000 (BBC, 2018).

- 64 per cent of home-educated Reception-aged children scored over 75 per cent on their PIPS Baseline Assessment, compared to 5.1 per cent of children nationally.

- The National Literacy Project assessment results revealed that 80.4 per cent of home-educated children scored within the top 16 per cent band on the normal distribution curve.

- The study concluded that homeschooled children demonstrated high levels of attainment and good social skills. Common to all families was a flexible approach.

(Rothermel, 2002)

In the US:

- There are around 2.5 million homeschool students in grades K-12.

- Home-based education has grown in the US so rapidly in recent years that it is 'bordering on mainstream'.

- A demographically wide variety of people homeschool, including 32 per cent Black, Asian or Hispanic.

- Taxpayers spend on average $11,732 per pupil annually in public schools, compared to the average homeschooling family which spends just $600 per child.

- Homeschooled students typically score 15 to 30 percentile points above public-school students on standardised academic achievement tests. Notably, a 2015 study found Black homeschool students to be scoring 23–42 percentile points above Black public school students (Ray, 2015).

- Importantly, home-educated children score above average on achievement tests, regardless of their parents' level of formal education or household income.

(Ray, 2020)

Story 5

Noughties Home Ed

by **Diane Westland**

• homeschool reflection • pros and cons • balancing work

I homeschooled my son Jamie between the ages of 7–11 and 13–16 during the early noughties. Home education was never something that I had imagined I would consider for my own child. I enjoyed my time in education and, in common with other children who have a less-than-satisfactory home-life, school was a place where I benefited from routine, stability, positive feedback and the opportunity to develop an independent sense of self. I gained a place at a local all-girls grammar school, with an amazing headteacher who knew all her pupils by name and took a personal interest in their progress (or lack of). I enjoyed a broad curriculum including Classical Studies and Music. Education provided an opportunity for me to explore and learn in a way which I believe is not so readily available in the target-driven National Curriculum of today.

Fast-forward to being a parent myself. I wasn't entirely satisfied with the Early Years education available, but we lived in a fairly isolated situation and

the opportunity for my son to mix with other children of a similar age was important, so we attended a number of parent and child groups together, and Jamie went to some playgroups in the area so that we had the option of several different primary schools when he became of school age. Ultimately, though, only one school seemed a realistic possibility, and Jamie commenced part-time attendance at the local small rural primary school at four-and-a-half years of age. I went back to work, having been a full-time parent up until that point.

Jamie attended Reception class and the first two years of primary school. I remember a parents' meeting just prior to his attendance when we were told that early education would be play-based. Unfortunately, my son's first teacher – Mrs H – seemed to be from the 'dark ages' of education, and it can't have been many weeks into his learning experience at school that I discovered Jamie was being kept in over break and lunchtime to finish work that hadn't been completed during lessons. Mrs H used 'traditional' methods such as shouting and shaming to manage behaviour in her class. This was not the sort of educational experience I wanted for my son. Add to this some bullying from older children, which the school failed to address (or even advise us had occurred), and a general lack of respect and sensitivity to the needs of individual children. We began to consider other options, such as a move to another local primary school, but realised that this would be disruptive and punishing for Jamie. It was at this point that we began to consider home education as a possible option.

I'm a student of social history, and know that the origins of state education lie in producing an educated workforce to keep the wheels of capitalism well-oiled; *not* to consider and support the needs and development of the individual as a free thinker. As I investigated homeschooling for my son, the artificiality of our education system seemed increasingly obvious to me, and counter to a model of rounded social development. How could it be beneficial to extract children from their home environment, put them with a large group of other children and practically leave them to sort it out (in terms of social development) for themselves? I wanted my son to be able to think and discover things for himself, and not just absorb information pumped into him that other people judged he should know. I wanted my son to have confident relationships with people of all ages. Remaining at school where bullying is inevitably 'part of the deal', whatever policies schools have in place, did not seem to me to be the best place for this to happen.

In my concern to get things right for Jamie, I probably failed to factor in the positives that I had found in my own education. I also failed to factor in that neither myself nor my partner had any experience as educators, in any sphere. I failed to consider that I'm not good at planning or organising, or that as the main wage-earner in the household, I had to continue to work for three days of the week doing a stressful job which ate into my time at home, too. Any creative energy I might have had for home education was mostly channelled into my work environment.

We started out hopeful and enthusiastic on this new chapter in our lives, though. I felt that Jamie needed to be able to relax and shrug off the stress of the school environment, and we did not attempt any organised education early on. We live in a very rural settling, and Jamie loved to spend time outside exploring nature. So we just let him do this, and I felt it was beneficial to him and that he became visibly more relaxed in the first days and weeks of home education.

On the days when I was at home, I tried to make sure that I offered Jamie a range of experiences – swimming, visiting museums, using activities at home as learning experiences. My partner explored the various home-education groups in the area in the hope that we would identify like-minded families. It was harder than we expected, and harder still to form the sorts of connections which we felt would be helpful for Jamie.

A home visit from a local authority inspector with her check-list of National Curriculum subjects that she felt we should be covering, and the recommendation of the use of workbooks, the death knell for creativity, as we felt obliged to ensure that Jamie did some of this in order to make sure we continued to receive a 'satisfactory' grading. Jamie struggled with concentrating on workbooks; he was bored and under-stimulated, and this led to some discord between the three of us. I did not favour the workbook approach, and felt that we weren't providing enough enjoyable learning opportunities for him, but didn't have the time or the creative energy to organise them.

It wasn't all negative, though, because Jamie was certainly able to pursue his own interests, too. He taught himself software programming and began to write some simple games. We were immensely proud of his abilities in this area. When Jamie went back into a more formal educational setting between 11 and 13 years of age, he was not educationally behind other children at all; in fact, he was ahead in several areas. He struggled, however, with the routines and pressures of the education system, and we therefore began to home-educate again.

Homeschooling during the teenage years was a different experience entirely. I paid for private tuition, and Jamie was able to attend some lessons via the local home-education group, which enabled him to take IGCSEs independently. Jamie's desire to engage with other young people of his age was intense, and it was difficult for us to achieve this satisfactorily. I managed to arrange for him to sit in on some classes at a local secondary school, and we supported his involvement in various drama activities. Jamie had a couple of regular friendships forged during his brief time back in formal education, and these were maintained at a reduced level after his return to homeschooling. Unfortunately, the contact these afforded was not enough though, and despite our efforts, Jamie lacked the opportunity to form closer relationships and connections with peers, which are so important during later childhood and teenage years.

I'd like to say that this story has a happy ending, but I know that my son does not look back on his homeschooling as a positive experience, and I believe that we let him down in many ways, particularly in terms of supporting him in being more socially connected. I believe I lost sight of the things which made my own education so rewarding for me. However, we are enormously proud of Jamie and know that he is an independent thinker, insistent on forging his own way in life. We hope in time that he may find things to value in his homeschooling experiences.

I'm still a fan of homeschooling. And in the context of an increasingly regimented and narrowing state education system I believe that organised, prepared, well-resourced homeschooling parents, in the context of a supportive homeschooling network, can offer a far more rounded educational and social learning experience than a mainstream school ever can. But I also know that homeschooling is a full-time job, a labour of love; not something you hastily put together on the back of an envelope whilst you have your morning cup of coffee on your day off. I can see that now.

Story 6

Autonomous Learning

by **Ceris Brewis**

- self-directed education • scientific family • being flexible

This morning, I sat down to breakfast contemplating what I might write for this chapter. Across the table, my eldest son was busy building a K'nex digger and asking my husband to help him find the 'red right-angled pieces', while our second boy was busy creating something out of Magformers, calling me over to look at the 'net' of his creation. Later, he announced that the shape had five sides, and his brother casually commented that it looked like half a hexagonal-based pyramid.

We have never taught maths formally, but still they seem quite fluent to us – 'us' being my husband Richard and me, plus our three boys: six-year-old Gabriel, four-year-old Ehren and 'baby' Christopher. It was a timely reminder of what I see as the core of our home-education philosophy; raising children who are creative, self-directed, strongly motivated and equipped to pursue their own interests independently.

Back in 2016, when we first discussed home education for my then two-year old, I would have laughed at the idea that a young child could direct their own learning. It is now April 2020, and my view has completely shifted on how children learn. At the time, I was disillusioned by my own experience of teaching in secondary schools. The students were largely disengaged and, at 16 years of age, were not even expected to take responsibility for remembering their school books. The rules put in place to maintain order in large classes of children who have not elected to be there created an environment where children were not respected as individuals. It is perhaps not surprising, then, that they were not respectful of each other or staff. So, I was concerned about the pace of learning and lack of challenge, but also about the emotional impact school might have on Gabriel, and the lack of motivation and responsibility I had witnessed in the young adults I taught. I thought we could do better.

The idea of home education was floated, and quickly gained appeal. Within the space of two evenings we were in full-scale planning mode. I purchased a copy of the forerunner to this book – *Free Range Education* – and was an instant convert. I had this vision of our children as teenagers, independently pursuing their interests, with assistance as needed from Richard and myself.

I had many thoughts on how we would home-educate, but ultimately our approach grew out of observing our eldest son in his preschool years. From the moment he could talk, Gabriel was on a quest for knowledge. I remember him bringing one of my mother's nursing anatomy books down from the shelf for her to read to him age three; and after some futile attempts to redirect him to something more age-appropriate, she found a picture of the digestive system and began telling him the 'tummy story'. For the next three months, he got the book out every time we visited, and before long was waving his little phalanges at us all. He was especially interested back then in steam engines, the human body, maps and Orca whales, and without any pressure to formally school him yet, it felt natural to simply explore these interests. He would ask question after question – his thirst for knowledge was insatiable;. I didn't want to curtail it by forcing him into preschool, where he would have so much less opportunity to explore and ask questions, nor did I want to force a curriculum on him which he would have to engage with. What would be the point, when he was already so readily engaged in learning on his own?

But I had my misgivings, too. I worried about social opportunities and the opportunity for developing friendships. Two years on, though, and these fears are completely assuaged. The boys have busy social lives and participate in weekly social meet-ups as well as group learning sessions. The abundance of opportunities on Facebook has made this simple. I joined our local Bedfordshire HE group, and from there was directed to a number of others, where weekly meet-ups and groups are advertised. Our problem is there are in fact too many things we want to do, rather than too few! The boys attend a weekly science session which I run myself, our local home-ed music hub, a French class, an after-school street-dance club, and a forest school. They have developed some solid friendships, as have I, and we often have playdates at each others' houses during the week. They play in mixed-age and -sex groups, interacting with adults and children, with no obvious hierarchy or peer pressure to conform to any particular 'norm'.

At the outset I hadn't heard about unschooling and the way in which children can learn without formal instruction. Despite my belief that we should continue to follow Gabriel's interests, I felt it necessary to start some formal learning in reading and maths. I bought a reception-level workbook, only to discover that he had already mastered everything in it without any formal learning at all! I wondered what the point was of looking at pictures of measuring jugs when we regularly baked together! And why we would read books on the seasons when we took walks and attended forest school each week? Our son was having *real-life* experiences, and his learning was based around that, providing purposeful tasks rather than abstract lessons.

Nevertheless, we tried the workbook. Back at that time, I was still thinking of maths as a linear progression that required a curriculum. Now, I would say that it is many progressions running in parallel, reinforcing each other. Children can learn to read numbers in the millions at the same time as they are working on their number bonds to ten; and they do not need to be fluent in numeracy to begin algebra. To be a successful mathematician, you need to approach problems creatively rather than applying a fixed formula, and this is better served by the explorations of play than the rigors of the curriculum.

Anyway, Gabriel hated the workbook approach. In fact, anything that resembled formal teaching seemed to raise his anxiety. Then, in December, we participated in a home-ed Christmas faire. The boys had a stall; they made magnets to sell and priced them at 5p each. To help them run the stall, I taught Gabriel to count in fives and – within minutes – he could recite the five-times table. I realised that all he needed to learn maths was for us to take advantage of the opportunities that arise in day-to-day life. The relevance of the activity made it easy for him – and his brothers – to learn.

Around the same time, we discovered Numberblocks on Cbeebies and the boys were hooked. I got some math link cubes for them to build the numbers while they watched. One day, having just watched an episode on square numbers, Gabriel came running into the room with a cube he'd built shouting, 'Mummy, Mummy! I discovered a cube number!' He'd just made his own mathematical discovery. This is how we encourage the boys to participate in the 'whole process' of the activities they do. Modelling for them any maths that they've not encountered before, and inviting them to give suggestions for more familiar problems. They learn well through observation, and the sporadic nature of this practice seems beneficial rather than problematic. I always find that when they are developmentally *ready* to understand something, they achieve it, purely from observing the world around them.

We focus on providing an intellectually stimulating environment, with many opportunities to discover new interests, rather than developing 'academic skills'. We take them to museums, for walks, visits to the library, the theatre, and generally embrace as many 'experiences' as we can.

Our week follows a loose structure formed by the groups we attend. When we're not out and about, I offer them choices of activities such as experiments, baking, or arts and crafts; but if they're actively engaged in play, I don't interrupt them. We provide resources such as books, games, magazine subscriptions and French audio stories. We have science kits, Lego and math toys. And we play cards and board games together. Gabriel loves chess and Pokémon. He has learned the basics of algebra from the Dragonbox computer game, and Scribblenauts is doing wonders for his spelling. Their academic skills have developed quite naturally through all these activities without any of the rigorous practice required in schools.

Whenever a country is mentioned we look it up on the map. If an historic event is being discussed, we plot it on the timeline that runs along most of the walls of our house. The dining table and dresser surfaces are covered in cardboard catapults, Viking long boats and clay bowls; the walls are decorated with Egyptian death masks and a life-size painted Orca whale, and there's a home-made marble-run, stuck to the side of the bunk beds.

This approach requires me to fully engage with the boys in their play and activities, answering their questions properly and in an open-ended manner – facilitating their interests, taking the time to explore curious facts we encounter along the way and providing new avenues of investigation. Conversation is essential to the learning process. I'm actively involved at all stages, and as there's no separation between learning and daily life, it can definitely be exhausting at times. Do you drink tea? You might need to! I'm creative about how to manage our time, though, and I make use of some childminder hours to have one-to-one time with each of them, exploring their individual interests more deeply.

All our best learning starts with a question. Even young children can ask some startlingly deep and observant questions. There are many times when Gabriel's questions have sent me swiping through Google for an answer! The wonderful thing about the internet is the speed at which you can acquire information on any topic. I once had a fascinating discussion with a microbiologist over Facebook while searching for an answer to a question about viruses. There is no need for me to play 'the expert'; I'm happy to say 'I don't know', and follow it up promptly with an enthusiastic 'Let's find out!' This teaches them *how* to learn.

Here is a sample of the questions that Gabriel has asked over the years:

'Why are there clouds going up from the teapot?'

'Why does a piece of paper fall slowly?'

'Can viruses infect the good bacteria in the body? And can the bacteria fight them off?'

'How does gravity pull things down?'

'If all the plants died when the asteroid that killed the dinosaurs crashed, how come there are plants around now?'

'Do bacteria age in the time it takes them to divide?'

Our discussions may go something like this. Gabriel recently asked why we don't often use the letter 'Z' in English. A quick internet search provided some information about the French/Latin origins of the 'ise' word ending. I managed to find a children's book on word origins on our shelves and we sat down to read it. We learned about the early history of the Britons, language families and roots, leading up to the origins of Anglo Saxon English, and looked at a sample of Beowulf in old English. This led to a discussion of the epic poem, and we found some children's adaptions on YouTube, which the boys enjoyed. Ehren then wanted to dress up as Beowulf, so we got out the dress-up clothes, made a Grendel mask and laid out a banquet with their soft toys, before play-acting the whole story. You just couldn't do this in a classroom – not in a million years.

Even things which do not immediately suggest learning may yield surprising avenues of investigation. A request to learn how to solve a Rubik's cube leads to a discussion of algorithms and computer programming. Watching a nature documentary leads to questioning how plastic ends up in the ocean and tracing the course of waterways joining a nearby lake to the sea. An advantage of this form of education is that you're constantly modelling how to find information. We use YouTube videos a lot to explore new topics. We search for information online, check books out of the library, visit museums and write letters to experts. It is all part of the learning process. Their interests are not confined to a specific area, either. I have become familiar with the expression on our librarian's face when we approach the desk to ask for children's books on viruses, canal boats and Norse mythology.

Home-educating this way has reshaped how Richard and I approach life. Without it, I doubt he would be retraining as a furniture maker next year, or that we'd be moving across the country to be near his course. We plan to travel extensively with the boys as they get older, and see this as the first stop on our worldschooling adventure. The world is advancing so quickly technologically, it's impossible to envisage what career options our children may have in 20 years' time. By following this approach, we feel they will be more able to keep up with the changes. And by focusing on *their* interests from the start, I hope that they'll have a unique skill-set that prepares them for whatever life and career path they choose, along with the self-motivation and determination to gain any new skills they need along the way.

People have certainly questioned our choice to give the boys so much autonomy, but without it, I doubt that my children would have developed in the way they have. If there's a class I think may interest one of them, I will always give them the choice. I tell them about it, and how far away it is, and they're able to weigh up whether the experience is worth the drive time. My eldest recently turned down a science activity 40 minutes away, but enthusiastically signed up for an archaeology dig over two hours away. All of their learning is interconnected, and I frequently see the boys apply something that they've learned in one context to a completely unrelated situation. Strangers comment on how well-spoken and confident the boys are. On several occasions, people have been unsurprised to discover that we home-educate. Something about how we are as a family must suggest this.

I come from a family of autodidacts. As far back as the 1950s, my grandfather was studying physics by correspondence with a local university, learning Greek and Hebrew in his evenings and keeping the library busy with book orders. I think he'd have been proud of his great grandchildren. In a time where information is freely available online, the most important skills for a child to learn are how to access the information they need and assess its reliability. Schools no longer have a monopoly on such information. Qualifications are only as valuable as the access they provide to further education and the job market, not an end in themselves. I hope my children never lose the joy of learning for learning's sake!

As I finish this chapter, the boys are busy designing and writing Easter cards to friends and family. The writing is not a chore, as it is purposeful and they've *chosen* to do it. Later, we'll take a walk to buy stamps and post them. There's no need to create artificial activities for practice, as they arise frequently enough. When you home-educate, each day is a life adventure – a quest for knowledge and an exploration of the world. It is a pleasure and a privilege to spend these years with my children.

Ceris produces the Homeschool Coffee Break podcast and tweets as @raisingautonom1.

Story 7

Pandemic Homeschooling

by **Simon and Tessa Osbourn**

- juggling work • school expectations • lessons from lockdown

We are a family living in the London suburbs; two full-time city workers and our two daughters. The way we look at these little ladies typically veers from heart-warming awe to genuine worry that they might pick up mummy's annoying knack of 'always being right', or daddy's delightful need to perform meticulous research when buying the most reliable energy-efficient light bulb. In short, we sail along just fine. But then in March 2020, their education journey and our high-pressure jobs in financial services were abruptly interrupted by COVID-19. Our homeschooling experience wasn't a choice; it was imposed on us. This is the story of how we coped.

For Simon and I, our own education journeys were very different, in different countries and cultures. Before this time, we didn't even reflect on, or appreciate how, our different backgrounds and upbringing would impact the way we approached education or homeschooling with our girls.

I was educated in rural South Africa, in an Indian-only community which placed the highest value on education. Educational value is part of the fabric of the community, alongside the value of family and hard work. I was driven by my parents to achieve the highest grades in school, as this was seen as the only guarantee of pursuing a university degree and securing a successful future. The importance of academic achievement far outweighed sporting or artistic interests. Both primary and secondary years focused on mastery of the academic curriculum.

Meanwhile, Simon went to an English public (yes, that means private) school. Again, pupils were expected to work hard, and parents expected results – and not surprisingly, given they were paying the fees! Yet pupils were certainly encouraged to think for themselves, and by today's standards, teachers were eclectic and eccentric. Often they were driven by personal interest in the subject, not by exam league tables. This could occasionally result in teaching methods that wouldn't be considered appropriate today. Teachers sometimes didn't show up to class, and there was a lot of emphasis on sport, drama, music and various extra-curricular activities – some of more value than others. Streamed classes meant that those with ability could shine.

So there we both were, on Day 1 of homeschooling. Before this moment, our greatest achievement was simply having the homework done before Sunday night (two days in advance of the due date... *woohoo!*), Now we were faced with weeks, or maybe even months, of *actual* homeschooling, combined with our full-time jobs. The night before, we'd printed a tree's worth of resources, set up close to 50 links to favourites on the home computer, plastered the dining-room table with activities ranging from planets to spring lambing, and we eagerly awaited the first morning of 'homeschooling'. What unfolded, though, was a scene of complete confusion. Our four-year old ran back to bed to seek comfort, and our six-year old just refused to engage in anything we'd prepared. This went on for weeks, in fact. In hindsight, we made the mistake of seeking to turn ourselves into their teachers, and our home into their classroom at school.

Then the school launched us into the virtual world of Google Classroom. *Oh my!...* The amateur approach we bumbled through initially soon gave way to specific, structured curriculum topics for each day, and each task had a deadline. The pressure was on to submit work daily as the teacher marked it and provided feedback that evening. Yet it was reassuring and familiar to be back in a daily routine. The dreaded but familiar daily commute to London had been replaced by the daily deadline of the teaching schedule. And it took over family life. Relaxing Sunday countryside walks were interrupted by a salvo of Google Classroom alerts as the teacher sent out the schedule for the week ahead, with our phones vibrating every time she posted a new piece of work. Any relaxation ended right there; we might as well cut the weekend short, get back home and try to get ahead of the rest of the class. Get all the tasks done, kids, and hopefully we'll make the cut for the class gallery at the end of week.

So yes, it's been tough. Obviously, a key challenge from the outset has been that we both have continued to work in demanding, full-time jobs throughout this process. Both of our organisations are dealing with considerable COVID-19 challenges, and so our workloads have actually been greater than in normal times; yet we also have the new responsibility of schooling our children. The suddenness of the situation also gave us very little time to prepare our approach, our tasks and our mentality. Homeschooling undoubtedly requires patience, and a steady frame of mind. Yet patience can be in short supply when you're thinking about the next conference-call in 20 minutes' time.

Where does this leave us on homeschooling, then? The opportunity to spend precious extra time with our girls has been invaluable and a true 'gift' of this enforced situation. Even though it has been an exceptionally tough few months, with the competing demands of full-time work, it has been an added bonus to be a part of their daily learning and journeys.

Overall, we see our homeschooling as having two benefits:

1. **Long-term benefit:** It has helped us become better at supporting the girls' learning. Before, we often struggled trying to get focused 'learning' time. This experience has certainly helped us understand their learning styles, abilities and interests, and how to adapt to them. We now understand better that our four-year old is not one to sit down and follow through with a structured activity, but she is happy to play alongside us, pays close attention, and listens in on what our six-year old is learning.

2. **Short-term benefit:** We notice that the home environment has recently provided a very safe setting for them to explore their thinking. They can get the answer wrong without feeling embarrassed, or tackle a difficult activity or craft knowing it's okay if it doesn't turn out as intended. Free of being assessed or compared to another child, they can feel proud of what they achieved – even if their rainbow turned out brown because they refused to clean the paintbrush.

If our situation were different and we were not both in full-time jobs, we could certainly see the attraction of being a part of their learning journey through homeschooling. We see the real value of one-on-one, safe, nurturing support where they can develop at their natural pace, encouraging their learning through creativity, adventure and beyond the confines of a desk. We 'get it', if you like. But it's just not a realistic option for us right now. For anyone currently homeschooling, or considering homeschooling who comes from our world of high-pressure deadlines and 10 p.m. meetings, here's our summary of how – with hindsight – to do it:

- Avoid trying to be professional teachers; instead, create your own home-learning environment that works *for you*.

- Don't devote everything to trawling through rigid classroom-type learning. Let your children explore their interests and hidden talents.

- Try not to push things when your child isn't receptive; follow their lead. Home-schooling offers that flexibility.

- Don't be over-ambitious, or try to achieve too much in a single day.

- Children learn best through creativity and play, so try not to overthink it and waste resources and printing.

STORY 8

Hometastic

by **Livvy Leaf-Grimshaw**

• my homeschool life • personal interests • daily routine

I have two older brothers and one younger sister; we are all home-educated. My brothers have learning difficulties, which meant it was hard for them to learn in a traditional school. So my mum took them out at the age of seven, when I was only three. After this, my mum decided that learning at home would be good for all of us. I played until I was seven because mum believes that playing is an important way for children to learn.

Each day we follow a rhythm. First, we start with maths because our brains are at their best straight after breakfast. Then we have our 'morning basket', which is a selection of books which mum reads to us and we discuss the topic. Then we 'notebook' the facts that we learnt and the parts we found interesting. We've covered topics such as activists like Harriet Tubman, Gandhi and Malala Yousafzai. When we learnt about the Georgians, I enjoyed the fashion and art, so we visited a local museum to see a real dress from the period.

Last year, we learnt about mechanics by using building sets to make cranes and levers. We watched videos, and visited the Wonder Lab at the Science Museum in London.

After lunch, we are free to do different things that we enjoy. Sometimes we do science experiments, go for nature walks, or learn crafts like sewing or knitting. Other days, we attend our Art Group or Book Club, where we write stories to share with the others. I like being home-educated because I can get all my academic work done in the morning, and then in the afternoon I can concentrate on the things I like the best. I want to be an illustrator, so this gives me an opportunity to spend time drawing and painting. Sometimes I watch online art tutorials or read about artists. I also love to read novels, and can spend more time reading than most children. I like homeschool because we learn about the earth, the environment and history, as well as lots of other things.

My mum runs a group called Hub Club where kids come with their parents, and I have lots of friends there. My mum sorts out what we do; normally we put games and activities on some tables and then we can choose what to do. Right next to the building is a park which my friends and I go in and play. My favourite day was World Book Day, because we dressed up and I went as a character from one of my favourite stories, *Little Women*.

I like to go to the Natural History Museum on the train and discover all the weird and cool things on earth. I also like to go to Tate Britain, which is my favourite gallery. We saw the Van Gogh exhibition there with our art group. My favourite painting was the 'Sunflowers'. All the older ladies who were visiting said how happy they were to see a young girl admiring the artwork, and how lucky I was to have seen it because lots of other children who go to school wouldn't have seen the exhibition. I had time to look at the artwork and admire the paintings at my own pace.

I love being homeschooled because I get to spend time on the things I want to learn, like maths and art. When we're learning, we don't have to rush, and can take as much time as we need on a subject. Sometimes we learn new things, and my mum learns them too; it's fun to know that we are all learning together.

Livvy's mum Emma can be found on Instagram @earthlovingfamily.

Philip is an American writer and child behaviour expert. His website www.philipmott.com provides support for gentle parenting and educational articles based on autonomous learning. Philip tweets as @PhilipMott1, and is the author of the forthcoming book *Kids Are People: The Surprising Shift That May Just Save Parent–Child Relationships.*

Interview WITH **Philip Mott**

1. **Why are the early years 0–5 so important in terms of child development?**
   Young children create the habits and values that will be the foundation of their development. They form a self-image that will be the basis for making many of their decisions throughout their youth. Some carry this self-image throughout their entire lives, for better or worse.

2. **Where does your approach to parenting come from, and has it evolved over time?**
   I've often referred to my parenting journey as my 'Four Conversions'; and each of them had a distinct and profound impact on my parenting style. The reclamation of my childhood faith showed me the importance of forgiveness. I learned about constructivism in college, which showed me the importance of inquiry. After those, I learned about choice theory; showing me the importance of respect between adults. And finally, I learned about respectful parenting, which taught me the importance of respect between adults and children.

3. **What was the most recent conflict you had with one of your children? And how did you resolve it?**
   Conflicts in our household seem to unfold over time and become more like long discussions, over weeks and months. The conflict we're in right now is over voice volume at the dinner table. Our children get so excited telling us about some of the things they're doing; sometimes it gets a bit much. We remind them that we'd love to hear their stories but it's hard to listen when they're all shouting!

4. **From your time working in schools, what do you think is the main failure of the school system?**
   I used to apply the hashtag #coercionistheproblem a lot on social media, and it still boils down to the problem to me. From my perspective, teachers are rarely teaching poor content (the exception being when history and economics are taught from a very narrow perspective) but rather, the method is counter-productive. The constant use of nagging, criticism, rewards, and even threats to get students to do things they don't see the value in actually creates far more problems than it solves.

5. **Why is homeschooling a good option for families who share your parenting ethos?**
   Homeschooling helps parents become intimately aware of their child's unique interests and challenges. Interestingly, people who have spent some time homeschooling and then go back to a familiar educational setting often have greater empathy for their classmates and teachers; skills they've picked up by being listened to and respected themselves, at home. Of course, some parents find that their children thrive way more in the homeschooling environment, so they never go back to a classroom unless, perhaps, they want to pursue higher education.

STORY 9

That's It, We're Done

by **Tammy Palyo**

• teaching background • trusting your instinct • saying 'goodbye' to school

School seems like a natural rite of passage for children, and it's something I never questioned as a young adult. However, shortly before the time came for my own daughter to begin kindergarten, and right after I finished student teaching, a friend of mine used the phrase 'adult convenience', and it really stuck with me. He pointed out that very often, schools operate based on what's most *convenient* for the adults who work there, and not what's best for the children. From that moment on, I couldn't help but find many instances of adult convenience in my daughter's school, and in the schools where I worked as a substitute teacher. My daughter would quite frequently come home with notes from her teacher stating that she was 'too social' that day. This outraged me; if one of the arguments *for* brick-and-mortar schooling is socialisation, *why* can't my daughter socialise? But as angry as the entire system left me feeling sometimes, I pushed my feelings aside, and was able to do so because my daughter is very compliant, and does well academically.

I was also in pursuit of my own teaching career at this point, and felt as if I couldn't have these negative opinions about school if I wanted to work in one. By January 2020, I found myself accepting a long-term substitute position, where I was filling in for a new mum for the remainder of the academic year. The school in which I found myself employed was new to me, and I'd hoped that it would be more student-centred than the other schools I'd previously worked in. Unfortunately, all I found were more instances of 'adult convenience'.

I desperately wanted to quit, and was toying with the idea of doing just that when COVID-19 hit. In the first few weeks of quarantine, I found myself to be – overwhelmingly – relieved. Being a teacher had become exhausting, and not for the reasons to which most teachers would attribute their exhaustion. Teaching is an authoritative role, and every time I walked into my classroom I felt as if I was playing a role I wasn't meant to play.

A few short weeks into quarantine, my daughter's school began sending lessons and work for her to complete. We would sit down every morning around 9 a.m. and work on what her teacher sent: maths lessons and worksheets, writing assignments, reading. During our six weeks of 'school at home', I watched my daughter become increasingly frustrated with her maths work; and she dreaded writing, and practically gave up on reading. My daughter, who's 'ahead' of her peers in all of those subjects, began to resent what she knew as 'learning'. She's only seven. Just a few years ago, she wanted to learn about everything under the sun; yet now, school had impacted massively on how she *felt* about learning. And while she is a compliant person who'd likely 'succeed' by traditional schooling's standards, I couldn't allow school to take more away from her than it already had done.

So there I was, a teacher who hated teaching, with a daughter who was beginning to despise learning. We'd already experienced so much change in such a short amount of time due to the global pandemic. Why couldn't we try something new? It felt like there was no better time to do so. I thought back to my friend who'd introduced me to the phrase 'adult convenience', and remembered him also speaking about unschooling; I needed to know more.

So I turned to Twitter, Google and my podcast app to learn as much as I could. The more I learned, the more I *wanted* to learn. And I found myself realising how much I was learning about unschooling because of how passionate I was becoming about it. What if that's how learning could occur for my daughter? What if I could allow her to – and even assist her in – following her passions?

After several long discussions with my husband, we made the decision that, going forwards, we'd give homeschooling or – more specifically in our case – *un*schooling a try. This is where we are now – brand new to home-educating, and loving every moment. We will live life more fully, allowing our child to follow her passions, and doing our best to nurture her interests. And I know instinctively that we're doing the right thing. I wish I had trusted my instinct a long time ago.

Tammy tweets as @mrspalyo21.

STORY 10

Scrapping the Vision

by **Frances Matthews**

• structure vs freedom • embracing Christianity • finding the right approach

As a young dating couple, Peter and I planned to work abroad. Home education was our 'practical option', if you like. Years before our children even existed, we started imagining their education, wanting it to be: flexible and child-led, textbook-free and based on creative, cross-curricular links and, importantly, high input and high expectation. When our eldest was born we managed to uphold this vision. However, since our second and third children arrived, we have had to pull back. We simply don't have enough hours in the day to manage an education that is flexible, child-led, textbook-free *and* creatively integrated for three small human beings. Much of our recent journey has been about learning to thrive within this scaled-down reality.

'You made the mistake of being *awake*', we would joke. 'Stimulation time!' This was how our first child's home-education journey began – immediately and enthusiastically. We started by attempting to create a loving, calm and kind environment by working hard at our marriage and behaviour patterns. We kept a daily 'God Time' with prayers, Bible readings and songs; and made regular space for simple family acts of generosity. We were also strict about healthy habits which included long-term breast-feeding, eating 'five a day', plenty of fresh air, zero screen-time, and so forth. We also made space for child-led socialising, hosting many events. We praised effort over result, and discussed emotions openly. These are foundations we still strive to maintain today.

Beyond this, we were impatient to introduce our child to the world. From birth, we'd watch our daughter's eyes movement and would discuss what she was looking at. The house was full of play, chatter and singing. We taught numbers, letters and blending letters into words in a variety of creative ways, before she could even speak. Instead of teaching nouns like 'flower', we would accurately name individual wild flowers, trees, mushrooms, fauna, dinosaurs, rock types, flags, countries, internal organs – in fact, anything we could explore. I was learning some of this for the first time, too; so our eldest learnt to navigate reference books alongside me.

As I speak some Mandarin and we'd planned to live in Asia, I aimed to raise bilingual children. My chosen method was joyful immersion. Every day, I read and chatted to my daughter in Chinese. Native-speaking teachers – who I knew in the local area – requested to act like 'favourite aunties' and soon became close friends, as we flung ourselves into dumpling parties and Chinese New Year celebrations.

Our living room became equipped with books and educational aids from which our daughter could select. We even squeezed in a piano, which she chose to start practising, aged three! And of course, frequent trips and visits were linked to our learning at home. Every morning, we'd prepare an exploratory educational activity on our coffee table to surprise our daughter as she woke up. She normally chose to dissect it immediately, but then again we didn't force her to do it, either. It was all a bit of an experiment for us, too.

So, with one child we had happily settled into a flexible, child-led pattern; our lives were slow and relaxed. But the arrival of our second and third children brought an expanding world of new interests and – you've guessed it – time pressure to pack it all in. We went from morning walks to the train station, naming the wild flowers and trees together, then home for breakfast and reading, to a different scenario altogether.

So in addition to our studious six-year-old, we now have a cute, cheeky four-year-old, and a savvy one-year-old menace whose primary desire is to throw shoes into the garden. Are you with me? There goes the daily coffee-table activity schedule! – for now, at least. But look, it is still possible to have high expectations, and to pursue a more structured education in this setting, so long as you're organised. I find that a tick-list helps.

Things to complete before noon:

1. **English** (*Eldest* – creative writing; *Middlest* – tracing and copying words, reading; *Littlest* – books, alphabet, blending, naming things)

2. **Maths** (*Eldest* and *Middlest* – 'Maths! No Problem'; *Littlest* – counting, number recognition, ordering)

3. **World** (*Eldest* – variety of exploration avenues, including 'Story of the World' (History) and 'My Pals Are Here' (Science); *Middlest* – non-fiction reading, physical exploration, trips; *Littlest* – interactive play)

4. **Chinese** (*Eldest* – Zhongwen writing curriculum, reading; *Middlest* – Read ten characters; *Littlest* – Chinese books and play; Everyone – speaking and listening together, or immersion crafts and games with native-speaking teacher)

5. **Music** (*Eldest* and *Middlest* – piano pieces and technique, creative musicianship; *Littlest* – action songs)

6. **Family Cuddles** – obviously! They are children, after all.

So yes, it's a busy schedule – and this is the way the children, Peter and I 'function' as a family. But by noon, the schoolwork is all finished and we have the rest of the day to enjoy socialising, fresh air, groups and clubs. I think you'd agree that we fit into a single morning what many classrooms couldn't achieve in a full term of study. This is definitely 'our way', and we know our children – they are thriving on it, and they're happy. They're the first to run up a steep river bank and suggest sailing umbrellas downstream.

But where is the time for genuine, child-led flexibility? – because this is still important to us. And where did all the textbooks come from? Well, it's actually more of a mindful process than it might at first appear. Bear with me, and I'll explain our approach.

When our lives hit a new level of 'crazy' after the arrival of our third child, we discovered that our initial aims for home education were simply not all possible to maintain at once. Something had to give, and the tension seemed to be between embracing true child-led flexibility, or adult-directed skills and knowledge – what I would call 'stuff'. We chose stuff. And guiding our decision-making were three key observations:

1. Our kids become best at what they do every day.
   But...

2. Our kids' most beautiful 'eureka' moments appear on unstructured, free days.
   And...

3. Our kids' eureka moments normally stem from what has been encountered during regular, structured learning.

Hmmm. Tricky? Or perhaps, not so tricky. Because in the end, we decided we needed two kinds of days: packed days and free days. Our packed days build key skills and muscle memory, while the empty days allow the kids to take ownership of those skills and learn to be themselves. So we maintain what I call 'protected free time', and the kids spend this time any way they choose – writing down freshly composed songs, reading, constructing historic buildings from Lego, making tepees, writing campaign letters, playing with friends, or paddling in our local river. It's a balance that works, I think. Without the weekday input, our kids wouldn't have the tools to attempt many of their free-day plans. Without the free days, there would be limited processing and connecting; family relationships would strain and all of us would burn out.

And I've also discovered there are some pretty fine textbooks out there. One great source is Singapore, a country which has adopted a nation-wide 'concrete-pictorial-abstract' educational method. All state-approved materials must explain concepts first with practical activities, next with pictures, and finally with words or symbols. We use Singapore-based materials for Maths and Science. Another resource is textbooks written by home educators themselves. 'The Story of the World' is still my daughter's favourite curriculum. Every chapter includes a narrative glimpse of history, colouring, map work, a choice of perhaps five practical projects, from crafts and cooking to outdoor role-play activities, plus a CD to recap in the car. We're in the process of broadening our resources, though, to include a wide spectrum of textbooks and learning materials from around the world. Our aim is to provide balance and understanding in our children's education, not the narrow focus of a white, Western curriculum.

If you're like me, you might even enjoy looking ahead to manage how parallel curricula can dovetail. I try to do a six-monthly planning schedule to make sure I don't have any unfeasible surprises lurking. So if I see two similar topics coming, I try to synchronise them. For example, when we reached the 'Mass and Volume' chapter in Maths, we jumped to the 'Mass and Matter' chapter in Science. Both included fun, practical activities. Since Mass involves weighing, we made pizza dough during Chinese immersion time. The kids love space so we recapped Gravitational Mass, and I left the home-made volume-measuring bottles in the bath for further exploration. Similarly, when we reached our first twelve-bar-blues in piano, we listened to blues from around the world and spent our 'world' time learning about the slave trade and the civil-rights movement. Trips and visits, too, can be linked. Curricula don't need to be rigidly followed. The joy of home-educating is that we can pick and mix. Curricula are simply a base upon which to create.

Let me see, then. Did our loss of total child-led flexibility and use of textbooks = failure? There's no concrete way of measuring child-rearing success, but my gut feeling is that our kids are okay. More than okay, really.

My eldest is an enthusiastic learner, a kind and empathetic sibling who is genuinely helpful to me. She is comfortably a year or more ahead in all her studies except Chinese writing – where, despite being non-Chinese, she keeps pace well with an ex-patriate curriculum. Her Chinese conversation is good. She's also a keen climate activist, enthusiastically attending marches and writing letters to politicians. Her life-plan is that mummy home-educates her children when she becomes Prime Minister and enacts radical environmental reform. My goodness! I asked her the other night what house she'd like to be in from the Harry Potter book series. She immediately replied, 'Hufflepuff'. 'Why?' 'Because they're hard-working and kind.' It took me at least 25 years to reach that level of maturity.

My second is also a climate activist, painstakingly tracing my writing in his campaign letters. He has amassed an impressive knowledge of hydraulics, high-speed trains, planets, South America, sea otters and orangutans. He may be around eight months behind his sister in reading and piano, but in every other subject he is matched, or ahead. I mean, seriously? He's four. And it is actually my second who initiated the weekly family tradition of running into the front garden to greet the rubbish truck team, who now bring us sweets! Our kids find lollipops inedibly sweet, but they love our rubbish truck team so much that they accept them gratefully and continue their welcome.

And our littlest one, the roving mischief-maker? Well, littlest has not achieved his first 200 words by 13 months, like his siblings, but I'm learning that this doesn't matter too much. This one has been my best walker, socialiser, problem-solver, bilingual speaker and 'perseverer'. He has so much to learn from growing in a five-strong family community, bringing empathy skills, love, liveliness and light to us all.

They are great kids; full of life, wise, skilled and empathetic. The gains we have made would be too much to lose now by sending them to school.

Frances can be found at www.francesmatthews.co.uk.

Story 11

The World is Our Classroom

by **Astrid Vijne**

- worldschooling • teens and travel • the global classroom

In a small dairy just outside of Parma, Italy, two men busily stir a large vat of milk. The milk contains rennet, a curdling agent which will turn the milk into lumpy curds and whey. From an observation platform above the floor of the dairy, my children and I watch as the liquid in the vat transforms, becoming lumpy and yellow. Slowly, the curds solidify into a large lump, which the men lift out of the liquid in a cheese cloth. My children and I watch on as the men transfer the large lump into a mould, to be aged into the type of cheese that this region of Italy is famous for: Parmesan.

For a typical family, an experience like this would be just another travel excursion to tick off on a vacation itinerary. But for our family, this dairy visit was part of a comprehensive educational unit on Italian food culture.

The day before, we watched a documentary on the process of making Parmesan cheese. A few days prior, we had taken a walking tour of Parma to learn about its food history. And we'd been visiting pasta and tomato museums, as well as making hand-rolled pasta at home. In the week after visiting the dairy, we visited museums focused on ham, salami and wine. By the last day of our time in Parma, sitting down to a meal of homemade pasta with prosciutto and a glass of red wine at an *osteria* in the hills, we fully understood the traditions, artistry and knowledge that went into preparing that delicious Italian meal.

This is what learning is like for our family. We refer to it, of course, as 'worldschooling'. Essentially, our brand of homeschooling focuses on using our global travels as the foundation for our kids' learning. To put it simply, the world is our classroom.

The origins of the term 'worldschooling' are fuzzy. Admittedly, many travelling families were already doing a version of worldschooling before anyone thought of putting a term to that type of education. However, since the latter part of the last decade, the popularity of worldschooling has taken off, aided by opportunities for families to work remotely, and the greater accessibility of travel. Today, worldschooling is a global educational movement – a distinct 'branch' of homeschooling.

At its crux, worldschooling involves finding opportunities for learning through real-life experiences in the world. Its underlying educational philosophy posits that children learn best through hands-on exploration. But another, less obvious component of worldschooling is an emphasis on a global mindset. Worldschoolers adhere strongly to the idea that the world is bigger than their immediate surroundings, and that valuable learning and growth happen when we step out of that environment and into the greater global community.

With this definition in mind, worldschooling can thus be seen not as a replacement for school, but as a supplement. Families who utilise Charlotte Mason, Steiner Waldorf or Classical curricula can still incorporate worldschooling into their lesson plans. Unschoolers, who do not adhere to one specific curriculum, can use travel experiences as a basis for unit studies or 'deep dives'. And even families in traditional schools can adopt worldschooling principles when travelling for vacation; seeking out travel activities with an educational component, rather than purely for entertainment.

For our family, worldschooling was a natural fit for the type of travel we wanted to do: full-time, slow travel. Travelling from country to country gave us ideas of what to learn about. And spending months at a time at destinations around the world offered us opportunities to learn about those destinations in a deeper way. But the path to becoming worldschoolers has not always been easy. In the past two years, we've faced our fair share of learning challenges.

Prior to travelling around the world, our kids attended traditional school. Since my husband and I both worked full-time, homeschooling was not at first a viable option for our family. Our then four-year old attended full-time childcare, while our then seven-year old did a combination of public school and afterschool care. When we dropped all this and began travelling, we had to learn how to homeschool as a family; how to be together.

Being new to homeschooling, we weren't sure where to start. Several homeschooling friends offered their suggestions for what they used for their kids: Time4Learning, Montessori-inspired lessons, or enrolment in a virtual academy. But ultimately, we opted for a more eclectic unschooling approach, reasoning that the unexpectedness of travel often makes sticking to routines quite challenging.

The transition from traditional schooling to homeschooling was rough. To say that we experienced culture shock during those first few months of worldschooling was an understatement. It wasn't so much culture shock from travel, but culture shock from homeschooling itself. Having only known traditional school, both my kids and I needed to take a step back

and examine just how to learn. We needed to determine for ourselves what homeschooling would look like for our family.

As the months of our time travelling progressed, we experimented with various approaches to learning. We settled on a mix of focused sit-down activities and physical exploration in the destinations we were visiting. My kids often resisted anything like 'focused lessons'. And often, during math and writing lessons my daughter would cry in frustration when she had trouble understanding an instruction, or couldn't execute a task perfectly. My son, on the other hand, was disinterested in any kind of 'lesson', and struggled against sitting down and learning.

The happy medium was often when we visited museums, or went on excursions. In those instances, the learning happened naturally. And our children were instinctively engaged in the activities. We learned to build these excursions more and more into our day, to break up the monotony of our more academic lessons. And over time, our kids learned on their own to balance the excursions with more of the sit-down learning. It wasn't me pushing them any more.

Now, with two years of worldschooling under our belt, we feel like we've found a mix that works for us. We still do excursions as much as we can, but we also do lessons with programmes like the Khan Academy. We read books together or separately on our Kindle apps; and we follow various educational YouTube channels for geography, social studies, science and history videos.

Hard days still affect us from time to time, but I now understand the unique ways that each of my kids learn, as well as how to cope as a family with adversity. Too many children are sheltered from this.

As we've met other families throughout our travels, I've learned that this uniqueness extends to almost everyone we know. Every family's approach is different. And every family's worldschooling experience is influenced by a variety of factors, from travel styles, cultural and religious backgrounds, learning styles, to social and emotional needs. Worldschooling, I've learned, is as diverse as the families who make it.

When it comes to travel styles, the speed and length of travel can affect how families worldschool their children. Quick visits to destinations aren't always conducive to deep explorations of the culture. But there are still ways that families can benefit educationally from short trips. Reading books about the culture and history of destinations can help give context to a trip, as does watching relevant movies. For longer trips, engaging in local community events can give families an opportunity to connect with the local culture, forming friendships and connections.

Cultural and religious backgrounds play another role in how families worldschool. When we travel in the world, we bring our own perspectives and views to the new experiences we encounter. Our travel experiences help to reshape and remould our views and perspectives. Families can expand their perspectives by finding opportunities for stepping outside of their comfort zones, even if just slightly.

Along similar lines, the learning styles of their children can influence how families worldschool. Children who are tactile learners may benefit from hands-on workshops or classes during their travels. Creative-minded children may gain more from their travel experiences by creating photo albums, movies, or stories about their experiences. By adjusting to children's learning styles, families can make their worldschooling experiences even more impactful.

Finally, the emotional needs of children – and of adults, too – shouldn't be overlooked. Long-term worldschooling can be a lonely experience, especially when families go through periods of time with little to no contact with friends or family back home. Being in a different culture may be exhausting, even when engaging in positive encounters with locals. Taking time to acknowledge the social and emotional difficulties that may come with worldschooling will help children adjust better to this way of learning.

However, maintaining a balance of social and emotional needs doesn't necessarily have to be hard. Connecting with other worldschooling families may help enormously. Additionally, alternating between culturally familiar and culturally new destinations may help ease some of the stress of culture shock. And allowing time for 'down days' makes the emotional aspect of worldschooling more manageable for families.

During our visit to Italy, for example, our experience was greatly impacted by the length of time we spent in that country, the biases and perspectives we brought with us, the learning styles of our kids, and the emotional needs of our family. Spending a month in one location allowed us to adopt some of the cultural habits of the Italians, like taking coffee after a meal and slowing down our pace of life. And our kids' preference for hands-on activities led us to seek out museums in our area and more engaging learning opportunities.

As we travel the world, we know that worldschooling isn't just a form of education, it's an entire life philosophy. We worldschoolers place value on learning from the world. And we use every opportunity we can to teach our kids life lessons through our travels. This is the legacy we are choosing to create for our own family, and this is how we raise our kids to become engaged global citizens. I wonder, what could be more important in today's world?

Astrid blogs at www.thewanderingdaughter.com.

Story 12

Pinky and the Brain Do Home Ed

by **Gemma Black**

- organic learning • unschooling • seeking the opportunity

Our home-education journey started before we had children. I worked with young children during this time and knew instinctively that I wouldn't want to leave someone that small to be looked after by anyone else. So once we came towards nursery and Reception stage with our eldest, we had already marked a 'different route', prompted by general hearsay that Scandinavian countries mostly started school a lot later. At this point, we intended on our children only starting school at the compulsory schooling age of five, although I still thought this was too young. We kept reading and kept thinking, and our second daughter was born.

I was lucky enough to have an old school friend, Sam. She started her family three years before we did and lots of her choices gave us names for the type of parenting we had already discussed. We knew we were going to parent in a similar way, and when it turned out that she felt the same about education and had already made some connections into the home-ed world, I knew this was my answer. My partner actually hadn't thought about anything away from the mainstream himself before he met me, and also hadn't had much exposure to babies and young children. He feels he learnt a lot from me, but my belief is that he was my 'co-pilot' from the start; he has experienced it all first-hand now, and is absolutely convinced by the path we're choosing. We are quite a yin–yang couple and can use our strengths to help the children, knowing that we can refer them to the other parent when we can't make it work. For example, my strength is being able to teach concepts and skills, but my partner is a designer, studied art and works with computers – all things in which I don't have such strong skill-sets.

It was motherhood itself that left me feeling I was swimming away from the strong current of mainstream life, but perhaps home education was the part of it that most helped me feel I wasn't just paddling at the edge, but climbing out of the river entirely and reaching for a towel! This was initially terrifying but – ultimately – it's what makes the journey so special: we 'homeschooling' families, whichever part of the 'river' we're in, have the opportunity to step back and observe life somewhat, to seek out the bits that work for us. We can watch the river run by and figure out whether we do – or don't – want to dip our toe in. And that goes for our kids, too.

My approach to home education is simply following the child, but in this adult-centric world, I sometimes find it much easier said than done! We have three children now, and they're all doing well, though.

- Our eldest cracked reading (in the sense of picking up any book and reading it purely for pleasure) when she was seven, but it wasn't a smooth, unhindered journey for her. I definitely interfered too much as I worried that her peers were practising, and perhaps 'achieving', more. I am so glad that I stopped short of trying to force her to do 'work' and let it come naturally in the end, with positive encouragement, as that became my most important learning point to date: trust and follow.

- Our second-born is currently benefiting from that lesson. She has just turned 7 herself, and I can feel that fluent reading is so close – but I won't be pushing too hard. We're just continuing with exposure to books and opportunities. Her baby sibling is being used as a positive here, as everyone gets turns to read to him.

- With the youngest, we're just getting to grips with the toddling, climbing, experimenting and talking non-stop phase, so it is fun to find the positives and work with them. For example, plenty of learning happens 'on the move' right now, with more concentrated time around naps. It actually works really well, but I'm not immune to that frazzled feeling on a day where I've had to help three people in three different ways for an extended time to help achieve their goals!

I constantly reflect on my practice as a home educator and regularly worry that I might be doing something wrong. What I've learnt over time, though, is that this fear is simply the result of being and 'doing' differently, and if we have a 'wobble', it can be helpful to take stock and make sure the approach still suits us, having considered all the alternatives. The answer is always a resounding 'Yes!'. And it's all an evolution, after all. I'm much more comfortable now to get my children to teach me, for example. Every now and then, I'll introduce an idea or topic: sometimes it takes off, and sometimes it doesn't. To move forwards, I might ask them to let me know how that went from their point of view, so we can understand each other better. This approach is helping at the moment with spellings: I've abandoned the method we were using and, through discussion with the girls, we have a new 'way' which seems to be working.

Social media has made the social side of home ed much easier, giving us a broad range of people to connect with, varying in approach, geography, finances, background, and more. There are people I don't get to see in the flesh so much, as they can afford to do more paid activities than us, or are confined to their local area a little more, perhaps without a car; but we can still connect regularly and easily when we want to make it work.

Diversity is key with homeschooling, but also being true to yourselves. For example, we have still occasionally come across bullying behaviour, but we can step back to understand it and learn coping techniques, as well as ultimately having the power to walk away and protect ourselves.

If I were to give any advice, I would say, 'Be flexible and embrace change'. Children are constantly changing, so you have the power to mould your weeks to match their needs; but it's also pertinent to realise that nearly all families can take that approach, and therefore groups may come and go. I would not really recommend any specific resources, as we are all so different. Just get to know people, join any groups that resonate (either on social media or through meet-ups), and simply borrow from the people who feel kindred in some way. It's a great starting point to finding your own family 'style' without trying to squeeze yourself into a programme that really doesn't suit. Homeschooled children are good at showing the way, and will take ownership of personal and home care once they're ready. I only considered this benefit recently after time with school children who hadn't yet mastered things like food preparation or tying shoelaces, for lack of time to do so.

But what happened to 'us', then? To Eoin and I – the yin–yang couple? Are we still full of big ideas and creative solutions? Actually, we really are, and we proved that to ourselves at the start of this year when we took the whole family for a ski-trip to Canada. Our snowboards – nicknamed Pinky and the Brain – stare at us every day from their mounting on the staircase, where they hang proudly along with the family mountain bikes, sports rackets, and a rather dazzling display of autumn leaves blowing in the breeze, which we never painted over. We aren't currently in a financial position to contemplate worldschooling, but we looked at each other one morning and decided 'let's do it!' Let's take our kids skiing – something requiring no shortage of planning and budgeting, but which ultimately would have been impossible if we were constrained to peak-time prices. Standing on top of those bright mountains, looking out over the snow with our fierce, fun, home-ed family, we felt like anything was possible.

I hope you find what you're looking for in your search; whether it be home education or something else that will make your world – and hopefully *the* world – a better place.

Gemma tweets as @gemmabelly.

STORY 13

Thank You, I Did It Myself

by **Maria Jones**

• single-parent homeschooling • managing my ex • rebuilding family

I have always said challenges are good in life, and then a big one came my way. In many ways, I think I ended up homeschooling my daughter Lani because of the break-up with her dad, not in spite of it. But let me take you back a bit and I'll explain how it happened.

Lani was three when we split, and it hit her hard. I find it painful to use the words 'emotional trauma', but if I'm being honest with myself, that's what it was. She was going to nursery five mornings a week during this time and almost straight away, I noticed her becoming increasingly clingy and tearful. It was like she needed to be with me all the time. Then came the start of Reception and the expectation of full-time schooling and, well, if I had thought things were challenging before, it just got a whole lot worse. We lasted a term. I'm a primary school teacher and I was actually working at the school where Lani was enrolled. It was a 'nice' school, and she was familiar with it from being at the nursery there. I knew that we were all coming through a difficult time with the separation from Lani's dad, but nothing could have prepared me for how she would react to starting full-time school. In the end, it wasn't a difficult decision; Lani came first. I quit my job and 'together' we quit school.

Sounds so easy, right? Well, it was and it wasn't. Don't forget I had my ex to deal with, and he wasn't at all on board with my decision. It wasn't as if we were in an easy place with our relationship either, so communication was exceptionally fraught, and this was definitely a 'problem area' to begin with. More than that, I was brand new to homeschooling, new to being a single mum, and had just upturned my life on an instinct... this gut feeling at that moment that school was the wrong place for my child. But there are a lot of people out there in a similar situation, and quite quickly I found two other families in North London (not far from where we lived) who were looking to form a small co-operative. We went for it, and things began to really change from there.

First, Lani was noticeably more settled and 'herself' now that she felt secure. And secondly, for the first time since the separation I felt a sense of real hope and optimism – like I could picture what the future could be for us. Our co-op was very small and friendly, with only four children across three families, all under 7. They got along well, and the adults supported each other and learnt from each other, taking turns to teach and manage the activities and resources for home learning. We carried on like this for nearly a year, with Lani and I driving down to spend four days a week living in the homeschool co-op, and the rest of the week at home in Hertfordshire. It was a good time and a healing process for both of us. Lani was able to re-root with me; she became less prickly and defensive, and I let go of a lot of the emotional baggage that I'd been carrying around. We felt united again – mother and daughter. In this time, when I least expected it, I also met the wonderful man that I would later marry.

People don't always think about how free home education is. I still think back now to afternoons spent tiling the bathroom, baking bread, or painting a huge mural in the lounge. We travelled, too, especially to Ireland; and as we wheeled our suitcases out of the front door we felt exhilaratingly like outlaws, knowing everyone else was at school. Keys? – check. Passport? – check. Lelli Kelly shoes? – obviously. Okay, let's go!

When you're homeschooling, time slows down, and the world seems to open up. Even Lani's dad was starting to come around to it, as he'd been doing research of his own and seemed satisfied that a significant proportion of top athletes, tennis players, film stars and so on were homeschooled. It made me roll my eyes at the time, to think that this was his take on it, but I guess in

a way he wasn't so wrong. Home education really gives you the opportunity to focus on what you're good at and – so important – who you are. This was great for Lani, and being a single parent actually gave me *more* reason to homeschool, not less.

The years have gone by and I am now happily married and expecting my fifth child! I teach in a unique new hybrid academy where home-ed families are supported with a curriculum and two days of formal education with tutor experience and guidance. All my children are homeschooled in this way, apart from Lani who, after five years of home education, has gone back into the school system as this was something she wanted to try. She's fine this time around and coping well with school, although she often comments that the children in her year group seem 'younger' than her and generally less mature. I think this is the homeschooling coming through; all those extra activities, work in the community, and interesting conversations with bus drivers and shopkeepers. School children don't get a lot of that.

We are so lucky in the UK that we have the freedom to remove our children from school, but at a later point, if it feels right, put them back in again. For some people, homeschooling has a personal or political ethos, but for others it might be something that gets them through a difficult time. I don't like to think where we would be now if I hadn't made the decision to follow Lani's lead and take us both out of school and into a new life. Again – through the challenges in life we have come out the other side much better for it!

Maria can be found on Facebook at 'Happy, Healthy with Maria' and on Instagram as maria.jacinta.pia.jones.

PART III
Further Support

'You get to see your friends more often and go to fun places, like bowling and Legoland. You can learn with them and have friends who aren't the same age as you. I have a 14-year-old best friend. You get to eat biscuits and feel more cosy because you're at home.'

Elijah, age 8

CHAPTER 4

Key Questions

Education is an admirable thing, but… nothing that is worth knowing can be taught.

Oscar Wilde

'Is Home Education Legal in the UK?'

In short, yes. The Education Act 1996 states that:

> The parent of every child of compulsory school age shall cause him to receive efficient full-time education suitable;
>
> a. To his age, ability, and aptitude, and
> b. To any special educational needs he may have, either by regular attendance at school or otherwise.

It is the term 'or otherwise' which makes home education a legal possibility in the UK, and many other countries, such as the USA, France and Canada, have similar legal terminology. It is important to note the term 'school age' which, in the UK, would refer to anyone from the age of 5 through to 18. The phrase 'full term' is also worth observing, as this indicates that there is some expectation of structure from a legal perspective. Regardless of your personal approach to delivering home education, therefore, it would be wise to maintain some paperwork or record-keeping, and to be clear in your own mind that your children are receiving an education consistent with your family ethos, but also with the law. Nobody has the right to simply disregard their children's education – this is neglect; and even radical unschooling should never fall into this category.

For a more general standpoint on homeschooling, we could look to the Human Rights Act 1998, which states:

> No person shall be denied the right to education in the exercise of any functions which it assumes in relation to education and to teaching, the State shall respect the right of parents to ensure such education and teaching in conformity with their own religious and philosophical convictions.

This is a moderate endorsement to embrace your own family values, culture and educational approach within your homeschooling. It does not, of course, encompass any method that is abusive, neglectful, highly restrictive or otherwise damaging to the well-being of the child.

Importantly, the law places responsibility for education squarely with the parents, whether the child attends a school setting or not (Dowty, 2000). Recognising this fact therefore shifts our horizons as parents, regardless of how we choose to educate. We can no longer throw our hands up and blame the school, because the buck stops with us. If our child is not thriving at school, it is legally our responsibility to be seeking a solution to that problem, either with the school, or via another school, or otherwise. As a home educator this has further resonance, and permeates all areas of daily life, encouraging a whole-family approach of enquiry and lifelong learning which is quite transformative.

'What Happens Once I Register as Homeschooling?'

If your child is below the compulsory school age in the UK then you are, upon the date this book has been printed (August 2020), under no legal obligation to register your child as homeschooling. You can simply choose not to apply for a school place, and continue educating your child at home. My advice, however, is that you might want to consider registering anyway. It is always advantageous to co-operate in a positive way with the local authority, especially when it looks increasingly likely that the rapid rise in elective home education could bring about some more stringent measures for parents to observe.

If you have decided to remove your child from a school setting in order to home-educate, then the standard process is that the school should contact the local authority to inform them that the child is no longer on their register and will be 'homeschooled'. Again, however, it does no harm to contact your local education authority (LEA) to inform them of this decision yourselves. Whilst some LEAs do not seem to be fully supportive of home education, this is not universally the case: many home-educating families do so successfully, and with the full support of their LEA.

In Bedfordshire, for example, the PLACE scheme provides a range of subsidised enrichment opportunities for homeschooling families with younger children, as well as teacher-led, seminar-style GCSE and A-Level drop-in classes aimed at providing targeted support for teenagers in home education looking to sit public examinations. Similar initiatives exist nationwide, and many hundreds of families use them every year as a useful accompaniment to their own private home-education.

Once you've been registered as elective home-educating, you can expect to receive a letter requesting further details about your child and your plan for delivering effective full-time education for him/her. The letter clearly states that you're under no legal obligation to respond; however, I would again urge you to write a short reply, professionally and without emotion about the circumstances which have provoked your decision. The role of the LEA at this stage is essentially to check that the child is not at risk in the home environment, and that the family understands their responsibility to provide an education. Think carefully about how you word your letter, and what you would like to share about your homeschooling ethos. It is not true that all LEAs are resistant to forms of learning that do not 'look like' school; however, because this is not the 'norm' in terms of education generally, you will need to feel confident in explaining your approach and methodology, if it is non-traditional.

It is less common for a representative of the LEA to request a home visit, but if that does occur, you are again at liberty to refuse the visit. I would simply caution you against being overly hostile towards an authority which is, fundamentally, providing an outreach for child protection – an essential function which we would all want to support. This is absolutely a personal choice, though, and of course we might well question why all families attending mainstream school don't receive a home visit as well, to iron out the same concerns.

Homeschooling Terminology AND Approaches

Homeschool (HS): Mostly used internationally, especially in the USA, this term describes any family educating their children from home, and is not, in itself, indicative of any pedagogical approach or identification with the traditional school model.

Home Education (HE): This is the term preferred by most home educators in the UK, again encompassing all families and/or legal guardians choosing to educate the children for whom they are responsible in a setting other than school.

Education Otherwise (EO): Taking the wording from the Education Act 1996 regarding the right to educate 'either by regular attendance at school or otherwise', EO is a charitable organisation promoting home education and listing registered groups and educators.

Deschooling: A term to describe the time-frame required to let go of our ingrained 'school way' of approaching education, such as: the idea of learning taking place during fixed hours, the division of subject areas, the use of terms like 'work' and 'get it done', and the attempt to create motivation through rewards and incentives. There is no 'end goal' for deschooling; wherever you are on the deschooling continuum is fine.

Unschooling: A child-led learning approach that advocates the benefits of autonomy in education. This, too, is a continuum ideology. Some families identify as 'autonomous' or 'semi-autonomous learners' which often means that they are conscious of the wider curriculum, but want to engage with their child's particular interests. However, families who fully embrace the unschooling ethos may allow their children freedom in every aspect of their lives, including food, bedtime, clothes, screen-time and more. The idea is to actively engage with your child's agenda, and help them to understand their choices and needs.

School-at-Home (Structured/Semi-Structured): Many families do this with great success. For structured homeschooling, you will be following a curriculum (or designing your own) and meeting self-directed targets throughout the academic year. Families might have a timetable, or a daily 'window' in which study happens. Many 'structured' homeschoolers prefer the morning, so that the rest of the day can be free for leisure and social activities. There might be plenty of resources such as workbooks, textbooks, online learning and even some private tutoring involved in this homeschool method, and children who have been educated this way often achieve top results in exams.

Charlotte Mason: Home educators use the name of this turn-of-the-century educator and reformer to refer to her educational philosophy. Many home-educating families will – knowingly or unknowingly – incorporate some elements of the Charlotte Mason approach, which states the importance of feeding children an intellectual diet of the 'best ideas'. Mason referred to this as 'mind food', and emphasised the importance of inspiring young people with incredible stories and awesome facts about the world. Her main focus was on the liberal arts.

Montessori: An educational philosophy that encourages rigorous, self-motivated growth for children and adolescents in all areas of their development. Because Montessori schools exist, particularly in preschool and primary settings, this differs from unschooling in that it can be achieved within a more structured environment. Again, the goal is to nurture the child's natural desire for knowledge, respecting autonomy whilst providing a wide range of resources and optional planned activities.

Steiner: Also known as Waldorf education, this model is based on the philosophy of Rudolf Seiner and emphasises the importance of children's spiritual, moral and creative-artistic development, alongside their intellectual progression.

Classical Education: This is an approach based on a three-part process to training the mind, called 'the trivium'. The instructional style builds on a method developed by Martianus Capella in the Middle Ages, and involves teaching based around three distinct stages of learning: Grammar, Logic and Rhetoric. When many people refer to Classical Education, however, they are simply referring to the use of traditional resources and texts considered to be 'classic' in today's culture.

Eclectic Homeschooling: This is a way of describing a homeschooling method that 'borrows' from a range of different techniques. A family might, for example, tend towards autonomous learning with a Charlotte Mason 'mind food' philosophy, but find that there are some excellent workbooks for Science that their kids love and spend half an hour a day working on after breakfast. This can work well for parents and children, as there's a lot of flexibility.

Secular Homeschooling: This refers to any home-educating family who do not identify with a religious belief or spiritual purpose.

Religious Homeschooling: These are homeschoolers who follow a faith. The home-educating community is generally supportive of religious families, the most common homeschool faiths represented in the UK being Christianity and Islam.

'Can Anyone Homeschool, Then?'

Broadly speaking, yes. In *Teach Your Own*, John Holt defined the 'special skills' required to be a home educator like this:

> We can sum up very quickly what people need to teach their own children. First of all, they have to like them, enjoy their company, their physical presence, their energy, foolishness and passion. They have to enjoy all their talk and questions, and enjoy equally trying to answer those questions. They have to think of their children as friends, indeed very close friends, have to feel happier when they are near and miss them when they are away. They have to trust them as people, respect their fragile dignity, treat them with courtesy, take them seriously. They have to feel in their own hearts some of their children's wonder, curiosity and excitement about the world. And they have to have enough confidence in themselves, scepticism about experts and willingness to be different from most people, to take on themselves the responsibility for their children's learning. But that is about all the parents need. (Holt, 2003)

Whilst this may appear a daunting definition, the point Holt is making is that you do not need to be specially qualified, or indeed a 'teacher', in order to homeschool your children. The fact that you are concerned about your child's education, and are holding this book, makes me fairly certain that you already fulfil most – if not all – of the qualities described here. They are, essentially, the attributes of a loving and engaged parent.

What this does not extend to, as touched on at the start of this chapter, are parents who would be putting their children at risk of abuse or neglect by home-educating. These circumstances are rare, but homeschooling would not be appropriate where the following exist: alcohol or substance abuse; the risk of domestic violence or sexual abuse; any form of emotional or physical neglect; or a severe mental-health crisis in either parent. In any case, a family in one of these scenarios should be closely followed by social services and would most likely not be seeking to home-educate, nor granted the right to do so.

There has been much talk recently regarding the importance of stricter surveillance of homeschooling families, following comments by Ofsted's chief inspector Amanda Spielman and, in the USA, Harvard professor Elizabeth Bartholet. When we interrogate these concerns, however, what we find is a perfectly valid concern for identifying the small minority of children for whom home is not a safe place to be. This demographic exists within the school system too, and nobody would disagree that at-risk children need to be protected; there is no need for a war over this. Home education and child protection are not the same issue, although unarguably, homeschooled children deserve the same rights as school children to grow up in a secure environment. We are all on the same page, in my view, and we must not shoot ourselves in the foot by confusing educational approach with safeguarding.

Finally, there may be families for whom homeschooling simply would not be possible due to finances. It is a big decision to home-educate, and there are many ways to juggle work successfully around homeschooling, such as working from home, running your own business, flexi-time and shift work, and splitting the week with your partner to 'tag team' part-time work with home education. However, I acknowledge that there are households for whom even creative thinking cannot change the reality of their working lives and financial choices, meaning that homeschooling is almost certainly not an option.

For anyone in this position, I would say that it is not impossible to incorporate the 'ethos' of home education into your lives and, significantly, to communicate clearly with the school what your educational principles are. There needs to be more dialogue like this, and schools will have to become more flexible and responsive to such requests, if they are to evolve and thrive in a world where more and more parents are choosing to withdraw their children from the school system.

'Isn't It Exhausting Being with Your Children All the Time?'

You know, I get asked this question all the time, and the answer is actually 'No'. Not at all. You will notice that none of the homeschooling families who've contributed to this book have mentioned finding their children difficult or exhausting, even though some of them have children who came into homeschooling due to challenging circumstances. Young people who are home-educated simply behave and interact with their families differently to those who go to school. They are not 'special', and there is no 'magic ingredient' here; but I will try to explain what the difference is.

Firstly, to address the concept of being with your children 'all the time', it is important to understand that these words would not ring true for most homeschooling families.

1. In their day-to-day lives, home-educated children quickly become independent in the way they manage their time and organise themselves. By the age of 5 or 6, the majority of homeschool children I've met with would be confident making their own snack, reading a book on the sofa, finding paint and paper to spend 20 minutes at the table by themselves, or choosing a favourite radio station or play-list to enjoy while reading comics. This is the sign of a child who has been nurtured and guided to understand his or her own needs, and is capable of a fair amount of autonomy in this area.

2. As parents settle into the homeschooling community they should certainly find themselves 'clicking' with some like-minded families, as well as attending a range

of groups and activities where their children can socialise. Over time, both trust in your children and bonds with other families strengthen, so that you might soon feel confident to allow your child to spend the day, or even sleep over, with another family, if they'd like to. The difference is that home-educating families *really* get to know each other – beyond a quick 'hello' at the school gates – which means that a careful parent can thoroughly check out a family, and get the measure of what their home set-up and parenting style are like, before allowing their child the autonomy to visit independently. This actually makes homeschooling an extremely social and autonomous experience for many children. Naturally, though, many of these opportunities are 'on pause' since the pandemic, and may take a while to re-establish; so my message here is to stay strong and give it some time, if you are brand new to homeschooling.

Secondly, I think all home educators would admit to sometimes feeling 'exhausted' – but not on account of their children. The homeschool approach, regardless of which methodology you choose, tends to change children in a very short space of time. If you are withdrawing your child from school in order to home-educate, you may soon observe that they're less angry, less hooked on screen-time, getting on better with their siblings, interacting more positively with you and your partner, and generally seem to have dropped a lot of the 'baggage' that goes with being a school child. This is because at the most basic level, children educated at home feel secure, relaxed, get enough sleep, and are given the time and space to feel 'switched on' and engaged with the world around them.

I will point out here that this positive change can take longer to occur, depending on circumstances. A child who has been severely bullied, or whose confidence has been broken by being labelled as 'dumb' at school, may take a long time to heal before you start to see the person they used to be emerging again. Similarly, if school was a battle for you when your child was attending, the bonds broken by emotional and sometimes physical coercion can take time to heal, and it is up to you to repair this damage by being present and open with your child at all times. There is more information about this in Chapter 3.

'But I Have a Baby, Too. How Does *that* Work?'

It's a funny thing, but the overwhelming majority of families I meet through homeschooling actually tend to have slightly larger families, often with a baby or toddler to incorporate. In fact, homeschooling your older children with a small child in the family is *exceedingly* rewarding, and enables you to view the way you engage with all of them quite differently. Crucially, it is important to recognise that we are home-educating *all* our children from the moment they're born – and making the transition to homeschooling brings this into close focus. Far from having less time with the baby, you might find yourself actually supporting that child much more effectively with their development and curiosities, whilst your older children will also benefit from the advantages of homeschooling in a mixed-age environment.

You can find more extensive notes on mixed-age interactions in Chapters 2 and 3, but I will summarise here the value of home-educating older children and teens alongside a small child:

i.   Babies and young children have a calming effect on older ones. They teach them empathy and kindness, and they help to keep the atmosphere playful and productive, providing everyone with the opportunity to have some down-time looking at a book or teaching the baby words, when they need space to recharge.

ii. The ethos of a homeschooling family generates an environment in which everyone is learning all the time. By having a baby or toddler in your family, older children are encouraged to think beyond themselves and to engage with the important learning that's taking place for their young sibling, too.

iii. Small children absorb all the complex information taking place around them, and having older siblings to look up to and imitate tends to have a powerful developmental effect on the youngest. This one may be the fastest at mastering basic skills, as well as the most strong-willed!

iv. Older children benefit from having a distraction in the house, as this gently pushes them to be more independent. When mum or dad are putting the baby down for a nap, or changing his nappy, the older children understand the situation and often end up answering that maths problem themselves, or inventing a good game together.

v.   By teaching information about the world to a baby sibling, older children also stretch themselves to process their own learning more fully, and consider exactly what they know and how best to impart that knowledge. This is a reflective process that aids their learning and progress, too.

One thing I would point out if you are homeschooling with a baby in the family is to be realistic about your expectations. We all have a vision of the kind of home-educating family we'd like to be, but the reality is that with a very small child, it's not always possible to tick all the boxes. The early years are a very labour-intensive phase! Give yourself a break with the cooking and have some freezer meals, or easy food like pizza and sandwiches ready to pull out when you don't have the time to cook properly. Ask your older children to help with food preparation and cleaning at least once a day. And if your ambition was to take an educational field trip every week (lots of families do this), then you might need to scale that vision down in order to cope with the here and now, but make a mental note of all the big adventures you'll have, once your youngest is a little older.

It is a wet start to the summer term. The trees are sodden – branches lolling under the weight of the water – and the 'all-weather' policy is now scrapped due to some particularly deep puddles causing trouble with Year 8.

Love
and the
Russians

Today is no exception. The canteen is shrill with the squeal of rain-slick shoes, and the dinner ladies are working flat out with Heads of Year to mop up the worst patches, exchanging frazzled looks and gesticulating wildly at any day-dreamer who bumps their bucket. Over by the steps, Leighann Haddon has 'accidentally' shaken her umbrella out, and Mr G is crossing the floor in quick strides to have it out with her. Such is the atmosphere in which love unexpectedly blossoms this year for Katya and Alexei, two of my most promising IB Diploma students. I can see them now, holding hands as they cross to the sixth-form building, stealing a kiss in the rain. The school rules, it seems, are for other people.

In truth, this is how the majority of their cohort behaves with regard to the laminated Code of Conduct at this inner London academy; they smile and carry on. The International Baccalaureate Diploma Programme attracts a certain sort. First, it's not a 'diploma' in the traditional sense, but rather a highly rigorous 'hexagon of learning', comprising six subject areas, as well as the notorious Theory of Knowledge essay and an integrated element of community service and personal development. It makes the A-Level look like a cheese sandwich. Secondly, the course consists largely of international students; kids who've been bounced through different school systems around the world and would normally be attending one of London's fee-paying international schools, but instead find themselves here – in a state secondary which, I was once told, 'works magic with a crap intake' – where they can do it for free. Katya waves at me from the library window, as I cross over in the downpour for their Literature lesson that afternoon. She's leaning on Alexei's shoulder and playing absent-mindedly with his long hair. I shake my head, but in truth I like them both a lot.

And I'm impressed by her choice of Alexei. Graceful, green-eyed Katya could have her pick of almost any boy on the course, and I had honestly expected it to be Bruno, or at least Yasin, with his hunched, handsome moodiness. But no. She has gone for the smallest boy in the class; slim-shouldered and uncomfortably intelligent, with rectangle glasses that keep slipping from the end of his long nose. Katya's no fool. And actually, Katya was the one who came to me at the start of September – before they were dating – hugging a stack of official-looking paperwork, and close to tears. I looked up at her, bemused. 'I can't read this, Katya', I said. 'It's in Russian.' And so she translated, line by line, the conscription letter, requesting Alexei's return to Russia for twelve-months' military service, unless it could be proven that he was in full-time education and had a place to study at a British university the following year. 'Oh *shit*', I said. And we got the documents signed.

In the library, the class are settled on beanbags rather than desks, and they all have their heads buried in Saadawi's *Woman at Point Zero*. Yasin. Bruno. The three Americans. Yamile from Colombia, who thinks my grasp of Marquez is laughable. Katya and Alexei. I fish around for my copy of the text, feeling what I always do with this group. That I am intruding on their thought process. That they don't really need me and my annotations, at all. I should, if only it were possible, simply sign the paperwork, and sit back.

'When Does "Schoolwork" Happen, Then, and How Can I Know Where My Child Is "at"?'

If you decide to homeschool, it is certainly important to move learning away from the school-based model of sitting at the kitchen table with pen and paper. All children are unique, and some will actually gravitate towards this style of learning as they relax into home-educating, but for many they will instinctively seek a more 'free range' approach to learning.

Here are a few ways to rethink teaching and learning for homeschooling parents:

- **Ways of Learning:** This is covered in more detail in Chapter 2; however we can summarise by saying that learning takes place all the time and in any variety of contexts. Painting can happen outside in the garden, on the floor, or standing up with a child-size art easel. Aspects of biology and geography can be discussed through conversational learning while you're out-and-about observing nature. An interesting book or TV programme might raise questions which can be further explored with an encyclopaedia or well-framed internet search. And the list could go on... As a general rule of thumb, try to remember that even in the classroom, teachers are aware that the more stacks of paper they have on their desk, the more they are 'evidencing learning' rather than focusing on the process.

- **How to Record Learning:** You will undoubtedly want to have some way of tracking your child's learning journey, so how should we do this? Having a drawer or shelf where your child can keep a folder of work and resources they're currently enjoying, such as workbooks and craft projects, is a good idea, and increases a child's sense of taking charge of their education. For older children, it might be appropriate for them to move this 'personal space' on to the computer, and to create a folder for their work, research and other projects. Structured and semi-structured home educators tend to create timetables for the week, and sometimes for the academic year, which support any concrete work that your child has produced; whereas child-led homeschoolers generally keep a retrospective daily log of the learning that takes place each day. Remember that photos, videos, leaflets from visits and tickets from events are also effective ways of documenting learning.

- **Avoiding the Temptation to Compare:** I do understand the desire to want to know where your child is 'at' compared to their peers, but research shows this to be unproductive, and even damaging to the learning process. Children all develop at different rates, and now that you're homeschooling, any examinations your child chooses to complete can be sat pretty much when they feel ready. Any time after the age of, say, 12 is the right time to be looking to your child to guide you as to whether they're ready – or even want – to take public examinations. A child who speaks another language at home might choose to take this subject very early on, in order to focus on another subject (or couple of subjects) the following year. Any attempt to measure your child and make them 'keep up' can have a detrimental effect on progress, and ignores two important points:

i. Learning isn't a straight line on a graph; it happens in leaps and bounds. One summer a child is not reading at all, and then by Christmas, they might have suddenly accelerated to the point of reading everything they can lay their hands on. In just the same way that babies around the age of one are typically *either* babbling really well *or* physically very mobile, so children also sometimes need space to develop one skill at a time. My son is really into numbers, and follows me around the house firing mental-arithmetic questions. He currently has no space for, or interest in, reading and writing, and I trust that we will work on that down the line.

ii. The actual content required for passing exam papers is not in itself strenuous, and can be acquired in six months or so of fairly focused study – even with zero previous knowledge – as and when a child is ready to make this commitment. I know this because I have done precisely that, many times, with children who've either missed years of school through illness or school refusal, and so require a 'crash course' before the exam. This also occurs regularly in schools where children might arrive in the UK at the start of their final exam year with very little English and no background in the UK curriculum. It is totally achievable. Much more important is the child's interest and willingness to engage with it, and see a value or purpose in setting their mind to take the exam. Don't worry yourself by focusing on your child's level, therefore, and instead just stay tuned in to how their day is going, what they've achieved so far and what they'd like to do next. It's a marathon, not a speed-race.

Although many homeschooling families do choose to cover 'academic subjects' in a window of time – usually morning or early afternoon – and then spend the rest of the day enjoying hobbies and socialising, when you're starting out it's well worth remembering that you're no longer obliged to keep to a school timetable. Because of our own inculcated habits of school and work, we tend to look at the clock and consider the hours of 9 to 5 as the 'homeschool day'; but this is simply not the case. From the moment your children wake up until they go to bed, they're learning, thinking, and processing constantly. This is a good way of relaxing around what your children are 'achieving' hour by hour, and instead observing what they're capable of when you back off a little.

My children often wake around 6 in the morning and are buzzing with energy; they're 'morning people' like me, and will happily sit down to a geometric puzzle or piece of writing at this time. Similarly, the tail-end of the day can also reveal flourishes of productivity, and is a good time to gently incorporate something that perhaps was missing from your day. For example, if we were playing with water and using the measuring jugs in the morning, we might find a moment before bedtime to snuggle on the sofa with the kids' illustrated encyclopaedia and look at the pages on materials, density and floating. This is the kind of focus that none of them were ready to give when they were running around in the garden earlier, shrieking and splashing in the sunshine; but now they're in their pyjamas, they are more receptive to thinking and talking this way about the learning that happened earlier. It is, of course, this kind of flexibility that's impossible to replicate in school.

'But We Haven't Enjoyed Homeschooling during Lockdown at All. We Certainly Don't Want More of This!'

Without a doubt, the Spring 2020 lockdown has been tough for everyone, but I think it's been hardest – in terms of parenting – for families whose experience has been dictated by the school. My sister-in-law sends her children to a grammar school, and began lockdown by phoning me daily, praising the school and offering to forward me the worksheets and online activities that her children were completing. Within a month, though, our roles were reversed, and it was my turn to counsel her on the improvement she might see in her two boys' motivation and engagement if she would allow them to pursue their own interests, and give them a break from the routine of 'logging in' and 'receiving an education'. Both boys are back to school now, and my sister-in-law remains resolutely negative about the experience of homeschooling and its suitability for her family. I blame the school for this.

Here's why I feel 'homeschooling' during lockdown hasn't really given families a chance to understand what it's all about:

- During the pandemic, the normal activities of daily life have ground to a halt, and all the liberating benefits of home education – museum visits, picnics with friends, Friday afternoon cinema treats, clubs and classes – have been temporarily lost from view.

- Families thrown into homeschooling during lockdown had almost no time to organise their working lives around educating at home, and in some cases, companies and employers have not been supportive in showing flexibility for homeschooling families.

- For the majority of families, learning has been 'delivered' in a strict timetable of online lessons, Zoom meetings and printable activities. This is the reason why many children have been passive and disengaged during this time, representing the very worst experience of learning at home.

- Additional pressures, such as loss of income and concern for the health of vulnerable family members, have added to a negative environment that is not conducive to learning, and is of course compounded by the public order to 'stay at home', which has been essential but claustrophobic for everyone.

I would add that there seems to be a clear purpose in the relentless 'bad press' that home education has received during lockdown. Nobody appears to understand what home education actually is, and yet we see newspaper headlines and public figures repeatedly announcing the 'dangers' of homeschooling, and the allegedly huge amount of learning that children have 'lost' during this time.

Fear-mongering is a classic propaganda technique used throughout history to keep the public 'in line', and I would put it to you that lockdown has shaken the core of the schooling system, exposing its poor methods and the general apathy of the students it serves. Many of the teachers I still work with feel apprehensive about the future, and fear being replaced by online learning, or more effective ways of self-educating. School, though, is a big business, and the message, like any form of advertising, is crystal clear: buy, buy, buy!

'You Mentioned a 'Rich Learning Environment' in Chapter 1. What Exactly Do You Mean by This?'

A good question. Although there are many superb learning resources out there (see p. 210), I think it's important to clarify that a 'rich learning environment' does not require shelves of expensive textbooks and activities. Of course, you'll purchase some of these along the way; and where you find something that works for your children, you might continue to buy second hand, or do exchanges with other families in order to access the full series of texts or workbooks. But this in itself is just an aid to learning, and is no replacement for the absolute basics: fresh air and access to 'real-life' learning opportunities, visits to interesting places, engaged and supportive parents and mentors, plenty of good books to read (the library is your lifeline here), paper and pens, and ideally safe access to a home computer.

It is important to look beyond the realms of stationary and 'stuff', though, in order to truly grasp what we are home-educating for. As a species, we humans are choosing to live increasingly limited lives. In every city, urban populations swell yearly around 'catchment area' postcodes, and children's lives quickly become dictated by spelling tests, entrance exams, gymnastics clubs, and even fake religious observance, if it means getting into the right school. Where is the time for lying on the couch watching the trees sway outside, and wondering what you'll make of your own life? Where is the time to go star-gazing on a clear night, or take a picnic and head out for the day on bikes? Their time – and ours – is often frittered away by a merry-go-round of 'meaningful' activities directed by well-intentioned adults. We have forgotten, I think, what it's all about.

I trained to be a teacher at the Institute of Education back in 2008, and I've been reflecting on my time there a lot while writing this book. Before I share with you some basic teaching methods (which you can feel free to discard, or simply use as a 'way in' to crafting your own homeschooling approach), I'll tell you what my supervisor would say, over and over again, during seminars: '*Who* are the learners, Anna, and *what* are they learning?' This lit a fire in me at the time, and I remember clutching coffee cups from the vending machine and babbling excitedly with other student teachers, as we walked down the steps to take the tube. Who *are* these people we will meet in our classrooms? What are *their* stories? What might we learn from all this?

Sadly, the reality of school is such that these questions rapidly dissolve, and the minds of the hundreds of children that any secondary school teacher might 'process' in the course of a week become 'buckets to fill' rather than people to know, or even fires to ignite. Don't lose sight of this problem, if you homeschool your own child. The very word 'teacher' brings with it a host of assumptions that can damage children's natural intelligence; and when the process is one-way, it becomes a self-fulfilling prophecy. Kids are smarter than the adult world gives them credit for, and they *get* smarter every day, when treated as equal partners.

'Are All School Systems the Same?'

In many ways, yes. A school is a school – but there are some educational models within the school system which provide an interesting contrast to what we typically associate with 'going to school'.

In Finland, for example, there is no Ofsted-style inspection, no streaming by ability, no fee-paying private schools, no school uniform and no school league tables; and yet a staggering 93 per cent of students graduate from either vocational or academic courses, with 66 per cent going on to higher education – the highest rate in the European Union. So what's going on here? The Finnish education system was revolutionised some 50 years ago as part of the country's recovery plan; and with the first PISA (Programme for International Student Assessment) test scores back in 2000, Finland was revealed to have the best young readers in the world. Three years later, they led in Maths, too. But this impressive ranking is barely on their radar. 'We prepare children to learn how to learn, not how to take a test', states Pasi Sahlberg, former director general of the Finnish education system. 'We are not much interested in PISA. It's not what we are about.' (Hancock, 2011)

Ultimately, this is a wise attitude to take regarding all league-table positions, but especially – from an ethical viewpoint – the PISA world ranking of education systems. The Finnish approach is unarguably a better method than ours, but nowadays China tops the leader board in global PISA scores across all subjects: reading, mathematics, science. Let's not speculate how

The very notion of 'teaching' goes against any autonomous learning model, so do feel free to skip this section if it doesn't fit with your home-education ethos. However, I have collaborated with a group of friends and colleagues from the world of teaching  here to put together a list of gentle and non-invasive 'teaching tricks' from which you can borrow, if you wish. It might help get you started.

- **Strewing:** This simply means 'putting out a selection of activities' to choose from. Notably, children always respond better to a task if they're given choice. This could be random (a sticker book, some colours, a good novel they haven't yet started) or it could have a topical focus. So if, for example, you were thinking it might be fun to do some baking, you could put a recipe book on the table and raid the cupboard for plenty of ingredients from which the children can select when picking a recipe to follow. For a maths focus, it might be a workbook, some dice, a bowl of pasta and an abacus. The key is letting the child bring their interest and direction to the activity.

- **Positive Praise:** 'What a great picture, Joe!' or 'That's sounding way better, Chloe; keep practising!' always works better than 'Stop that!' or 'No, I don't think so, Mister...'. Unsurprisingly, kids don't really want to be in trouble, and they like feeling the warmth of your praise. If you're having a difficult morning, focusing on any small achievement, or praising the efforts of a younger sibling who might be behaving in a more positive manner that day, can shift the atmosphere from 'No, no, no... *don't!*' to 'Yes, that's great; well done!'. You can't spoil a child with praise. Try to occasionally make your comments constructive, though, such as 'Oh, that's lovely. How did you mix that colour?' rather than just 'Wow, great!'.

- **Short Tasks and Rolling Projects:** Which is another way of saying 'variety is the key'. Make sure you have a range of activities and ideas for your children from which they can select and which are always available to them, such as: Top Trumps, books, magazines, paper and colouring pens, an atlas, a calculator, and plenty more besides. These can provide useful 'short, sharp' bursts of activity which might fill a gap between walking the dog and lunch, or some quick-fire brainwork after breakfast. Don't throw away their projects, though! Make sure you have a shelf or cupboard where you put abandoned projects such as a book that never got written, or a cardboard rocket that never really 'took off', so that the kids can return to and complete these items a few days later, or even weeks and months later – bringing a renewed vision to an old idea. This teaches some key skills: tenacity, evaluation and the satisfaction of completion.

- **A Note on Timetabling:** You might not want to consider any form of timetabling or structure – and certainly not if you're embracing the unschooling approach. However, if you would feel more comfortable home-educating with the reassurance of a timetable, remember that you'll need to look at the long- and short-term plan. What do you aim to have covered by the end of the year, and how will you break this down month by month? What will you do on a weekly basis? Try to keep this fairly loose and general, as the amount you can cover with a small group of children is astonishing; you might be setting your goals too low! See where it goes. Also, try to bear in mind the body clocks and natural habits of your children, considering when they are usually most alert and the times when they're likely to need chill-out space, or some fresh air and exercise. You are uniquely placed to do this successfully for your kids, as you know them so well.

- **Structuring Activities:** If your child announces that they want to write a letter, for example, you might consider whether or not you will help to 'scaffold' it for them. You'll likely not want to do this if you're following child-led learning; but not all children are the same and you know what will work best for yours. If you think they might be 'lost' with the task they have set themselves (and this could be anything from making lasagne to drawing the solar system, or planting tomatoes in the garden), it can sometimes help to provide your child with a few tools to help them 'access' the task, rather than simply telling them what to do. With the letter, for example, you could suggest that they begin by looking at a letter you received recently, to observe how it is laid out and how this form of writing tends to be structured. You could then ask a couple of questions, such as 'Who's the letter for?' and 'What's the purpose of your letter?', to help shape your child's ideas. Less is more, but there's no harm in modelling and scaffolding as a way of exposing your homeschooler to the tools they need to access the task.

- **Differentiating:** This is a fancy way of saying 'getting different outcomes from the same task', and it is an essential skill if you're home-educating with more than one child. Let's say you're doing maths in the kitchen. Your eleven-year-old might have a maths workbook that they enjoy, and be happily absorbed in a page or two from that, stopping to ask you for help every now and then, as they go. Your eight-year old, however, doesn't like sitting down for too long, so you're using dry pasta twirls to demonstrate division and multiplication on the floor, where the baby is plunging his hands into the pasta and laughing at the noise it makes. All of your children are learning and gaining something from this half hour, and you're able to support each of them differently because none of the tasks are entirely adult-led or supported. It's also a nice atmosphere to learn like this, and you'll notice a really fun sharing of ideas between your children as they grow into this approach.

- **Floating Ideas:** My kids are fairly autonomous and increasingly know what they want to do with the free time they have during the homeschooling day. We might have a club late morning and then friends in the afternoon, but for the first couple of

hours they're free to play and learn, mostly as they choose. This works well for us, and we often discuss over breakfast what they would like to do, which helps me to ensure I'm supporting each of them in achieving their goals. Like any family, though, some mornings we're all a bit tired or 'flat', and I can sense that they could do with a hand to help shift the mood. This is when I might 'float' an idea. 'I was thinking...' or 'Do you know? It's been a while since...'. The reason I use this terminology of 'floating ideas' is because this is an approach that always has more success than giving a direct instruction, such as 'We're going to do geography after breakfast' or 'I want you to finish your map this morning'. Nobody likes feeling dictated to, even adults, and it works better to frame your suggestion as a conversation, rather than set yourself up for a battle.

- **Shaping Learning with Language:** You can do this at any age, but in many ways it becomes more obviously constructive with a slightly older child, say above the age of 7 or 8. This is the age when most children start to show an interest in developing their minds and abilities in a conscious way. Even if you're taking an autonomous learning approach, you will find that children appreciate being given the 'adult' language to identify what they've just achieved through an activity or completed project. We all say 'Wow!' and 'Well done!' to our children, and in spite of some criticism which runs contrary to this, I think it's instinctive and nurturing; it does no harm. But what you could add to your appraisal are a few comments which help your child to consolidate their learning. 'Hey, that's such a great *inverted pyramid!* You've managed to get it to balance by getting the *centre of gravity* just right; nice one!'; or 'Oh, your poem, let me see... yep I really like it. Short and sweet. Almost as short as a Haiku. *Do you know what a Haiku is?*' In truth, you don't need to know lots of technical terminology to make this effective, though. If you're stretching their thinking beyond the immediate act of finishing the task itself, you're already pouring fertiliser on their minds for the way in which they will approach their next project.

- **Collective Behaviour Support:** It would be surprising indeed if you never had to deal with behaviour issues between siblings, even if they mostly get on well. Sometimes, though, it can feel like one member of the family is always in the 'dog house', and this will have a negative effect on their self-esteem, mood and concentration. You need to figure out how to change things. If you've exhausted all the usual conversations and measures to curb negative behaviour (things like pushing a younger sibling, not sharing, shouting a lot, or finding it very hard to come off the TV or computer), then it might be time for *collective behaviour support*. This is where the whole family unit sit down together, and discuss how everyone can help this person to feel better and behave in a more positive way. Such intervention can have quite surprising results! Far from creating conflict or another flare up, it can often bring everyone together and siblings who previously seemed at war often stick up for each other, making useful suggestions and showing the child at the centre of all this their love and support, rather than animosity.

- **Raiding the Cupboard:** 'Out of sight, out of mind' really is true, especially when it comes to younger children. You can use this to your advantage, though. Aim to have a cupboard or storage box where you keep things that haven't been popular for a while (activity books, word searches, maths dice, glove puppets), and be sure to turn this box out every now and then to explore what's inside. Your children might spend a month or so intensively drawing and working on comic-strip animations, which leads to other resources being neglected and forgotten. Simply suggest one morning that you all have a look in the resources box and allow them to take their time going through it and selecting materials; it's very rewarding.

- **Self-Assessment:** Such an empty buzz word in the world of education, but nevertheless an important life skill when done correctly. I would suggest a non-invasive approach to this, such as keeping all folders of 'work' (writing, drawings, theatre tickets, projects) in one place where your children can access them freely and, if they want to, spend time looking back on what they've achieved over the months and years. This is often a favourite activity and can inspire new ideas and topics of interest, as well as natural reflection on personal progress.

- **Routines and Expectations:** Much of the joy of home education lies in flexibility and allowing your children to lead the learning with their own directions of interest. However, many children also enjoy some sense of routine, and this can be an enjoyable way to see progress on a particular theme or topic over time. For example, we have some friends who devote every Tuesday afternoon to recycling; a family project which began in the home but has evolved into a weekly volunteering project. 'Baking Monday' or 'learning visit Wednesday' could also work well. In our family, we have 'letter-writing Friday' which we simply did two weeks in a row, and this has now become a 'thing'. The kids love receiving letters in the post and, over time, this weekly routine has evolved from writing personal letters to friends and family, to contacting local MPs and entering magazine competitions.

such astonishing results came to be. For anyone seeking academic excellence, though, and who turns to PISA for answers – be careful what you wish for.

But we need not worry with the Finns. Indeed, far from the current Western model for state education, Finnish students only begin school at age 7, and there was until recently no compulsory schooling past age 16, forming a total of nine years' mandatory education compared to almost 15 in the UK. It's as far as post-industrial schooling has come to a perfect system, and it looks like there is even a move to disband the division of separate academic subjects, which would be revolutionary indeed! This really is worth looking into, if you're keen to see how a 'school' model can have better results *and* less academic pressure than we currently place on children in the England.

Another interesting one to watch is the Sudbury School Model, which defines itself as 'a self-directed, democratic setting for students aged 5–18'. This highly distinctive prototype first began with the Sudbury Valley School, and has since gained popularity as an autonomous and self-governing system of education. There is even a recently opened Sudbury School in Kent, in England. Students are in charge of their own learning in this setting and freely mix among ages, with adults sharing equal rights and responsibilities with the students. No formal teaching takes place unless a child directly requests information from another student or adult mentor, and there is no curriculum. All students have unlimited access to a wide range of learning resources and materials, and older students operate an 'open campus' policy, meaning they're free to leave for visits to parks, museums, cafés and libraries in the local area whenever they want.

In his book *Free to Learn*, Peter Gray discusses a study he conducted into the success of the Sudbudy Valley School. By contacting the majority of 'ungraduates' from a single academic year, Gray discovered that 75 per cent had gone on successfully to higher education, and reported no difficulty with 'getting into the schools of their choice or doing well there once admitted.' (Gray, 2013). The majority of graduates (82 per cent) also claimed that their preparation at the Sudbury Valley School was beneficial for their future lives and careers, equipping them with a relaxed attitude, high motivation to learn and significant independence when it came to pursuing their goals as adults. It is certainly one to watch; and if I lived in Kent, I would definitely be considering this as an option for my children, if they ever wanted to return to a 'school' setting.

Montessori and Steiner schools are also popular alternative models, although they tend to have a bigger presence at preschool and primary level. The Montessori method of education is a child-centred approach, based on the scientific observations of Italian physician Maria Montessori. You will find many nurseries and some primary schools claiming adherence to the 'core values' of Montessori; developing the child holistically and following a child-led curriculum. Go and check it out, though, because the promises of the website and the vibe of the classroom don't always match up. Waldorf education, also known as Steiner education, is based on the educational philosophy of Rudolf Steiner and aims to cultivate pupils' intellectual, artistic and practical skills in an integrated, holistic manner.

The terms 'Montessori' and 'Steiner' have quite different meanings when implemented fully and correctly within school settings. However, the frequent mislabelling of educational institutions for the purpose of attracting a 'well-to-do' demographic has led to the two definitions being, in some contexts, interchangeable bywords for 'schools looking to boost their image'. Read around the subject if you're interested, to be sure that the school you visit is the 'real deal', and understands the philosophy they are headlining.

'What Do I Say to Friends and Family about Our Decision to Homeschool? I Don't Think the Reaction is Going to Be Entirely Positive'.

No, it may well not be. People find it very hard when someone they know steps out of mainstream expectations and choices. There is an obvious reason for this; it places an unspoken question-mark over *their* decision-making, and nobody appreciates this feeling of scrutiny. Moreover, we are all naturally defensive of our life choices. Nobody is likely to hold their hand up and say, 'I know school damages my child's psyche and destroys their desire to learn, but I do it anyway because it's convenient for me'. Similarly, no home educator is going to start the discussion saying, 'I'm honestly winging it a lot of the time, and some days I have doubts about whether this is the right thing to do'. And so, we all mount our 'soapboxes' to justify our positions, and tension can arise between people who were previously on the same page in their values and life choices.

The best advice I have ever received in this area was to drop my own defences. It's easier said than done, because for many of us, at least the first few years of home-educating are a constant process of review and justification for what we're doing. We care. But the truth is that you're not going to convert everybody; and in fact, the likelihood is that most people don't want to hear your educational philosophy at all. It messes with their view of the world and their own life plans, and so as a result, you'll almost always get a negative reaction. Remember that it is *you* who has chosen to take your family on a different path, and that a consequence of this is that you might occasionally need to be the 'bigger person' and let go of your worldview in order to create harmony with your neighbour (whose children all go to school), or the grandparents (who might not be convinced by what you're doing).

Instead of trying to explain or prove anything, I recommend this simple course of action for friends or family who are uncertain, or even critical, of your choice to home-educate:

- Compile a shortlist of the best books you've read on home education, and communicate those titles to the person in question at the start of your journey. The Further Reading section at the end of this book can help you with that.

- Disarm any negativity by being overwhelmingly friendly and engaged in their lives, rather than focused on explaining yours. Asking questions, showing interest and reserving judgement is key here.

- Find other outlets for the powerful evangelism that comes with understanding the importance of home education, and how deep this philosophy runs. Of course it's political. Of course it's life-changing. But not everyone is ready for it, or even wants to hear it. Moreover, it is something most people need to discover – if ever – by themselves, rather than being led.

- Where there is persistent negativity or criticism of your educational approach, you may choose for a time to distance yourself from some friendships or even family members. Your children deserve warmth and stability, which you cannot provide if you feel harassed.

Another way of looking at this tricky area is with the English teacher's hat on. Every year, when it comes to creative writing we say the same thing to students: 'Show, don't tell.' It's a great mantra for life, though, and one of the positive things that came out of my time as a teacher and examiner. With respect to your home-education journey, therefore, try to focus on what a glorious transformation you see in your own children, and trust that the people who spend time with you will *see* the positive effects of homeschooling with their own eyes, and don't require a lecture on it.

'How Do I Find Other Homeschooling Families in My Area?'

Very simply and online, at least initially. Most of the home-educating parents I know tell me that everything is on Facebook. Simply join the groups that appeal to you and are relevant to your area, and then you can start attending some of the clubs and activities that are taking place. A good way to start might be your weekly home educators' meet-up, as this tends to be relaxed and without a focus, such as a sport or a trip to a museum. You'll have more time to chat with the other parents you meet in this environment. Be sure to be as bold as you can, and introduce yourself to people, explaining that you're new to homeschooling, and sharing some of your own story. You'll find most people extremely welcoming, and you'll soon be swapping numbers to arrange activities or visits with other families independently.

One thing I've learnt from experience, though, is to begin cautiously with the process of homeschool socialising. If you have withdrawn your child from school, it's tempting to want to 'replace' the network that you previously had with a new network and a new set of friends. This will happen naturally over time; but what you will come to learn about the world of home-educating is that families generally operate slightly differently from those within the school system, and tend to be more self-sufficient and comfortable spending a lot of time within their family unit. So you might not find a family which wants to meet with you every week – even if, initially, you might be seeking this kind of structure; but you *are* likely to build, bit by bit, a group of same-minded families with whom you enjoy spending quality time, when the opportunity arises. This idea may seem scary now, if you're at the start of your homeschooling adventure, but it's actually a very empowering and liberating way of living, once you've adapted from the relentless social expectations of mainstream school.

Finally, avoid abandoning all school friends and contacts straight away. It is absolutely true that withdrawing your child from school represents an implicit criticism of what goes on there, and this may well drive a wedge between your family and some of the people you were friendly with before. But not *everyone*. In fact, for our family I would say we have built our homeschool network significantly over the past year, and 'lost' just over half of the friendships we'd made from the local school. The families we *do* stay in touch with from this time now feel closer than ever, though, as I think we mutually feel the benefits of staying in touch and seeing our children remain friends. These families tend to be open-minded and genuinely keen to hear more about homeschooling: we're a useful contact for them, and our children teach their children to think and play differently compared to the majority of their school friends. But they are good contacts for us, too, and I enjoy hearing their perspective on the pros and cons of what's happening in the classroom, as well as seeing my children come home bubbling with playground songs and phrases they've picked up.

It is like keeping a finger on the pulse of mainstream life and – I expect this works both ways – it helps us to appreciate our own choices even more.

'How Can I Help My Child Learn to Read without a Teacher?'

Very easily indeed; let's take a look.

1. **Forget the school books:** Most children aren't at all interested in these basic phonics stories with repeated sentence structures and vocabulary (such as Biff and Chip, or Topsy and Tim); so just let your child have a go at anything they're interested in, from newspaper headlines to non-fiction books on topics like Ancient Egypt – whatever grabs their curiosity.

2. **Don't force reading aloud:** Schools always require children to read aloud – usually with volunteer 'reading assistants' – as with 30 in a class, this is the one way you can get around everyone and find out where they're all at. But actually many children don't like reading aloud, and develop skills much more rapidly when simply left alone to browse books. They might appear to flick through the pictures at first but then, bit by bit, most children begin reading. You can tell by their eye movement across the lines whether or not they're following the words, and if it feels appropriate, you could ask a few gentle questions later on to check comprehension. Try not to meddle, though; they can do this better than you think.

3. **Make reading special:** To encourage independent reading, it can be useful to make 'book time' feel fun and special. Sometimes we'll put up a tent indoors and get the kids to fill it with books and toys to enjoy in their own private space; or else I might just grab a couple of beanbags and put them in the corner of the kitchen with a big blanket over the top to create a 'reading den', where they can hide away with books and magazines. You might also find that playing chilled background music at a low volume can boost attention span and concentration.

4. **Model reading:** I know it's difficult to fit this in, but if you can, aim to model independent reading at least once during the day to show your kids how adults enjoy reading, and to encourage them to do the same. I have three small ones, and I do sometimes find this hard to fit in; but I always make sure I have a newspaper or magazine at the breakfast table, and if an article interests me I'll read it, and sometimes tell the children about what I'm reading, if they ask me.

5. **Read as much as possible to your children:** I'm sure you do this already, but the more exciting books you can fill their heads with now, the more of an appetite they'll have to become fluent readers themselves. Reading aloud, even when children are able to read independently, is also useful in helping children to understand pace, intonations, accents and expression in reading.

6. **Sibling reading:** You might find that asking your child to read a story book to a younger sibling will get a better response than you sitting with them to 'listen in'. This is a chance for them to step up and demonstrate 'how it's done'. It's also a good way to encourage your children to spend some quality time together and both make progress with reading, as the reader will sound out difficult words for younger ones to follow – a mutually beneficial exercise.

7. **Avoid correcting words too quickly:** It's very natural as a parent to step in and help your child to make the correct word sound as they're reading, but this actually means that your brain is doing all the work putting the connections together, not theirs. If they sound a word out and it doesn't come together correctly, leave it and see if they can figure out independently what the word could be. This develops neuroconnectivity, and helps the learning experience to stick.

8. **Don't over-stress phonics:** Research shows that the phonics method is ineffective – and can even be counter-productive – when it comes to achieving reading fluency (Pattison, 2013). Put bluntly, the phonics approach is good at herding large groups of children towards literacy, but at the expense of 'dumbing it down' to administer reading skills like a pill, or 'baby puree' – forgetting that our children have 'teeth', and should be encouraged to use them. The basic message is not to worry about using phonics, unless you're encountering real problems accessing reading beyond the age of 7 or 8. For most children, they'll make far better progress if you allow them to draw the connections between letters and whole words themselves.

'Maths Is the Area I Feel Most Concerned about Delivering at Home. Do You Have Any Suggestions Here?'

I have handed this question over to Charlotte Stanford, a colleague and good friend who makes Maths accessible and fun for ages 11–18. Charlotte currently works at a grammar school in Shropshire and tweets as @charlottepegram.

One of the most off-putting things about Maths for parents is the method. Even those parents who feel reasonably confident with everyday Maths can feel flummoxed by their kid's primary-school homework when they're faced with the 'bus stop' for division or 'the grid' for long multiplication. None of these formulaic methods are actually necessary, or even particularly helpful, beyond a classroom setting.

The best thing about learning at home is that you don't have to juggle differing or confusing methods; simply apply the same approach you use in day-to-day life. For what the majority of people are aiming for in Maths is confidence, not necessarily fluency. Confidence must come before fluency, and if we have parents looking worried, scared or bored in the face of Maths, then it's a massive obstacle for the children involved. Let's see how we can change our thinking here.

First off, what *is* Maths? In the early years, Maths is defined as the ability to count, measure and compare. We want to be talking to our children about 'how many?' and 'how much?'. Most people naturally count stairs as they climb them with a child, but you want to also give your child confidence in the 'how-many-ness' of a number, i.e. the 'three-ness' of three means that a child recognises the number three whether they're looking at the spots on a ladybird or the dots on a domino. The key, then, is to use the language of Maths in as many settings as possible, counting things of different size, or counting things that can't be seen or written, like sounds or gesture.

All children enjoy learning through song; and while some homeschoolers dislike traditional or rote methods for learning, the essence of song is that it imprints easily on to the mind and is fun to pick up. I also think it's rather hard to learn the core elements of Maths (such as times tables) without trying in some way to 'cement them' in the mind. There are plenty of online sites that help children to master these essential skills, such as the ever-popular Times Table Rock Stars (see https://ttrockstars.com/), and I would definitely advocate using sites like these: they're the equivalent of practising scales when learning to play a musical instrument – except that these sites make the process a great deal more lively.

It may be stating the obvious, but Maths is really all around us. Or rather, Maths is our way of describing the world around us. So, a child's natural attraction to mark-making grows into drawing shapes or representing space through small-world play and model-building. A child can design a garden by using a tray filled with sand, twigs and small building blocks, and in doing so can start to talk about objects being 'in front of', 'behind' or 'on top of' – as a result thus developing a sense of perspective. Or they start to consider the repeating pattern of bricks in the wall of their home, or on the print of a piece of fabric, or even the repeating pattern of words in the lyrics of their favourite rhymes; and in doing so, this sets children up for the (seemingly) scariest of topics – algebra.

Try getting your children to make patterns with the things they collect on a walk, and then 'model' using mathematical language by talking about how it is 'coded'. Talking about the relationships between objects, 'two leaves followed by a pine cone', helps them to build confidence in observing (saying what they see), but also in starting to verbalise generalisations. So, a leaf–cone–leaf–cone pattern becomes a simple ABAB structure that the child could then re-create using toys, shoes or the food on their plate. And as children get older, they will naturally work out the relationships between more complex repeating patterns, and feel happy playing around with the numbers until they can make a generalisation. For example, for a party or barbeque in your back garden, you might need their help working out how many chairs are required (see Figure 2).

Figure 2: Real-life Algebra – via Tables and Chairs!

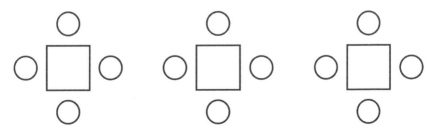

If you have five folding tables and each table has four chairs round it, you could either say 'we will need 20 chairs', or you could find a formula to represent the mathematical equation, such as $T = 4C$ (i.e. one table is equal to four chairs – thus, two tables would be equal to eight chairs, and so on). Providing real-life learning in this way grounds simple concepts that are the foundation of everything that is tested at examination level.

Of course, most of us won't need to write down algebra in our jobs, but nearly all of us would benefit from the life hacks that mathematical thought can bring to our lives – stacking, cutting, sorting and making. Mathematical minds use logic to find the quickest solution to a problem. Basic confidence in numbers is surprisingly easy to establish if you take advantage of family activities like baking, shopping and scheduling. Ask your child to work backwards from a fixed time, like getting them to count back from 5 p.m. (if that's the time they want to be sitting down to watch their favourite programme), or ask them to work out the difference in price between a single and a multipack item in a supermarket, and you suddenly have them thinking in ratios.

The bottom line is that Maths might have once been scary, because there were 30 sets of eyes on you and the sound of a ticking clock when you had to answer that question about circle theorems. But in real life, you can take your time, and mostly use the calculator on your phone. What's more important is being interested, asking questions and, if in doubt, fielding your questions to other people.

Finally, Maths is all about problem-solving, and that is almost always more interesting when done in a group; so if your son or daughter is interested in studying higher Mathematics, then you'll probably want to reach out to your homeschooling community to see what groups are already established.

With thanks to Charlotte Stanford, who tweets as @charlottepegram

'What about Taking Exams?'

There is currently no legal obligation for your child to take examinations in order to gain qualifications such as GCSEs or A-Levels. Many home-educating families put no pressure on their children to do so, and find that their children either choose to take a limited number of qualifications in certain key subjects, or else forget exams altogether. With plenty of support in making applications and finding work experience, as well as a clear vision for what they'd like to do in adult life, this approach can work out just fine.

Anecdotally, you will also hear many people tell you of homeschoolers who ended up in top universities with no qualifications whatsoever, based on a unique personal statement supported by relevant experience and skills. Given that exam boards set the academic benchmark fairly low and are indisputably over-generous with their marking, universities are often at a loss to make choices between identical candidates, and welcome something rather different to read. Home-educated students also tend to perform well at interviews, as they're used to talking to adults as equals, often have rich and interesting life experience to share, and generally don't exhibit the same performance-based anxiety that many school children face.

If your child doesn't want to pursue higher education, then work experience is the key; and it will be through this that they'll discover whether any qualifications or training are necessary in order to launch a chosen career path. Help them to form industry connections, and to draft an acceptable letter requesting work experience, making it clear that they are home-educated and are requesting this because of serious intent on pursuing a career in this area, as opposed to fulfilling the school's Year 10 work experience schedule and just copying a letter template provided by their tutor. You'll be surprised how many positive responses your child gets once people realise the initiative is their own.

If you wish to follow a traditional exam path, however, then you'll need to begin planning for this when your child is around the age of 12 or 13. Your tasks will include:

- Discussing the subjects that your child would like to take by the age of 16 (you can then look to the examinations at age 18, in a few years' time).

- Considering whether it would be best to sit all papers in one summer, as at school, or to split it over a couple of years, taking perhaps two or three qualifications per summer.

- Choosing the exam board carefully, looking at the syllabus to make sure your child is happy with the content they'll have to cover and the nature of the final assessment. Many home-educating families choose IGCSEs with Cambridge Exam Board, rather than GCSEs, which use boards such as OCR, Edexcel and AQA.

- Registering your child with a Registered Examination Centre in order to be able to sit the exam papers. This is often a local school, but it really depends – look it up online.

- Paying the fee to the exam board for each subject your child takes. This usually comes in at well under £100 per unit, but it does vary for each subject and paper. Again, this information is all available online under the 'fees' section.

As your child prepares to take an exam, there are several things you can do to help. First, read through the specifications carefully, noting all the skills and information that will be tested and, especially, the structure and assessment scheme for the exam papers. Remember that exams are essentially a test of how well you can feed back information and deliver what's wanted on each section of the exam; so keep a level head when you're going through the information. There are a lot of words there, but the actual content is manageable; and there's also plenty of support available, not least from the exam board helplines.

You should definitely invest in some of the recommended workbooks and textbooks which accompany a specific qualification, and as soon as possible you should get hold of past exam papers and model answers (all usually available online through the exam-board website, but again call the helpline if you have any trouble accessing these). Your child will want to know from the word 'go' what they're aiming for and where this is going. If your child is struggling to access this new way of learning and feels overwhelmed, don't panic. A few sessions with a private tutor in a couple of subject areas might well put them on the right track, and many LEAs run state-funded local projects aimed at helping homeschooled children through exams with the help of voluntary classroom teachers working in small groups. The CLIMB and PLACE schemes are examples of this. Contact your LEA for further information on what's available in your area.

As a rough guide, I would say set aside a year to prepare for an exam session, with no more than six subjects taken in one summer. Spread the content out over the course of the year and factor in at least two months of revision and past paper practice under timed conditions prior to the date of each exam. If your child keeps a level head and sees this for what it is – a hoop to jump through – they'll do just fine.

'My Child Has Special Needs and Receives Extra Support in School. I Honestly Don't Know if I Could Cope Managing This Alone at Home.'

I do understand your concern, and I wonder whether a part of the problem for parents of special-needs children can be that they have exhausted so much energy battling the school and local authority for the support they need for their child, that the challenge of home-educating can appear more overwhelming than it actually is. Some schools do a great job adapting the curriculum and finding appropriate support for children with neurodiversity; but many do not, and this places a child with Dyslexia, Autism, ADHD, Sensory Processing Disorder and many others in a stressful, frustrating environment. Your child may be 'down', withdrawn, disengaged or lashing out because they feel like a failure every day in school. Home education can turn this around.

Children with neurodiversity often feel more secure in their home environment, and frequently – but not always – benefit from taking things at a slower pace. If your child has Autism, Down's Syndrome or Auditory Processing Disorder,

Engaging properly with your children is the key to a happy home, and it is naturally a crucial aspect of home-educating. We all know how to show our children respect and give focused attention, but life is so busy

that it can sometimes feel hard to carve out these moments. The following quick guide to connecting with your children aims to provide you with a basic checklist for how to engage fully with each other throughout the day.

Stop! When your child comes to you with something to say, aim to stop what you're doing and give them your focus. If this takes a moment (like turning the tap off and drying your hands, or wrapping up a phone-call), let them know that you'll be with them – and they'll shortly have your full attention.

Look! When you have smaller children, especially if they are upset or wound up, it can be respectful to crouch or kneel at their level. This means you can give them proper eye contact and also be available for a hug, if that's what they want. This face-to-face interaction is also essential for language development and emotional education; a reason why it would be preferable to minimise the amount of time small children spend in car seats and outward-facing pushchairs.

Listen! It's so easy to brush off much of what children come out with, especially when they're in the babbling and constant chattering phase, which lasts a long time! Let's try not to do that, though. Let's remember these are little people, and whatever it is matters a whole lot to them. If you didn't hear properly, or you don't quite understand what they're talking about, let your child know and ask them to repeat it.

These are the absolute parenting basics; however, I will add two more specific parenting tips below, which I have personally found helpful over the years.

Be playful and affectionate (especially with a girl): It is beneficial to be playful and affectionate with boys and girls, of course, but girls *really* need this kind of attention! We all typically observe our little girls growing up much more quickly than our boys, and they soon appear independent – mature, even – and tend not to be constantly hugging our ankles and crawling into our laps, like their brothers. That's why it's so important to keep an eye out for when your girl is seeking this kind of contact. She may not want to say, 'Can I read the book on your lap?' or 'I want to play at wrestling, too!' because she feels that she's 'too grown up' for this, or else fears not being heard. Pull your girl in and get her involved in the tumbling and cuddling of family life – if she's wanting this, and on *her* terms. Find gentle ways to tease her and play slapstick fighting – just like we all do so naturally for boys – because this is the stuff our girls desperately *need* to reduce anxiety, boost positive endorphins and grow up well.

Set firm boundaries (especially with a boy): Our boys are so cute, aren't they? And cheeky, too! We all seem to have a different threshold with boys and that is, in part, because we can sense – quite correctly – that they're developing at a slower pace compared to their sisters. A slightly wild four-year-old boy can really seem quite adorable in the way that a moody and demanding girl of the same age isn't. We are right in assuming that our boys are more 'childish' and therefore need a different approach, but we mustn't let them become disrespectful and aggressive. Play-fighting is fine, within the proper boundaries. But many little boys struggle to contain their rage or excitement, and can tend towards pushing, biting, kicking and throwing things around the house in a bid to burn off excess energy. It is wonderful if you understand the biology of your boy enough to appreciate that this is largely beyond his control at this early stage; but it's essential not to allow aggression or disrespect for other people to become a habit. Be firm, be consistent, and make sure your partner backs you up, every time.

they may for different reasons benefit from shorter tasks and more visual or kinaesthetic learning. A multimedia curriculum and resources can work well, especially when counterbalanced by plenty of fresh air and connection to animals and nature. With the best will in the world, this is not a balance that almost any school can hope to achieve within the inevitable constraints of the school environment. Children with Autism especially can find the perpetual strip-lights, and long corridors of block colours and echoing noise, highly stressful. It can be better to take them out of this setting, where you might notice your child 'come back' straight away.

Other special needs are more subtle – such as Dyslexia, which has an obvious impact on spelling but tends to impact a child more globally, affecting the way they structure ideas and process information. Back when I was at school myself, I remember extremely bright and creative students being held back by an entire academic year due to Dyslexia – a devastating blow to their confidence and a move which lacks any acknowledgement of the many gifts that come with Dyslexia. Although thinking has moved on since then, the reality is that the curriculum isn't written for dyslexic students, and the best schools can do is differentiate, offer extra time and perhaps a teaching assistant in some lessons. They cannot reshape the direction of the course, and the fundamental *way* learning takes place, for just one or two students. At home, however, you certainly can.

By home-educating your neurodiverse child, you can achieve some important goals which will set them up well for life:

1. Create a supportive, consistent environment in which they can thrive.

2. Avoid any chance of harassment or cruelty.

3. Network with other families who either understand your child's special needs, or within the home-educating community generally.

4. Find out what your child is good at and thrives on, persuing new opportunities wherever possible.

5. Set up a learning environment at home which works for your child in terms of resources, attention span, content and areas of interest.

6. Carefully consider the options available as your child moves towards their teenage years. Will they sit standard exams, or any exams at all? Would they benefit from work experience or volunteering in an area that engages them?

Homeschooling can be an extremely beneficial choice for your child, with or without special needs. Every child and every family set-up is unique, however, and you are best placed to make the decision as to whether you feel that you and your partner would be able to effectively manage home-educating around your working lives and your child's special needs. It can be an easy decision, but it's not one to be taken lightly. If you're still unsure, you could try talking to the Special Educational Needs Coordinator (SENCO) at the school, to focus your thinking about your child's requirements within an educational context. The school SENCO is usually very approachable and well-informed, and will likely be honest with you about what the school can and cannot offer for your child.

'My Children Are Constantly Distracted at Home. I'm Not Sure that They Would Actually Learn Anything.'

So long as your home environment is safe and supportive, there is no question that any form of distraction around the house pales in comparison with what goes on in school. I have seen teachers spend half of an entire double period (that's about 35 minutes) simply drilling the class in lining up quietly without shoving, shouting and so on. The old 'pin-drop' test is still alive in many classrooms. And the trouble is, this is a huge waste of time, especially for the majority of the class who simply want to sit down and 'get on with it'. In his recent article 'School's out', Tobias Jones portrays a familiar dynamic when he describes how 'the kids misbehave and the teacher yells, and soon everyone is shouting over each other' (Jones, 2020). Because of this common scenario, many classes are forced to sit in absolute silence during several lessons of the school day, as well as assembly, queueing for lunch, and listening to notices during form time. An unhealthy oscillation exists between total repression and reckless abandon, and we should remember in this context that sitting quietly facing the front is not at all synonymous with concentration.

For many children, therefore, the school day is quite straining, and represents a lot of human effort for minimal daily progress. Even once they're in the classroom, the process of taking the register, answering questions, delivering notices and generalised feedback – all take up a significant portion of the lesson, and again, this is irrelevant for many children who simply drift off and daydream for much of it. I would estimate that the actual amount of schoolwork children achieve to be approximately 25 per cent of each 'lesson'. In a secondary school, therefore, which might be divided into as many as eight 40-minute periods, this could be translated as approximately an hour and a half of *real* learning within a six-hour school day.

Put bluntly, if your child is putting in a couple of hours study (teens and older children) or play-based learning (under tens) a day, plus a range of other hobbies, social engagements, domestic chores and 'down-time' activities, this represents a far more productive day than one spent in the captive chaos of school.

Let's also observe here that procrastination is a natural and healthy aspect of human productivity. In school, timetabling dictates that a child might cover a topic and must then – on command – have to immediately 'summarise their learning' through some kind of written or oral presentation task. For a homeschooled child, however, it's quite natural to look at the same topic and then go to play Lego, or racket ball in the garden. It might be several days before they've processed what they want to 'do' with a topic, and this more accurately mimics the way adults would operate in semi-autonomous employment, and also in the wider decision-making of adult life.

An essential aspect of engaging properly with home education, therefore, is understanding the importance of *intrinsic motivation* – the desire to do things of our own accord, without coercion or bribery. All children are easily distracted, and it takes some time for the innate drive to learn concrete 'subjects' to develop. Before the age of 9 or 10, children often engage in what looks like play, but is actually of fundamental significance in terms of forming the way that they think and operate. Children who initiate their own learning and, from a young age, are encouraged to follow their interests tend to have high levels of competence and self-motivation. When they eventually fall in love with an area of scientific knowledge, or a fascinating historical era, they will be capable of directing their research and devouring information for pleasure – there is no battle. In this way, home-educated children don't 'cover' a topic; they *own* it. Failing to teach children *how* to learn, therefore, is a self-fulfilling prophecy, and highlights one of the most damaging conundrums in our modern lives. Parents – who were typically never taught how to learn themselves – feel they lack the skills to deliver an education at home for their children. I wonder whether this personal anxiety forms the basis of much mainstream resistance to home education; for it challenges everyone to question their own capabilities, and what they 'got' out of school.

Finally, on the subject of children's willingness to engage with learning and our management – or mismanagement – of it, I would draw your attention to the fact that we're coming towards the end of the book you're reading without once (I think) formally discussing *discipline*. This is a major deviation from school-based learning and its impact on dynamics in the home, and might take your child a while to get used to. Children are subjected to strict *behaviour management* throughout their time at school, via a system of rewards and punishments. From lining up quietly, to submitting homework on time, to copying from another student – the minutiae of personal conduct is dealt with through some form of discipline (detentions, removal of privileges, public chastisement, threat of exclusion...); and of course we then enforce this at home when we use the TV like a carrot for getting schoolwork 'done', or when we side with the teacher over an issue and in some way 'punish' our children (emotionally, or physically – such as being 'grounded'). Operating outside this familiar structure can at first feel like an uncertain process.

Although I understand that schools are to a certain extent 'forced' – because of the size and nature of the institution – to 'run a tight ship' in this way, I certainly don't think the outcome of even the most 'effective' Behaviour Management techniques is a well-rounded, moral and highly motivated person. There's a better way to get there. What, after all, *is* 'Behaviour Management'? I think discipline in schools (and at home) comes down to three things:

1. How we process our feelings

2. Understanding safety matters

3. Cultivating empathy

In the case of a child being 'constantly distracted' and lacking the motivation to pursue learning, therefore, we might typically see this addressed in school through a series of detentions, phone-calls home, parental meetings and, perhaps, an adult-devised action plan for the child.

At home, we can and *should* do better, though. Why is the child feeling this way? What exactly is the problem with their course of action? Given the same predicament with my own child, I might ask myself, first, whether I need to give him or her space to have total autonomy in this area for a while (perhaps they're reclaiming some of the personal direction that was taken from them by school), and secondly, are the activities that they're 'distracted' by entirely meaningless, or am I imposing an unhelpful agenda on my child's choices and interests?

'Do Home-educated Children Have Much of a Social Life?'

This is the bugbear of all homeschooling parents – the question we get asked all the time. The answer is a resounding 'Yes!'; but let me offer you a bit more insight.

Our understanding of what friendship is and the nature of human connections have changed immeasurably within the past 20 years. The rise in social media interactions and 'screen-time' (especially mobile phones) has rapidly taken us to a place where we've developed unhealthy ideas about what socialisation should look like. These include:

• Being 'connected' and 'available' all the time

• Measuring our self-worth based on the number of social media followers we have

• Consequently, treating friends as 'followers' rather than real people

• Needing to amass a large number of friends, rather than a few important ones

• Allowing the culture of 'likes', hash-tags and trolling to infiltrate the way we deal with actual people, at work and in the playground

The misunderstanding of socialisation is part of the problem when it comes to understanding the way socialising happens in home education. Regardless of evidence which points to the importance of 'unplugging', there's an increasing tendency for families to be 'constantly social' – in person and online. It's now considered normal to spend all day in a large group, either at school or work, and to arrange 'playdates' and further social time after school, including at the weekend. Even when we are travelling to and fro, we're constantly available on our phones, exchanging WhatsApp messages and Tweets with a frenzied concentration, as if this was of the highest importance. It is very hard to step back and imagine doing things another way.

Most homeschooling families will, for the most part, undertake the majority of structured or autonomous learning together at home or in the local area, with a few classes and activities to punctuate the week, as well as 'real-life' tasks (shopping, dentist, post office, library...). Children who are home-educated are no angels, but they quickly form strong family bonds, learning to rely upon and respect each other, as well as seeking friendships outside the home.

An interesting aspect of this is that, for example, when the recent pandemic took us all into lockdown, I don't recall a single homeschooling family complaining about 'missing their friends'. The home-educated children we messaged, wrote to and did video chats with during this time seemed almost universally to accept the situation, and to be rather *enjoying* kicking around at home. Fundamentally, the homeschool family unit is strong, and isn't seeking constant contact and reassurance from fleeting friendships. This might seem hard to comprehend, but if you think about it, this mentality forms the basis of most solid relationships and households in the adult world. This is, surely, what we want for our children when they grow up and have a family of their own? To be happy in each other's company? To be talking face-to-face with their partner, not sitting next to each other on their phones?

When homeschooling families *do* socialise in groups – either for 'family days' together or, as children get older, increasingly independently and on their own terms – it tends to look quite different from the way school children typically mix. We had a real problem when my daughter was at school, with friends coming over to play and immediately going into my daughter's bedroom and shutting the door on the boys. 'Big girls, only.' 'No boys and no babies allowed.' This happened so frequently, and is such a contradiction to the way that we have raised our children, that my husband and I began to wonder whether we were the strange ones. Until, that is, we discovered homeschooling.

There are no 'big ones' and 'babies' in the homeschool community; there are just people. A 14-year old boy will not ignore the request of his eight-year-old sister and her friends to help build their den. It is an opportunity to share his skill, and to feel the power and wisdom of his age; it's good for him, and he knows he'll get many admiring looks as he does so. Similarly, babies are not just left to the parents, but are quickly absorbed within the larger group of children playing, with the older ones usually responsible for the safety and rules of the game, while the younger ones fool around teaching the baby words or playing 'peekaboo'. The parents get to keep an eye from a distance, and have a well-earned cup of coffee!

Because the quality and general atmosphere of mixed-age homeschool play tends to be so positive and enjoyable, the time spent together is also totally different. Children need far less 'micro-managing' when their play is naturally regulated by a healthy mix of ages and genders, all keen to be involved and keep the game going. Rather than arranging a rather stressful playdate after school, which might last two hours and has to be broken into several times to resolve disputes, a homeschool family might arrange to come over to our house on Wednesday and – I now know – we'll set aside the whole day for them. This is because the really good games won't even begin to get going until a couple of hours in; and just at the point when you'd usually be saying 'Goodbye-and-thank-goodness...' is the point at which the children seem to dive into another level of play and creativity. It's wonderful to observe whilst – importantly – keeping a respectful distance; for this is their time. Small disputes are naturally resolved, the game evolves exponentially, and we usually end up inviting everyone to stay for dinner.

'My Child Has Experienced Bullying at School. I Am Thinking about Homeschooling but I Don't Want to Teach Him to Run away from His Problems.'

This is a common concern, and one which I will address by responding to the two crucial fallacies that underpin this thinking.

1. **Children need to learn to 'toughen up' and face their problems:** There is a feeling among parents that school is a miniature version of the adult world, in which children must either sink or swim. We all hope our child will swim, of course! But in fact, nothing could be further from the truth in terms of the 'model' that school represents. Adults are not generally forced against their will into a constrained environment, where they have to ask permission to use the toilet, speak and even drink water, and where their performance is pushed and measured on a daily, sometimes hourly, basis. If they are and they don't like it, they're free to leave. School creates a toxic bullying culture because of the unnatural pressure of this environment, but also because the children trapped within it are undergoing major developmental change in a 'moral vacuum' where there simply aren't enough adults and positive older mentors to curb unpleasant behaviour and help students to respect each other. In the same way that a bully in Year 9 is still on a learning curve and may well grow out of this behaviour as they enter adulthood, so a child who is victimised doesn't need to be told to 'toughen up now, or they never will'. In fact, when a child is pushed too hard to 'be tough', it can have the opposite effect. Being 'tough' and 'facing problems' isn't a lesson that everyone, universally, has to swallow; and it's also a lesson that can be taken on board later in life, when we're older and wiser.

2. **Walking away from bullying is weak:** Many parents tell their children that violence is wrong but, out of concern for their child, they might add, 'If he hits you, though, hit him back!'. However, few of us would actually do this ourselves, faced with the same problem. Fighting is a waste of time and energy, unless it is for the purpose of real, immediate survival. Even if a child is pushed over in the playground in an act of bullying, an intelligent child will be quickly calculating the consequences of a range of different responses, as he stands back up. The fact that he may not choose to hit back doesn't show that he is weak; he's just thought it through. That same child backed up against a wall with someone holding a knife to them might demonstrate surprising strength and combat skills, because the scenario is totally different. But let's hope it never, ever comes to that. Choosing to leave school, therefore, due to a systemic bullying problem within a particular year group is not a sign of weakness. It shows, instead, that the family are 'wised up'; that they see the hopelessness of the problem, and don't want to be involved with that.

I am very sorry if your child has been bullied, and I wish I could say that it will be tackled in school; but the reality is that none of the innumerable measures that have been recycled over the past 50 years or so seem to work. School is simply an environment that perpetuates bullying, in the same way that the prison system and countries operating under military dictatorship are fraught with bullying and 'thuggish' behaviour (Gray, 2013). For more on this, see the 'Freedom from Bullying' section in Chapter 3 (p. 71).

'My Partner and I Both Work Full Time and Have a Mortgage. I Don't Think We Can Afford to Home-educate.'

Many homeschooling families started out just like you. It is definitely daunting considering a way forward with home-educating, when finances play such a major role in our modern lives. Most of us have high mortgages or rent to pay on our houses, and aren't in a position to just 'live on less' if we home-educate. The money has to come from somewhere.

The scope of this book can't cover the full ramifications of negotiating work and finances alongside homeschooling. Perhaps I should write another book just on this topic! I've ended this chapter, therefore, simply with some short personal stories that I've collected from home-educating families during my research for the book. I hope they will be of help to you in shaping your ideas.

> Maggie and I started homeschooling our girls a year ago. We travel a lot because of my work, and they were both really unsettled at school. The problem was that Maggie was working full-time too, and had clients calling her all day as well as tight deadlines to meet, even though she was working from home. It wouldn't be possible to home-educate like this! In the end, we looked at the situation and realised that, because of my job which takes us all over the place, we were spending less than a third of the year at 'home'. So Maggie quit her job and we rented the house out, which covered her lost income. It was quite emotional for all of us, but in the end it has worked out really well. Maggie absolutely loves homeschooling, and both of our girls are thriving. We live a very nomadic life right now, but it works for the time being. We're always ready for the next challenge (or, in my case, contract). and we see life as one big adventure.
>
> *James*

> It's actually kind-of serendipitous how we came to home-educating Finn and Georgie. Darren and I had both started retraining the year before Finn started school, taking online courses and gaining qualifications in order to move out of jobs that we both felt were uninspiring. I started practising as an Aromatherapist last summer, and Darren began his online business around the same time: we both began working from home in a

shared office space. So when it was almost immediately obvious that Finn wasn't at all coping at school, it was such an easy decision to make. We are both at home anyway, so we just worked our schedules and clients around our new homeschooling life and... – *boom!* It worked out well for us. Of course, Georgie wants to do everything Finn does, so I don't think she'll ever even set foot in a school!

Thea

My husband and I are both paediatric nurses, so we do shift work. The logistics aren't difficult, and we've had time to plan, because we knew from the start that we didn't want to send our children to school. We had to reduce our hours a bit, so there's less money to go around right now – but we cope. There's always someone at home to focus on the children, and when we occasionally get a couple of days off all together, it really feels like a holiday.

Sarah

Well, you really want to know the story? Here it is.... I was a single parent when I started homeschooling, and I felt so strongly about it, I didn't actually mind being on benefits because the quality time I had with Archie was something money couldn't buy. But yeah, we had no money, no holidays, and I sometimes wondered if I was making the right choice. Then we met Dina and George at a local home-ed group. They were brilliant and I clicked with Dina right off. She was a single mum like me, but she was running her own business from home three days a week. I think her parents helped out with childcare at this point, or something. Anyway, the boys clicked, too. George is two years older than Archie and they immediately acted like brothers, even squabbling over the remote control, but mostly getting on really well. We sort of formed a plan around Christmas time, when we realised both of our ex's weren't that interested in helping out with the homeschooling. We actually went and rented a house together. Well, this changed everything. Now, we could split the week and share the home ed. I went back to retail and picked up a part-time job two days a week, and Dina carried on with her PA business, working from the attic, which we turned into a study.

It's been about three years now and we're all doing great. The boys are so happy and get up to lots of mischief together, and money isn't so tight. Dina now has a partner called Sean, and he is a great addition to the home when he spends the weekend. We are all taking it slowly, but I know our lives will change again if Dina and Sean decide to move in together. I think this will impact mostly on the boys, who are the best of friends, and that's something we'll have to work on to make sure they still see each other regularly. I've managed to save money since living in this arrangement, though, and I feel established enough with other home-educating parents now that I think I would be able to continue working part-time by creating another shared homeschool arrangement with a different family to cover those days. We certainly have enough money to get our own place now, and that's a start.

Polly

We have two boys and a girl, who were all deeply unhappy at school. My daughter is the youngest; she is very shy. Our next son is also shy and doesn't seem to fit in with other children of his age. Our oldest boy was diagnosed with ADHD at school and we had problem after problem with him. It was exhausting, and we didn't understand because he wasn't like it at home. In the end, I sat down with my wife Imani one evening, and we talked for a long time about the future, thinking a lot about what we really believe in. We are both risk-takers, and would like to educate our children beyond the curriculum of just one country. We want them to be global citizens.

So, we did a lot of calculations over the next few weeks, and in the end we decided to try worldschooling. We didn't really have a plan at this stage – just the feeling that nothing could be worse than the situation we were in, and that our children's happiness was all that mattered. We were renting a house in Tooting but we had plenty of savings, so we just ended our contract and went, really. This was two years ago. At first, we travelled a lot, but now we tend to stay in one place for around six months and make some real friends. One of us will pick up contract work, or some online paid jobs for the time we're there, and then we move on.

I think the children would like to settle at some point, so we're thinking of finding a business opportunity, like a café or a book store, that we could run together in a place where we want to put down roots. I have my eye on this amazing small premises on the island of Ithaca, but Imani thinks this is another one of my crazy ideas! We shall see.

Karim

CHAPTER 5

101 Activity Ideas

Knowledge which is acquired under compulsion has no hold on the mind.

Plato

This list is only a starting point; a way of looking at learning across a wide spectrum of ages and abilities, if you choose to homeschool. It does not represent a comprehensive curriculum, nor would I recommend structuring your day around getting your children to 'do' these activities. Think of it simply as a reference point – a source of ideas and inspiration, as well as subtle guidance regarding the breadth and creativity that is permissible within home education. Note that your children are likely to click with some, but not all, of the suggestions here. And if the idea of formal 'activities' doesn't resonate, please just skip over it.

101 Activity Ideas

1. **PLAY PIRATES:** Turn the sofa or duvet into a pirate ship; dress up, pack for your voyage, use the globe or atlas to locate where you're going in the world, and finish with a treasure map or the secret diary of a stowaway.

2. **CLOUD-SPOTTING:** Lie on your backs in the garden, on the balcony or in an open space, and look at the sky. What shapes do you see in the clouds? Get the paint box out and turn this into artwork; or check out a geography book or documentary to learn more about cloud formation.

3. **STORY CUBES:** Either use story-cube dice, or else take turns giving each other a task to tell a short story with three ingredients and a location. For example: 'Tell me a story involving a hippo, a chocolate bar and a pack of cards which takes place at the beach.'

4. **BACKGROUND MUSIC:** Whatever your children's ages and academic level, a bit of calm music often helps concentration and the flow of ideas. Try something relaxed and non-invasive like Classic FM, Scala Radio or BBC Radio 2.

5. **PASTA MATHS:** Get out the pasta or even use grains of rice, dried beans or buttons, to have a maths game with younger children. Take turns asking maths questions, and use the props to demonstrate how to add, subtract, multiply and divide.

6. **YOUR TURN TO COOK:** Hand over responsibility for the family meal to your children and be sure to get them started with a recipe book, so that they can enjoy the process of looking through the options, reading the recipe, measuring and searching for the ingredients.

7. **STUDY DEN:** Let them build a den or nest behind the sofa or under the kitchen table using duvets, throws, cushions and scarves. Once the den is ready, they might find this is a great space to snuggle up with books, or even do a bit of creative writing.

8. **PUT ON A PLAY:** As big or as small a task as you want it to be. This could use puppets and/or toys, or you could make sock puppets – and you might tell a story that's familiar, or invent one. Older ones may want to write a script, or create

tickets and a poster to advertise the play.

9. **COLLAGE:** Grab all the old magazines and newspapers and put together a collage, cutting out pictures and headings (or key words) that catch your attention. Explain the idea of a 'topic' to your children. Do they want to group their ideas in this way? What are the pros and cons?

10. **STILL-LIFE ART:** A fruit bowl, flowers, or even teddies set up around a pretend picnic would serve as a good stimulus for still-life art. Try different materials, such as paints, and then another picture using crayons or felt-tips.

11. **AUTUMN CLEAR-OUT:** Why not get stuck into a big organisational task? Tip out all the toy boxes in the living room and let your kids spend as long as they like looking through everything and sorting the items. You'll need a box for the charity shop and, probably, a rubbish bag.

12. **LANGUAGE IMMERSION:** If you want your children to speak another language, home education is the ideal environment. Why not begin every morning with a short TV episode such as Peppa Pig or Dogtanian, available on YouTube in the language of your choice?

13. **DANCE PERFORMANCE:** Ask your children to choose one of their favourite songs and let them listen to it on repeat. Give them, say, 20 minutes to prepare a dance recital, which they can make extra-special with costumes and props, if they want to.

14. **PEN AND PODCAST:** We do a lot of drawing or writing whilst listening to a podcast. From scientific shows such as 'Wow in the World', to ethical debates like 'Short and Curly', or even podcasts in another language such as *Les Odysees* which we listen to in French – the choices are endless.

15. **WALK AND TALK:** Conversational learning, especially in combination with movement and fresh air, is a powerful learning tool. From talking about nature, to discussing the news, listing favourite movies or quizzing each other on tricky maths questions, walking can be the perfect time to get your brains buzzing, too.

16. **FLIP-BOOK:** Watch an old Disney such as *Snow White* or *Fantasia* and explain how these animations used many thousands of hand-drawn images. Use the corner of a notepad to create a flip-book for a moving image. You could go on to look at stop-time animation, if your children are interested in this topic.

17. **GIANT CARDBOARD MODELLING:** Don't throw away those big cardboard boxes! You can spend a morning making a castle, pirate ship or space rocket. Go ahead and paint or decorate it, if you're feeling creative. To develop the task, you could suggest starting with a labelled plan.

18. **HOME-MADE MARBLE-RUN:** There's nothing you can't do with some toilet-roll tubes, empty cereal boxes, sticky tape and a few books (they make great tunnels and stairs). This is satisfying brain work, and can take five minutes or most of the day, depending on how your kids take to the task.

19 **WRITE A BOOK:** We make books out of folded paper, usually no more than 20 pages long. Prolific writers might want their own ringbound notebook! Help them if necessary with a title, page numbers and chapters, then just allow them to work on it when they want to. It might take several days or weeks to complete.

20 **EXERCISE SCHEDULE:** As we are all adjusting to the new 'normal' following lockdown, what better time to give your kids the autonomy to arrange a family exercise plan? This can be informal, or written down on a timetable, and could include looking up new ideas like yoga and martial arts on YouTube for inspiration.

21. **FREE BAKING:** An immersive task and great fun for the kids. Allow them to choose a baking recipe to follow and – other than making sure they don't burn themselves on the oven – give them total freedom to do it on their own. Don't worry – making mistakes is part of the process.

22. **SINK OR FLOAT?:** Run a bath of cold water and collect at least ten different items from around the house. Do your children think they will sink or float in the water? You could discuss your ideas and create a table to record your results, or do further research into your findings.

23. **MAKE A MUSIC VIDEO:** Time to sit down with a laptop and show them a load of fun and age-appropriate music videos, then discuss what song they will lip-sync to and how the video should be filmed. Think: costumes, locations, turn-taking, who will film it on their phone etc.

24. **DIY:** If you have a wall that needs painting, or a table that requires sanding down, now is the time to get the kids involved in physical activities around the house. Put on some music or an audiobook, and enjoy the time together.

25. **FASHION SHOW:** Children grow so quickly, don't they? Next time you know that a clothes shop is needed, why not encourage your kids to turn out their drawers and put on a fashion show, as you decide which items will be handed down, you go to the charity shop, or they can be recycled as rags and textile projects around the house? Disco ball and music, if possible.

26. **MUSICAL EDUCATION:** Make every day of the week dedicated to a different type of music – for example: Rock Monday, Pop Tuesday, House Wednesday, Country Thursday, Classical Friday, Disco Saturday, Reggae Sunday. Be sure to immerse yourselves in the genre each day.

27. **INTERVIEW A RELATIVE:** Home education is all about expanding your children's horizons regarding where information comes from. Why not come up with a list of questions about the past for grandma, or another elderly relative? This could be a personal study, or linked to a wider historical topic.

28. **MODEL HOUSE:** Do you have creative kids? Keen to develop their maths brains in creative ways? Why not suggest your older ones take the full dimensions of your

In his article 'Being Highly Sensitive: recognising its virtue and maximising its potential' (House, 2005), Richard House looks at the emerging recognition of a  highly sensitive personality 'type' in the context of his own experience of counselling and psychotherapy. The article is based on his study of Elaine Aron's seminal book *The Highly Sensitive Person* which first appeared in 1999. Aron's key points, and House's reflections on the implications for highly sensitive children, can be summarised as follows:

- Up to 20 per cent of the human population can be defined as congenitally 'highly sensitive'. This has major implications for parenting and the way we medically treat our children.

- Thousands of people die every year due to faulty medical diagnosis and thus, the clinical-scientific 'medicalisation' of distress in a highly sensitive person represents a gross oversight in this area.

- If around one-fifth of patients seeking help from their doctor can be defined as 'highly sensitive', then failure to recognise this phenomenon can lead to chronic misdiagnosis and 'iatrogenic' treatment (where the treatment offered actually makes you worse).

- Recognition of the highly sensitive personality 'type' can be hugely beneficial for highly sensitive parents, or parents of highly sensitive children, whereas failure to acknowledge your child's sensitive nature can do considerable damage.

- Being a highly sensitive person is not a 'condition' or 'syndrome', but rather a part of the continuum of human experience, and it is essential to present it to and think about your child in this way.

- Lack of sensitivity is not a desirable state of being and, indeed, some degree of sensitivity is an essential part of what enables us to lead a healthy and meaningful existence.

- Far from being a malady or negative 'diagnosis', highly sensitive people have historically made huge contributions to human culture. The key is to understanding how to realise the potential of your highly sensitive child and to avoid any misunderstanding which may stunt or fatally compromise their development.

Please consult Further Reading and References for details of Elaine's book and Richard's article.

house (this can be as detailed or as basic as they want) and creating a cardboard scale model? This task requires technical skill, calculations and tenacity.

29. **BUG HUNT:** How many different kinds of bugs can you find in your back garden or in a green space outside your house? Make a note of all the different creatures you see, with photographs or drawings to accompany your notes. Your kids could also look up their proper names, or study their habitats.

30. **MUSICAL RECITAL:** What's everyone's favourite song right now? Can your kids learn the lyrics and sing it? Would it sound better if you add musical instruments? If you don't have loads at home, upturned saucepans and tupperware can work as drums. For older children, figuring out how to play a tune on the piano or violin is hugely beneficial, as well as fun.

31. **BINGE-READING:** If your child is a bookworm and enjoys reading independently, home education provides the time to let them just disappear in a book for hours on end. Be sure to buy the entire series of whatever they are into – normally available at a reasonable price second hand, or ask at your local library.

32. **BIKE RIDE:** Getting outside, using your bodies, and feeling free is why we all do this. Bikes are an absolute must, I think. You might occasionally plan a bike ride with an agenda or topic to pursue (such as seasonal changes), and collect items along the way to bring home for a collage or painting.

33. **MAKE YOUR OWN KITE:** There are some great tutorials out there for this activity, and you don't need much in the way of craft items. You could even find light sticks or twigs from a recent walk or bike ride to use as the central-cross structure.

34. **FAMILY DANCE ROUTINE:** Oh, this is a favourite in our house! You could look up something fun on YouTube to learn (like 'how to Dougie' or a barn dance), or have a go at your favourite dance sequence from a movie. Just be careful with the lift from *Dirty Dancing… – ooouuch!.*

35. **MAKE YOUR OWN BOARD GAME:** This one needs planning and is great for uniting older and younger siblings, as the big ones inevitably take the lead but you can get everyone involved by delegating tasks like making the dice, writing the rule book, colouring the board, and more.

36. **THE MINDFUL MENIAL:** In our house, we mostly wash the dishes by hand rather than use the dishwasher, and this is just one example of how we get everyone involved in helping out around the house. It's a great excuse to listen to music or a podcast, discuss and feel united as a family.

37. **WRITE A JOKE BOOK:** Another bonding activity that unites older and younger siblings. Remind your older ones this is a family joke book; they can save the really rude version for their friends. Extend the task with a front-cover design, blurb, reviews, price, and so on.

It's mid-winter, and we are invited to play at the house of a local family who home-educate, as we do ourselves. We are relatively new to this life, and enormously grateful for the invitation. Having been used to school interactions, I was

Aladdin's Cave and Homeschool Houses

anxious for this 'playdate' to go well for all the children – but I needn't have worried. Almost immediately after our arrival, the eldest child – a long-legged early teen with a mop of curly black hair – comes into the living room and introduces himself. Aaron is five years older than his sister, and seven years older than my eldest. At 14, he stands with his hands in his pockets, talking easily with the grown-ups, and I'm finding myself forced to 'come down' from my usual 'matey' teacher-mode when engaging with adolescents, and speak to him with my natural voice. Our youngest wanders over to him and he scoops him without blinking, telling me about his guitar practice while letting the baby hold his finger. I am out of my comfort zone, and questioning everything about how we've have raised our kids thus far.

All the children – apart from the baby – are now upstairs playing in Aaron's bedroom. My middle son immediately wanted to see his guitar, and the girls ran off together to hide under the duvet and 'surprise them'. Aaron has, his mum says, about half an hour before his friend is picking him up for swimming club; and he smiles broadly – in the way kids sometimes do – to tell their parents that they don't need the reminder: he knows his own schedule. And now I have time to look around. The living room seems almost like a movie set and bristles with curiosities, from the packed bookshelves and life-size dolphin mural, to the photography project taking up most of the coffee table. Half of the entrance hall is occupied by a giant cardboard time-machine designed by Aaron's sister, Sasha – complete with dials and buttons, as well as a simple electric circuit which activates a sensor to turn on the light when you open the door. The baby is fascinated by this, and keeps peeking his head in, saying, 'Oh!'.

But by early spring, I am used to this kind of set-up. Mountain bikes suspended above staircases. The entire original collection of Agatha Christie, dog-eared and much loved, piled up in the reading corner. Chess boards, dismantled radios, paint pots and Rubik's cubes cover the surfaces. In the garden, elaborate dens and ziplines not only beat anything you could purchase online, but are also designed and constructed by the children themselves. One family actually had a climbing wall running from the kitchen up to the first-floor landing. At first I am quite gobsmacked; who *are* these people? And then, bit by bit, our home too becomes more eclectic, more full of wonder, and less of a pristine crash-pad for passing a few hours at the end of each day.

I think I prefer it this way.

38. **AMBITIOUS PUZZLING:** Everyone loves a good jigsaw, but now that you have the time and space to engage in more deep learning, it's time to dust off that thousand-piece train puzzle and have a go at it. Think teamwork. This might take several days, or even weeks.

39. **PHOTOGRAPHY COMPETITION:** A good way to introduce this is to look at photography categories and ideas online, then discuss as a family the rules and – possibly – category for your own photography competition. Of course, if photography becomes a 'thing' in your family, you'll need to invest in a decent camera.

40. **WORLDSCHOOL ZOOM SESSION:** There are some fantastic educators out there, such as Blake Boles, uniting home-educated teenagers from around the world in interactive group web-chats. If your children are the right age for this, they might also want to look into worldschooling adventures and projects aimed at older teens and, sometimes, families too.

41. **FREE WRITING:** This is a hit in our house, and always good for a laugh or some real imaginative flow. It can be fun to provide a time-limit – five minutes, for example – and the only rule is that you all must keep writing and not stop. Give regular indications of remaining time ('...Three minutes left!') to keep the pace and the energy up.

42. **STAR GAZING:** Why not make the most of the fact that you don't have to get up early and, on a clear night, see if you can spot some of the constellations in the night sky? It's worth reading up on constellations beforehand, and even if you're in the middle of a city, it's definitely an interesting experience and can be linked to history, geometry, mathematics and the creative arts.

43. **DIY WEATHER STATION:** Pinterest is all over this. All you need are some empty bottles and a few other bits to create something really unique, which will mean there's now officially no need to be tuning into boring BBC weather forecasts, because your kids are on it.

44. **GAMING GENIUS:** Sites like Buildbox and Sploder provide basic software to enable your children to try coding their own game. And why not? This is much more relevant and useful than allowing them to spend hours just playing video games. Set aside a whole day for it, and see what they can achieve.

45. **POT PLANTS:** Order seeds or small shrubs for your pots and spice up your garden, balcony or communal area. You could even start growing herbs, salad leaves or vegetables to throw into a salad or sauce at some point.

46. **TEACHER ROLE-PLAY:** After covering a topic with your kids (this could be a discussion, or from a magazine article, or TV programme), ask them how they would teach the information. When they're ready, sit on the floor with your legs crossed and play the student.

47. **CHARADES:** A fun family game, but also great for thinking skills and dramatic expression. Do it in a pair, or teams if you have a larger family. If you don't have a box of charades, you can invent them as you go along, or create a longer task by making your own box of charades.

48. **BALLOON TENNIS:** Grab your rackets, find a bit of space and knock a balloon about for a bit of exercise and co-ordination skills. It can just be a bit of fun; or rules can be established and scores kept, with younger ones volunteering as ball-boys/girls and some epic Wimbledon-style grunting!

49. **BODY PAINTING:** So messy, but tons of fun! If you don't mind a bit of craziness, spread out a load of newspaper and do full head-to-toe body painting with non-toxic paint. If this initially seems a bit daunting, limit it to tattoo sleeves or face paints only.

50. **PLAY-DOUGH MODELLING:** Make an imaginary world from play dough and use your camera phone (even better if you have a Polaroid) to try out a short stop-time animated story. Don't be too ambitious! – it's really tricky. Then watch Wallace and Gromit.

51. **MAKE AN ASSAULT COURSE:** Inside or outside, depending on weather and what you've got available. Duvets make great tunnels, wooden steps for hand washing can become jumping platforms, and piles of cuddly toys are shark-infested waters to wade cautiously through.

52. **HEADS, BODIES, LEGS:** An old school classic, but if you haven't played this with your kids before, give it a go, as it can be quite a hit. Fold a piece of paper into three sections and pass it around, with one person drawing the head and then folding the paper to hide what they've drawn, before handing it to the next person, and so on.

53. **THE WORD GAME:** This can be done with any set of alphabet letters, from foam bath letters to fridge magnets, or your own homemade letters. Spread all the letters out on the table and take turns to form words. Can be competitive (longer words score higher), or just for fun.

54. **PLAY-FIGHTS:** Don't underestimate the value of this activity. Studies suggest that children who regularly play-fight in a safe environment are calmer, happier and have better concentration than those who don't. Do be careful, of course (see p. 48); but a bit of play-wrestling, throwing on the bed, and pillow-bashing are great fun.

55. **MAKE A POP-UP BOOK:** Not difficult at all (I'm sure you did this when you were a kid?), but hugely satisfying to take the time to create properly. For children who really get into this activity, the task can obviously develop into a longer story with more detailed illustrations, and even moving pop-ups. Plenty of videos online to generate extravagant ideas.

56. **TEDDY-BEAR ZIPLINE:** A classic which I stole from 'The Five-Minute Mum'. Can be done indoors or outdoors, and it's best achieved when you don't get involved at all for the first few minutes. Let them really think through what needs to happen to make this work.

57. **RE-WRITE SONG LYRICS:** A great lesson in syllables and iambic meter. Mine love 'Rockstar' by Nickleback, and we've re-written the lyrics based around Harry Potter, *Star Wars*, Pokemon, and more. Fun, but very engaging too; this can be a quick family activity to get brains warmed up over breakfast, or a more detailed independent task.

58. **PAPIER-MÂCHÉ:** Look, we went overboard with this and spent a week making a papier-mâché solar system; so please take my advice and keep it simple – it's very labour intensive! All you need, though, are some old newspapers and PVA glue. Begin, perhaps, with a hot-air balloon, or a mask, to give yourselves a manageable project to 'master the process'.

59. **HAIKU POEMS:** These are super-short Japanese poems consisting of three lines only. Another perfect warm-up activity or task to summarise a topic you've covered. Challenge the adults to produce one too, or write one Haiku a day, and put together an anthology at the end of the week.

60. **KEEP A DIARY:** What better time to begin a diary than now, if your family is embarking on home education? Buy a nice notebook online, or just tie together scrap paper with a ribbon, and decorate it. This is private, though, so don't upset your child by reading it and correcting their spelling. I'm sure you know that.

61. **MAKE A DOCUMENTARY:** Have a think about what topics and themes your life right now lends itself to. Could you do a day in the life of the cat, for instance? Or a nature documentary in the garden? Planning this is half the fun; consider locations for filming, interviews with experts and so forth, if you want to do it properly; and for older children, there are plenty of free editing programmes they could use to make it look professional.

62. **PEN PALS:** My kids have a couple of families with whom they exchange letters. Why not get that rolling now, if you haven't already? Sometimes I find it quicker and easier to screenshot the letter and send the image for the other parent to print out at their end, although I know that removes the magic of receiving a handwritten letter in the post.

63. **CHARITY PROJECT:** Is there a charity that your kids would like to support this year, or a family challenge that would be good to sponsor? Have a look online at what different charities do, discuss how you might like to help out or raise money, and short-list options before making the final decision.

64. **AUDIOBOOKS:** A CD player and a couple of audiobooks are a great investment.

If you can have this available in the kitchen or the living room, you have a constant source of entertainment which isn't just more screen-time. Also great for car journeys and, when the CD player breaks (it will), get a screwdriver and take it apart to see how it works.

65. **BOOK DOCTORS:** Who knew this would be such a hit? We have tons of very battered books which we sometimes decide to mend. But what we actually find is that sitting down with a pile of books and some sticky tape to repair damaged books is actually a great opportunity to do loads of reading. So, get stuck in!

66. **GLOBE-TROTTING:** If you have a globe, a world map on the wall or an atlas, this is a great opportunity to copy it out on to paper, and mark the route you'd take if you were planning a trip around the world. Where would you go? What oceans would you cross? What would you need to pack to go there? This can be more concrete if you're actually planning on worldschooling as a family, or connecting with families who do.

67. **FILM EDUCATION:** I would always rather my children watch films/movies, rather than junk on TV. Good films are artistic, creative and provide wonderful story-lines to feed children's imaginations. You could use resources such as the BFI to expand your children's cinematic knowledge by looking at different genres, classic and retro movies, as well as foreign-language films.

68. **GCSE BITESIZE:** There are hundreds of short video clips and information summaries available via GCSE bitesize, on a huge range of topics. Although this is shallow learning, it provides a great way to kick-start interest in a topic for further study, or simply a more educational way to spend ten minutes of screen-time before lunch.

69. **TED-ED:** Another good source of information covering a broad range of topics, with succinct videos or keynote speakers if you'd rather just listen to the audio. We sometimes use this as a 'way in' to a topic, then discuss afterwards what we found out and what questions we still have. For older children, there are more complex topics discussed on TED talks.

70. **COOKING MATHEMATICS:** The next time you're cooking and have a little person dipping their finger in the sauce, why not quiz them on some maths linked to real life? This could be simple, such as, 'I usually put one egg in but we're going to double the recipe, so how many do I need?'; or a more challenging calculation like, 'This recipe has a 3g spoon of salt. There are seven people eating – so how much salt is each person having?'.

71. **TEXT TRANSFORMATIONS:** A typical creative writing task for late primary/ early secondary stage. You could turn a newspaper headline into a poem, or suggest transforming a topic from the book they're reading into a leaflet or poster. There are a lot of variations here.

Heidi Steel is a former primary school teacher, turned unschooling mum of four. She has worked in education for almost 20 years. Heidi can be found on Facebook  *at live.play.learn and tweets as @liveplaylearn1. In this section, I asked Heidi to compare the typical day of a Key Stage 1 pupil with an unschooling day.*

A typical day for a Key Stage 1 pupil is always timetabled. Each school may have a slight variation on how that is implemented, but is legally obliged to complete a set number of hours for each curriculum subject during the course of an academic year. Each morning is usually divided into literacy and numeracy sessions, with added daily phonics instruction, mental-maths sections and group/guided reading. Afternoons are normally reserved for other subjects, such as history, geography, science, music and PE, and are often approached via topic work. The day also includes an assembly, break and lunch times, and commonly ends with story-time.

A typical school day might look like this:

8.45–9.15 – Registration
9.15–9.45 – Phonics
9.45–10.30 – Literacy

BREAK

10.45–11.00 – Assembly
11.00–12.00 – Numeracy

LUNCH

1.00–1.30 – Guided Reading
1.30–2.15 – Topic Work

FRUIT SNACK

2.30–3.00 – Topic Work
3.00–3.15 – Story Time

In contrast, an unschooled child of similar age rarely has a typical day. Each day is different and new. It is filled with different questions to ask, and fresh lines of enquiry to follow. A child is supported as they follow their own curiosity and pursue their own interests, in their own time. A family might spend an entire day devoted to one interesting activity, and another day engaging in several different things. There is no standard format. Individual children will develop their own passions and daily, weekly and annual rhythms and traditions, but they are always flexible. Family culture is crafted around respectfully meeting everyone's needs, and making room for each person's activity.

One day in our house might look like this:

9.00: The girls watch *Small World Barbie* play on YouTube after breakfast, followed by dressing up a selection of dolls, each ready to go on swimming adventures. The acting and story-telling continue until they're hungry. The boys are playing chess, which they're getting good at, and my eldest later practises his guitar.

10.00: The children decide to make their own smoothies. Today's experiment is bananas, ice cream and melted chocolate, which is a success. Sitting in the garden as we drink it, the girls notice the birds and butterflies. We talk about the different butterflies, look up what they are in our *Wildlife Encyclopaedia* and name them. Then two of the children settle to some reading in the hammock, while the others play on the trampoline. They are practising gymnastic moves, flips, turns and tricks.

11:00–12:00: We have friends over for lunch, because one of the boys goes to a homeschool gymnastics class in the afternoon with this family. The children play freely. Before lunch, some of them come downstairs to show a dance routine they've choreographed.

1.00: In the afternoon, we do craft together before collecting their older brother from gymnastics. Today's chosen activity is collage, freely chosen by the children. We listen to their favourite podcast while we work, and learn about dinosaur bones.

3.00: We stop at the gymnastics class and stay a while, catching up with friends. The children talk extensively about how they think raspberry slushies are made blue. Some of the older children suggest science-based theories. They also discuss condensation on the cups.

4.00: On the way home, the children decide that they would like to go on a bike ride, so we take our bikes to the park for an hour. Conversational learning happens all the time here; today they're discussing how to build a strong bridge.

6.00–8.30: The evening is spent playing card games together, and then preparing food. The children cut vegetables and write lists of their favourite things to eat. They are also in the middle of a film about ancient Rome, which they finish after dinner.

Unschooling is not governed by timetables or curriculum. Adults partner with their children in their day-to-day activities, facilitate their children's interests by doing more of the things that they love, and help them discover and explore their passions further. Learning happens all the time, not in scheduled allocated sessions. Practically, this means that children play and learn in a seamless way.

Heidi Steel

72. **SOUND CUPS:** Two blunt-cut tin cans (or even paper cups) attached with a piece of string create a cool home-made walkie-talkie system, and is a good introduction to talking about how sound waves travel and other basic physics principles.

73. **SHOPPING LIST:** I do this all the time, and the kids love it for some reason. When getting ready to do the weekly shop, put them in charge of writing the shopping list (you might need to edit it...); or even ask older ones to prepare a meal plan for the week and list the ingredients needed.

74. **PICTIONARY:** Another classic family game. If you don't have a Pictionary box, perhaps look it up online to see what the categories tend to be and then create your own Pictionary card set. Laminate with sticky tape and they should last for a while.

75. **HOME LIBRARY:** Organise those bookshelves into alphabetical order, or by topic. This is a sure way to get your kids reading and focused on a quiet task for a good half-hour. We have a 'topic of the week' shelf which they decide upon themselves – selecting books for the topic shelf also works well as a prompt for wider reading.

76. **LEARN A NEW SKILL:** From yoga to a musical instrument or a foreign language, make homeschooling into an opportunity to expand your own skill-set, and model for your children how to commit to something which perhaps you wouldn't previously have had the time for. We are currently following a series of YouTube martial arts videos – perfect for rainy days.

77. **THE STORY WHISPER:** Tell a short story to the person sitting next to you and pass it round the room until it gets back to you, when the last person should say what they heard aloud. How has the story changed? Does it still make sense? A fun five-minute game.

78. **GIANT FLOOR ART:** Watching an episode of Art Ninja is great for ideas here. Whether working on a giant mosaic or blow-paint project with straws, if you don't mind your kitchen being upturned for a few days, giant floor art is an ideal long task which is satisfying for the whole family to help out with.

79. **VEGETABLE DISSECTION:** So long as the food gets eaten at the end, this can be an engaging way to look at fruit and vegetable structure. Cut anything from apples to courgettes in half, and discuss what you see. Can you draw and label the different parts of the fruit or vegetable?

80. **GET CRAFTY:** Have a go at making a craft, based on a country or culture you're studying. For example, take Chinese pottery, or if you're doing a topic on the ancient Egyptians, you could get the kids to plan a delicious pudding using figs, dates and honey.

81. **MAKE A MINI WORLD:** Using a shoe box or empty cereal packet, ask your kids to make their own 'mini world'. This could be based on a topic you're studying, or it could be imaginary. The inside of the box can be coloured or painted to form the background, and objects can be found in toy boxes to set the scene.

82. **SEASONAL WILDFLOWER PROJECT:** Using paper or card, why not make a chart for identifying the different flora and fauna you see when you take a walk? Bring some samples home with you (or photograph them) as a stimulus for a painting later.

83. **TOILET-ROLL ART:** Honestly, what *can't* you do with an empty toilet-roll tube? From rockets to octopuses, keeping hold of the cardboard tubes rather than putting them straight into the recycling gives you a constant source of inspiration for short creative tasks.

84. **TRAIN-SET CHALLENGE:** If you have a box of wooden train track, this is a very immersive task. A simple challenge could be to plan a route all the way round the sofa; but if you also have older children, you could extend the range of the task by overcoming obstacles such as cushions, as well as creating a landscape of tunnels and mountains from household objects.

85. **MAKE A BRIDGE:** Lolly sticks are perfect for this task, but you can also be creative and use cardboard or small wooden sticks collected on a nature walk. It's a superb education in engineering, and teaches children about forces and angles in a natural, hands-on experience.

86. **HISTORY INTERVIEW:** Whether studying a unit from history or looking at a current political or environmental topic, choose someone to dress up as a famous figure, and get ready to interview them, with a list of questions and a clipboard to record their answers.

87. **GEOMETRY GAMES:** You could use a box of Magformers, or simply cut out and flip shapes on paper. Either way, engaging children in geometric rotation and visualisation is great mental stimulation for all ages, and can be accessed at basic and higher levels, depending on their ages.

88. **MAKE A WORD SEARCH:** Fun and simple, help them to draw out a square grid and initially list the words which will be hidden, before filling up the rest of the grid with random letters. This takes some time, and is a satisfying task which can be developed into a more challenging activity for older ones.

89. **TOP TRUMPS:** Oh gosh, do you guys play this? We were introduced to Top Trumps by homeschooling friends a while back, and now we have at least ten different sets for various topics and interests. Great for reading and number skills, as well as a fun warm-up or wind-down family game.

Children should be in school

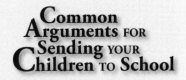

Common Arguments FOR Sending YOUR Children TO School

This is actually a very recent argument. Historically, most children did not go to school, but learnt the skills they would require for adulthood from their parents and the people in their community. Even ancient civilisations that did operate a system of schooling – the Greeks and Romans, for example – bore no resemblance to the monstrosity of modern schooling. Check your understanding of human history.

Home-educated children are being controlled by their parents

Whilst controlling parents exist, both within the school system and outside it, I am yet to meet a home educator whom I would describe in these terms. The overwhelming majority of parents choose not to put their children into school precisely because they place a high value on their children's freedom, and this is palpable in their interactions with their children, and the way their homeschooling operates.

Still, homeschooled children have no idea of the real world

The opposite is probably the case. School children spend the vast majority of their time in a bubble of academic pressure and adult expectations, which bear little resemblance to what adult life is really like. The only adults whose working lives are governed by dinner bells and lining up are teachers and prison officers. By spending much more time in the 'real world' – visiting interesting places, volunteering, travelling and meeting people of all ages and walks of life – home-educated children are often exceptionally 'switched on' and savvy about the real world, compared to their school peers.

Okay, but they have no social life

Homeschooling – if you want it to be – can be so overwhelmingly social that you end up doing little else. Rather than passing notes in class and grabbing a half-hour chat on the walk back from the bus stop, home-educated children can indulge in entire days playing freely with their friends, uninterrupted by adults who mostly understand the importance of allowing children space to play. Because there is such a busy social life attached to homeschooling, most families begin with too many commitments, and so learn to scale it back in order to balance the week.

What about exams? That's really important

Is it? As someone who has marked examination papers for two different exam boards, I would put it to you that the exam system is a total farce. Since exam boards are private companies, their agenda is making money, and keeping schools (their customers) happy with reasonable pass marks for cohorts. Moreover, as all students are forced to take an almost identical path through education, the grades that they end up with don't actually mean an awful lot, as they're the same as everyone else. How do universities and employers even begin to distinguish between applicants? The worlds of higher education and employment are becoming increasingly aware of this problem, and there is a growing number of students entering higher education, professional training, or going straight into active employment with no formal qualifications whatsoever. Even if you insist on following the exam route, the content can easily be covered in the year leading up to the exam paper(s), and there's plenty of support out there in terms of resources and study groups.

Adults who were home-educated will surely stand out a mile in the working world

They probably will – and for all the right reasons. Adults who were home-educated tend to be highly skilled at what they do – the opposite of a 'Jack of All Trades'. They are typically mature, reliable, confident and empathetic, engaging with tasks because they want to and because their area of work interests them. Having been raised outside of the competitive culture of the classroom, homeschooled adults are generally good team players, open and approachable, with subject-specific wisdom that dates back to a childhood immersed in the topics they enjoyed.

But still, isn't it boring, sitting at home all day?

Well, first we need to remember that homeschooling and lockdown 'crisis schooling' are two separate things. Most home-educated families are out and about a lot, attending clubs, workshops, visits and playdates. But the second thing to point out is that homeschooling provides a fresh perspective on how we all spend our time, including 'down-time' at home. Children raised this way quickly become skilled at managing their own time and projects, meaning that being at home is certainly not 'wasted time' or boring in any way. In our garage, my son has dismantled a car engine and has been working on cleaning it and trying to reassemble it. My daughter loves 'home days' because she can get on with reading, her favourite pastime. Lost in a fantasy world and without interruptions, she can read from breakfast through to lunch in the indoor hammock we have set up in her bedroom. Most kids would give anything for that kind of autonomy.

90. **TEACHING HISTORY 100:** I like this website, which lists 100 historical artefacts found in museums, with an image and brief thumbnail description for each item. Great for browsing, art inspiration, or igniting an interest to explore the topic further.

91. **SWEET STATISTICS:** Interview your friends and family to find out what their favourite sweet treat or pudding is, and then help your kids to transform their results into a bar chart or pie diagram. The topic could be anything you like, of course, and there are other mathematical ways of representing statistical information.

92. **HANGMAN:** The traditional guessing game which involves spelling skill, memory and some topical knowledge, depending on how you play the game. It's always worth agreeing on a category to enable the players to really think it through, and not just shout out random letters.

93. **DIARY IN THE LIFE OF...:** Create a diary entry for a historical or literary character that you've studied, or know about. Your kids might enjoy adding pictures, or developing this into a series of creative writing entries, if the topic you're studying is ongoing for several days or weeks.

94. **FOREIGN LANGUAGE RADIO AND PODCASTS:** Whether you're just starting out, or you already speak a second language at home, the only way to really get your children speaking naturally is total immersion. Have the radio playing a station in the language of your choice during breakfast every day, or tune into a podcast in that language aimed at children.

95. **COMPUTER SKILLS:** Do your children know how to do a Google search, or send an email? Do they understand the results the search throws up and which sites are useful sources of information? Now is the time to show them how it's done, then test their new skills with a task or research project.

96. **MEMORY GAME:** Time to test the kids' memory – and your own! Gather 20 objects that can be found in the home and lay them all out on the table. Have a look together and then cover everything with a blanket or a sheet after one minute. How many can you remember?

97. **MAGAZINE COMPETITION:** Check out your subscription magazines or look online to see if there are any good competitions for kids to enter at the moment; I'll bet there are. Encourage yours to enter a creative writing competition, or submit their environmental art project to earn a Blue Peter badge.

98. **PEER ASSESSMENT:** In the world of homeschooling, most of us are not about putting grades on kids' work. However, if you feel assessment is important, then a more effective way of providing feedback is to get your children to look at and comment on each other's work, rather than you doing everything. This way, everyone is learning.

99. **TV TIMES:** Got a TV addict in the house who would rather chill in front of their favourite programme than read a book? Don't worry – it's quite common. Why not pick up a copy of the *Radio Times* each week and get your child to check the TV schedule with a pen, highlighting the TV shows they want to watch? Don't tell them they're reading, though!

100. **DANCE TOPIC:** Link your study of history, geography or the environment to a physical activity by learning a form of dance from a particular culture or nation. There are plenty of videos available on YouTube and lots of fun, as well as exercise for everyone.

101. **'PEACE OUT' BEDTIME:** There are tons of meditation and mindfulness options for kids, but I love Peace Out and their guided relaxation for families. Mental health is more important than ever for our children, so take time to unwind and find peace at the end of the day.

AFTERWORD

So, why this book; and why now? And why have so many of the stories told here been about school, when this book is supposed to be looking at home education? To even begin to address these questions, I would have to reveal to you my motivation for writing in the first place, which began the day we removed our daughter from school. Home education was nothing short of a revelation for parents like us who had never really given it a second thought. I felt immediately compelled to write, to capture the freedom and exhilaration of this journey, and to evaluate the educational benefits I see unfolding every day. Far from being 'alternative', home education feels like the very definition of being 'woke', and our former lifestyle now seems like another era that belongs in the past, along with sandwich boxes and book-bags and homework. I also felt a lot of anger, to begin with, and disappointment. And after that dissolved, I had to consider what was left.

Plenty of teachers leave the profession each year, and plenty – like me – decide to homeschool their own children. This is a significant trend that the government appears to deliberately ignore, perhaps because it says so much. It is astonishing – incredible, really – the number of teachers I've met along the way who despised school themselves, just as I did. And yet we come back to it; apparently 'choosing' to spend the rest of our working lives governed by changeover bells and despotic leadership, like some form of school-based Stockholm Syndrome. We inflict on our students, year on year, what was done to us. And I realised, mid-way through this project, that we need to stop the cycle. So I came down from my anger and re-wrote the book, saying what I wanted to say this time, and putting my disappointment on the shelf where it belongs. Here are my conclusions:

1. Teachers and home educators share fundamentally similar beliefs about education. Most classroom teachers understand the value of homeschooling, and feel constrained by what they can realistically offer in a classroom setting. Most homeschooling families recognise that they are making harsh sacrifices in the name of their educational beliefs – sacrifices they know not everyone would be able to make.

2. You don't have to be a teacher or an educational psychologist to home-educate your children, but it helps that so many people with this kind of career background choose to homeschool their children and make a point of speaking out on it. There are many strong voices within the community, all saying the same thing about education.

3. For society to become a fairer and happier place, we need to listen to these voices and bring about unprecedented change in the established model of public education. As it stands, the school system is the basis for all emergent 'adult' problems: low

expectations, social rigidity, discrimination and poor mental health. It is standing in the way of our progress as a species.

These conclusions appear modest, and yet it seems beyond the grasp of mainstream society to acknowledge the problems with school. In an interview with the *Guardian* newspaper, Labour's deputy leader and former Shadow Education Secretary, Angela Rayner – whose own experience of school involved systemic poverty and bullying – nevertheless presses the urgency of getting all children back to school in September coming (as I write) – failing to recognise that this is the same educational system that failed her mother, who cannot read or write, and even her grandmother, who worked three low-paid jobs to be able to cover basic amenities (Hinsliff, 2020). And I'm not picking a fight with Rayner here – inspiration for succeeding against the odds that she is, and rightly, a powerful role-model. Rather, I am commenting more generally on so many people's dogged loyalty to a system which, when you look closely, has actually done them no favours. It's an ingrained mindset. In a sinister echo of nineteenth-century subservience, we still show resounding gratitude for what the state 'provides' for our children. We ask no questions – nor are we given the 'tools' to do so – and we silence, or side line, those who do.

Yet more and more families *are* choosing to homeschool. What once felt like an eccentric luxury has now gained mainstream traction, and thanks to more flexible employment options, this feels increasingly like an achievable goal. The experiment of home-based 'crisis schooling' through lockdown has only served to unveil the outdated methods and the toxic pressure of the education system.

Don't call it 'homeschooling'; it's not. Elective homeschoolers shouldn't be the only ones to benefit from the message of this book and the many books on home education that came before it; those ideas should make it through the school gates and into the staffroom. Homeschooling is the first step for families like ours, but if we truly value children, we must be seeking to radically alter the establishment that blindfolds them. The current climate is tough and it seems unlikely that school reform is at the top of government's agenda; but still, we must make our position clear – keep writing, keep lobbying, keep sharing our thoughts on education – not just for our own children, but for *all* children. Their thinking, and their *ability* to think, are what's going to shape the future.

Finally, real solutions *do* exist for improving educational practices in our country, and I will leave you with these final thoughts:

• Make school more clearly optional;

• Improve the experience of school with greater autonomy, less testing, and smaller class sizes;

- Recognise the value and financial sacrifice of home education by providing tax allowances/reductions for home-educating families;

- Increase flexibility in the work-place, to allow for permanent remote working and flexi hours; and

- Create a fair and universal system for checking in with school and homeschool families, to ensure vulnerable children are identified and protected.

INTERVIEW: *Why We Homeschool*
With Anna Dusseau

'What was your reason for withdrawing your child from school?'

AD: A number of things, really. I should say, to begin with, that I struggled with putting my eldest into a nursery when I went back to work. That was a difficult time, and when we figured out a way for me to work from home after the birth of our second child, it was a huge relief. So I never looked 'forward' to my children starting school; and although we were supportive and involved in the life of the school, I always had a critical eye and would regularly offload in private about the things I didn't like. Some safeguarding issues worried me, as well as the fact that a year of school had apparently taught my child to loathe reading. I also saw a few mismanaged situations involving other people's children, as well as – twice – physical manhandling of a child. And so when, quite out of the blue, my daughter was verbally and then physically assaulted by an older child, it was a no-brainer for me. We withdrew her immediately; and although we met with the Head to hear the school's nonsense policy on bullying, I knew before we even sat down that there was absolutely nothing that could be said to change my mind. This stuff is all just 'what happens in school', and that one incident made me realise that it wasn't for us.

At what point did you think that homeschooling was the right thing?

AD: That's a good question because, at the beginning, we were certainly open to looking for a school that might be a 'better fit' for us. We were thinking along the lines of Steiner, Montessori or the Kent Sudbury School. Initially, though, we simply registered our children as homeschooled with the LEA and spent about a month hanging out and trying a few groups in the local area. By the time October had been and gone, the children had changed beyond recognition. Our eldest had taught herself to read fluently, and was making her way methodically through anything interesting on the shelves: Philip Pullman, Enid Blyton, Marjane Satrapi. It was like a light had been switched on. Our son was similarly influenced by the change in dynamic, and rather than trailing me around the house complaining about nursery or wondering what to do, he began taking anything he could open with a screwdriver up to the kitchen table, and disassembling it. I was quite astonished. And this was when we first thought seriously about homeschooling as a long-term prospect.

How would you describe your homeschool style or method?

AD: The National Curriculum was never something we considered. We felt quite relaxed, and agreed that our children were young enough to just 'try' unschooling for a while, before bothering with anything more structured. It's funny that unschooling – something I was sure *wouldn't* be right for us – has proven such a game-changer, and seems to fit in with the natural way we do things. We make listening to the children and helping them to achieve their personal goals our top priority, which means we now have a four-year old who can mix tracks on my husband's turntables, a baby whose first language appears to be French, and a six-year old who wakes up daily with an ambitious project in mind (writing a book, making a chess board, designing clothes for Harry Potter dolls), which we bend over backwards to help her realise. We love the diversity, the challenge, and the fact that no two days are ever the same.

Do you feel anything has changed about your approach through lockdown?

AD: This time has actually forced me to reflect on my years in the classroom and consider my own teaching practice, much more than is comfortable. The outpouring of parental stress and overload in response to what they have – mostly – been fed by schools during lockdown is at once understandable and important, as parents have been made to struggle with the same overwhelming pressures that their children usually absorb every day. This got me thinking about teaching and learning; the 'ingredients' of a solid lesson plan. *Clear instructions. Smooth transitions. Differentiated learning objectives.* All jargon for getting kids to 'do the work'. This doesn't feel like learning to me – not any more; and perhaps it never did. Lockdown has therefore encouraged us to strip our own homeschooling down even further, making it more child-led. We feel clearer about what makes home education special for us, and what we don't want to replicate from the school system.

What advice would you give to someone considering home education for their child?

AD: Many people feel under pressure to 'get going straight away' when they make the decision to homeschool, and are looking for tangible, curricular progress which feels quantifiable. I do understand; however, such pressure is unnecessary. Whatever educational approach you adopt, it's worth recognising that actual learning doesn't happen particularly effectively or rapidly in school. Every day is hectic – sure; but for any individual child within this system, there is a lot of wasted time and waiting. Even without commenting on the wider directed structure of the school day, in lessons alone, at least half the time is absorbed with 'admin', and the pace of learning is hampered by the impossible diversity of the class. This reduces the 'take-away' from each lesson to a very basic objective – something that could be covered in five minutes at home – and renders the experience of learning mundane, as topics and assessment grids are revisited again and again.

I hope you have the confidence to enjoy homeschooling, set yourselves free from all this, and '*trust* your child, as you were never trusted'. (Holt, 1967).

Further Reading and Resources

Books

Elaine N. Aron, *The Highly Sensitive Child: Helping our Children Thrive when the World Overwhelms Them*, Thorsons/Harper-Collins, London, 2002.

Julie Bogart, *The Brave Learner: Finding Everyday Magic in Homeschool, Learning, and Life*, Penguin, Harmondsworth, 2019.

Blake Boles, *Why Are You Still Sending Your Kids to School?: The Case for Helping Them Leave, Chart Their Own Paths, and Prepare for Adulthood at Their Own Pace*, Tells Peak Press, Loon Lake, Calif., 2020.

David Didau, *What if Everything You Knew about Education Was Wrong?*, Crown House Publishing, Carmarthen, Wales, 2015.

Ted Dintersmith, *What School Could Be: Insights and Inspiration from Teachers across America*, Princeton University Press, Princeton, NJ, 2018.

Linda Dobson, *The Homeschooling Book of Answers: 101 Important Questions Answered by Homeschooling's Most Respected Voices*, Prima, Roseville, Calif., 1998.

Jan Fortune-Wood, *Doing It Their Way*, Educational Heretics Press, Shrewsbury, Shropshire, 2000.

John Taylor Gatto, *Dumbing Us Down: The Hidden Curriculum of Compulsory School*, New Society Publishers, Gabriola Island, BC, Canada, 2005 (2nd edn 2017).

Sally Goddard Blythe, *The Genius of Natural Childhood: Secrets of Thriving Children*, Hawthorn Press, Stroud, 2011.

Mary Griffith, *The Unschooling Handbook: How to Use the Whole World as Your Child's Classroom*, Prima Publishing, Roseville, Calif., 1998.

David Gutterson, *Family Matters: Why Homeschooling Makes Sense*, Harcourt, San Diego, Calif., 1993.

Matt Hearn (Foreword by Ivan Illich), *Deschooling Our Lives: Kids, Communities and Self-design*, New Society, Gabriola Island, BC, Canada, 1995.

Richard House (ed.), *Too Much, Too Soon?: Early Learning and the Erosion of Childhood*, Hawthorn Press, Stroud, 2011.

Richard House, *Pushing Back to Ofsted: Safeguarding and the Legitimacy of Ofsted Inspection Judgements – A Critical Case Study*, InterActions/Wynstones Press, Stroud, 2020.

Alfie Kohn, *Punished by Rewards: The Trouble with Gold Stars, Incentive Plans, A's, Praise, and Other Bribes*, Houghton Mifflin, New York, 1999.

Martin Large, *Set Free Childhood: Parent's Survival Guide to Coping with Computers and TV,* Hawthorn Press, Stroud, 2003.

Jean Liedloff, *The Continuum Concept: In Search of Happiness Lost,* Duckworth, London, 1975.

Grace Llewellyn, *The Teenage Liberation Handbook: How to Quit School and Get a Real Life and Education,* Thorsons / Lowry House Publ., 1998.

Roland Meighan, *The Next Learning System,* Educational Heretics Press, Shrewsbury, Shropshire, 1997.

Pat Montgomery, *The School That's Inside You,* Clonlara Press, Ann Arbor, Mich., 2017.

Thomas Moore, *Care of the Soul,* Piatkus, London, 1992.

Ross Mountney, *Learning without School: Home Education,* Jessica Kingsley, London, 2009.

Sarah Ockwell-Smith, *The Gentle Parenting Book: How to Raise Calmer, Happier Children from Birth to Seven,* Piatkus, London, 2016.

Eloise Rickman, *Extraordinary Parenting: The Essential Guide to Parenting and Educating at Home,* Scribe, London, 2020

Carl Rogers, *On Becoming a Person,* Constable, London, 1974.

Sebastian and Tamara Suggate, *Reclaim Early Childhood: The Philosophy, Psychology and Practice of Steiner-Waldorf Early Years Education,* Hawthorn Press, Stroud, 2019.

Alan Thomas, *Educating Children at Home,* Continuum, London, 2000,

Websites

The Institute for Self-Directed Learning – www.selfdirect.school

Self-Managed Learning College – http://www.college.selfmanagedlearning.org/

East Kent Sudbury School – https://eastkentsudburyschool.org.uk/

Learning Begins in Wonder – https://www.facebook.com/groups/learningbeginsinwonder/

Oxford Home Schooling – www.oxfordhomeschooling.co.uk

The PLACE Programme – https://place-programme.org/

The Free-Range Education Website – www.free-range-education.co.uk

Education Otherwise – www.education-otherwise.org

Home Education Advisory Service – www.heas.org.uk

The Islamic Homeschooling Advisory Network – https://www.home-education.org.uk/articles/article-he-muslim-community.pdf

Schoolhouse – www.schoolhouse.org.uk

The Home Education Website – www.home-education.org.uk

The HE-Special UK website – www.he-special.org.uk

National Bullying Helpline – https://www.nationalbullyinghelpline.co.uk/

Home Education UK – https://en-gb.facebook.com/HEUKadmin/

Simply Charlotte Mason – https://simplycharlottemason.com/

Waldorf Education – https://www.waldorfeducation.org/

Christopherus Homeschool Resources – https://www.christopherushomeschool.com/

Well-Trained Mind – https://welltrainedmind.com/

Leadership Education – https://tjed.org/

John Holt GWS – https://www.johnholtgws.com/

Living Montessori Now – https://livingmontessorinow.com/

Home School Legal Defense Association (HSLDA) – https://hslda.org/

The Coalition for Responsible Homeschooling – https://responsiblehomeschooling.org/

Oak Meadow – https://www.oakmeadow.com/

Moving Beyond the Page – https://www.movingbeyondthepage.com/

Khan Academy – https://www.khanacademy.org/

Academic Earth – https://academicearth.org/

Simple Homeschool – https://simplehomeschool.net/

Special Needs Homeschooling – https://specialneedshomeschooling.com/

Highly Sensitive Person website – http://www.hsperson.com/

REFERENCES

Biddulph, Steve (2013). *Raising Girls*. London: HarperThorsons.

Biddulph, Steve (2018). *Raising Boys*. London: HarperCollins.

Booth, R. & Duncan, P. (2020). 'Nearly 1,500 deaths in one day: UK ministers accused of downplaying Covid-19 peak', *The Guardian*, 19 June; available at https://tinyurl.com/yd3mjgl2 (accessed 20 July 2020).

Clanchy, Kate (2019). *Some Kids I Taught and What They Taught Me*. London: Picador/Pan Macmillan.

Cohen, Lawrence J. (2013). *The Opposite of Worry: The Playful Parenting Approach to Childhood Anxieties and Fears*. New York: Ballantine Books.

Dowty, Terri (2000). *Free Range Education: How Home Education Works*, Stroud: Hawthorn Press.

Dweck, Carol (2012). *Mindset: How You Can Fulfil Your Potential*. London: Robinson.

Eden, Aaron (2020). 'Aaron Eden on rehumanizing education' Off-Trail Learning Podcast; available at https://tinyurl.com/y63k44oj (accessed 20 July 2020).

Gray, Peter (2013). *Free to Learn: Why Unleashing the Instinct to Play Will Make Our Children Happier, More Self-reliant, and Better Students for Life*. New York: Basic Books.

Gray, Peter (2020). 'The case against the case against homeschooling', *Psychology Today*, 16 May; available at https://tinyurl.com/y4zt4zof (accessed 20 July 2020).

Hancock, LynNell (2011). 'Why are Finland's schools successful?', *Smithsonian Magazine*, September; available at https://tinyurl.com/y6ppzpwd (accessed 20 July 2020).

Hinsliff, Gaby (2020). 'Life of the party: Interview with Angela Rayner', *The Guardian Weekend*, 20 June; available at https://tinyurl.com/yy998acv (accessed 20 July 2020).

Holmes, Edmond (1911). *What Is and What Might Be*. London: Constable & Co.

Holt, John (1964). *How Children Fail*. London: Pitman Publishing.

Holt, John (1967). *How Children Learn*. London: Pitman Publishing.

Holt, John & Farenga, Pat (2003). *Teach Your Own: The John Holt Book Of Homeschooling*. Cambridge, Mass.: Hachette Books/Perseus.

House, Richard (2005). 'Being Highly Sensitive: recognising its virtue and maximising its potential', *The Mother* magazine, 13 (Spring), pp. 12–14.

Jones, Tobias (2020). 'School's out: Italian lessons: what we've learned from two months of home schooling', *The Guardian*, 24 April; available at https://tinyurl.com/y92wktna (accessed 20 July 2020).

Lockhart, Paul (2002). 'A mathematician's lament'. Washington, D.C.: Association of America; available at https://tinyurl.com/lrqzoz4 (accessed 20 July 2020).

Palmer, Sue (2006). *Toxic Childhood: How the Modern World Is Damaging Our Children and What We Can Do about It*. London: Orion Books (2nd edn, 2015).

Pattinson, Harriet A. (2013). *Rethinking Learning to Read: The Challenge from Children Educated at Home*. Birmingham: University of Birmingham, September; available at https://tinyurl.com/yysmo8ch (accessed 20 July 2020).

Ray, Brain D. (2020). *Homeschooling: The Research*. Salem, Oregon: National Home Education Research Institute, 23 March; available at https://tinyurl.com/yda5z6y2 (accessed 20 July 2020).

Robinson, Sir Ken (2006). 'Do schools kill creativity?', TED Talks, February; available at https://tinyurl.com/y84drvev (accessed 20 July 2020).

Rothermel, Paula-Jane (2002). 'Home-Education: Rationales, Practices and Outcomes'. Durham: University of Durham, D.Phil. thesis, November; available at http://etheses.dur.ac.uk/1005/ (accessed 20 July 2020).

Santos, Gabriel (2020). 'Experience: I built the first skatepark in Syria', *The Guardian Weekend*, 19 June; available at https://tinyurl.com/y4a6gnf6 (accessed 20 July 2020).

Schore, Allan N. (2017). 'All our sons: the developmental neurobiology and neuroendocrinology of boys at risk', *Infant Mental Health Journal*, 38 (1): 15–52; https://doi.org/10.1002/imhj.21616.

Turner, Camilla (2019). 'Britain has biggest primary school classes in the developed world, report finds', *Daily Telegraph*, 10 September; available at https://tinyurl.com/y376px9j (accessed 20 July 2020).

HAWTHORN PRESS
HOME EDUCATION RESOURCES

Kindergarten, Play, Child Development and Parenting

Reclaim Early Childhood

The philosophy, psychology and practice of Steiner-Waldorf early years education

Sebastian and Tamara Suggate

Reclaim Early Childhood presents a lively overview of Rudolf Steiner-Waldorf early years education as adaptable, creative and dynamic, informed by a profound respect for the uniqueness of each child.

200pp; 234 × 156mm; paperback;
ISBN: 978-1-912480-10-4

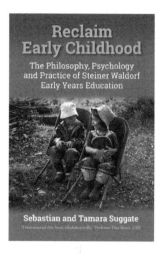

Movement: Your child's first language

Sally Goddard Blythe
with music by Michael Lazarev

This book explains why movement and music are essential for healthy brain development and learning, and the 2 CDs within the book include songs, stories, nursery rhymes and exercises.

This invaluable resource is suitable for parents, teachers, paediatricians and health-care workers.

192pp; 234 x 156mm; paperback;
ISBN: 978-1-907359-99-6

The Well Balanced Child: Movement and early learning

Sally Goddard Blythe

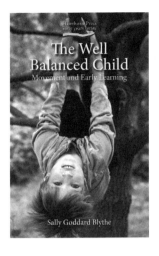

This practical, inspirational resource will help parents and educators to understand: why movement matters; how music helps brain development; the role of nutrition, the brain and child growth; how to help children with learning and behaviour problems.

304pp; 216 × 138mm; paperback;
ISBN: 978-1-903458-63-1

The Parenting Toolkit
(paperback edition)
Simple steps to happy & confident children

Caroline Penney

Caroline Penney explains clearly how to help your child become confident, capable, caring, and able to reach their full potential. This book also offers tips on how to ensure that you are getting all the self-care that you need in order to be a good parent.

164pp; 250 x 200mm; paperback;
ISBN: 978-1-912480-11-1

Simplicity Parenting
Using the power of less to raise happy, secure children

Kim John Payne

This is a title for parents who want to slow down, for families with too much stuff, too many choices and too much information. Here are four simple steps for decluttering, quieting, and soothing family dynamics so that children can thrive at school, get along with peers, and nurture well-being.

352pp; 234 x 156mm; paperback;
ISBN: 978-1-912480-03-6

Too Much, Too Soon?

Early learning and the erosion of childhood

Edited by Richard House

In 23 hard-hitting chapters, leading educators, researchers, policy makers and parents advocate alternative ways ahead for slowing childhood, better policy-making and, above all, the 'right learning at the right time' in children's growth – learning when they are developmentally ready.

376pp; 234 × 156mm; paperback;
ISBN: 978-1-907359-02-6

You Are Your Child's First Teacher

What parents can do with and for their children from birth to age six

Rahima Baldwin Dancy

A book that advocates a 'slow parenting' approach so parents can enjoy the magical first years of raising a child. Practical advice will help parents to understand their child's unique needs, enjoy storytelling, crafts and musical activities, and value their own ability to understand and care for their child.

400pp; 234 × 156mm; paperback;
ISBN: 978-1-903458-65-5

Seasonal Festivals and Crafts

The Children's Forest

Dawn Casey, Anna Richardson, Helen d'Ascoli

A rich and abundant treasury in celebration of the outdoors, this book encourages children's natural fascination with the forest and its inhabitants. An enchanting book where imagination, story and play bring alive the world of the forest. Full of games, facts, celebrations, craft activities, recipes, foraging, stories and Forest School skills, Ideal for ages 5–12, it will be enjoyed by all ages.

336pp; 250 x 200mm; paperback;
ISBN: 978-1-907359-91-0

All Year Round

Ann Druitt, Christine Fynes-Clinton, Marije Rowling

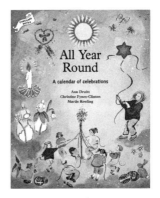

Observing the round of festivals is an enjoyable way to bring rhythm into children's lives and provide a series of meaningful landmarks to look forward to. This book is brimming with things to make, activities, stories, poems and songs to share with your family.

320pp; 250 × 200mm; paperback;
ISBN: 978-1-869890-47-6

Festivals, Family and Food

Guide to seasonal celebration

Diana Carey, Judy Large

This family favourite is a unique, well-loved source of stories, recipes, things to make, activities, poems, songs and festivals. The perfect present for a family, it explores the numerous festivals that children love celebrating.

320pp; 250 × 200mm; paperback;
ISBN: 978-1-869890-47-6

Festivals Together
Guide to multicultural celebration
Sue Fitzjohn, Minda Weston, Judy Large

This special book for families and teachers helps you celebrate festivals from cultures from all over the world. This resource guide for celebration introduces a selection of 26 Buddhist, Christian, Hindu, Jewish, Muslim and Sikh festivals, and offers a lively introduction to the wealth of different ways of life.

224pp; 250 × 200mm; paperback;
ISBN: 978-1-869890-46-9

Making the Children's Year
Seasonal Waldorf crafts with children
Marije Rowling

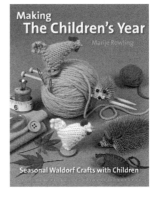

Drawing on the creative ethos of Steiner Waldorf education, this is a full-colour second edition of The Children's Year. Packed with all kinds of seasonal crafts, for beginners and experienced crafters, this book is a gift for parents seeking to make toys that will inspire children and provide an alternative to throwaway culture.

120pp; 210 x 200mm; paperback;
ISBN: 978-1-907359-84-2

Making Woodland Crafts
Using green sticks, rods, beads and string
Patrick Harrison

This book is guaranteed to get children out and about and enjoying nature. Through a series of stunning hand-drawn illustrations, *Making Woodland Crafts* provides the basic knowledge and skills to complete a range of both simple and more advanced craft projects.

120pp; 210 x 200mm; paperback;
ISBN: 978-1-907359-84-2

Making Simple Needle Felts

40 inspiring seasonal projects

Steffi Stern

A back-to-basics guide to making needle-felted objects, this book contains chapters on techniques, materials, tools and accessories, as well as projects organised by season. All the projects are suitable for a beginner, with some for little fingers (no needles involved), for beginners, as well as those who have more experience.

176pp; 250 x 200mm; paperback;
ISBN 978-1-907359-69-9

Making Peg Dolls

Over 60 fun, creative projects for children and adults

Margaret Bloom

Coming from the Waldorf handcraft tradition, these irresistible dolls encourage creative play and promote the emotional and imaginative development of young children. Easy to follow, step-by-step instructions with beautiful colour illustrations for children and crafters of all levels and experience.

192pp; 200 x 210mm; paperback;
ISBN: 978-1-907359-77-4

Making Soft Dolls

Simple Waldorf designs to sew and love

Steffi Stern

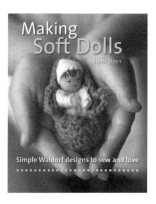

From the simplest rag doll to more complex characters, this book gives straight-forward instructions, a guide to buying your materials and upcycling materials you already own. A lovingly hand-made doll makes the perfect present, and these dolls are easy to make and will be much loved for generations.

128pp; 200 × 250mm; paperback;
ISBN: 978-1-912480-05-0

Learning Resources for Children aged 7–14

Creative Form Drawing
with Children Aged 6–10 Years

Angela Lord

Designed to be used with the Steiner/Waldorf curriculum from classes one through three, this workbook will also be valuable to home-educating parents using the Steiner/Waldorf ethos as their base. Creative form drawing helps children develop hand–eye co-ordination, spatial orientation, observations skills, confident movement, drawing skills and the foundations of handwriting.

136pp; 297 × 210mm; paperback;
ISBN: 978-1-907359-98-9

Creative Place-Based Environmental Education
Children and schools as ecopreneurs for change

Jorunn Barane, Aksel Hugo, Morten Clemetsen

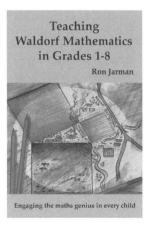

This book presents the why, what and how of creative place-based education. Design tools for developing place based educational curricula are made globally relevant, with case studies from Britain, Norway and Tanzania. Teachers from kindergarten to high school, teacher trainers, environmental educators and forest school educators will find this an invaluable resource.

172pp; 234 × 156mm; paperback;
ISBN: 978-1-907359-73-6

Teaching Waldorf Mathematics in Grades 1–8
Engaging the maths genius in every child

Ron Jarman

Ron Jarman shows how children can easily grasp math principles without the drudgery of endless worksheets. He draws on Pythagoras, the ancient Greeks and Rudolf Steiner for re-imagining the vital importance of mathematical learning for human growth. The techniques and exercises in the book have been tried and tested by Waldorf teachers around the world.

304pp; 234 x 156mm; paperback;
ISBN: 978-1-912480-25-8

Writing to Reading
the Steiner Waldorf Way
Foundations of creative literacy
in Classes 1 and 2
Abi Allanson and Nicky Teensma

This theory- and practice-based book outlines the
foundations for creative literacy and teaching children
how to write and read in Classes 1 and 2, or UK Years
2 and 3. The child discovers their own voice through
movement, form drawing and story-telling.

352pp; 246 189mm; hardback;
ISBN: 978-1-907359-88-0

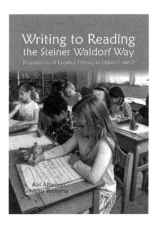

The Natural Storyteller
Wildlife tales for telling
Georgiana Keable

Here is a handbook for the natural storyteller, with story
maps, brain-teasing riddles, story skeletons and
adventures to make a tale your own. This diverse
collection of stories will nurture active literacy skills, and
help form an essential bond with nature.

272pp; 228 x 186mm; paperback;
ISBN: 978-1-90735-980-4

Storytelling with Children
Nancy Mellon

Children love family storytelling and parents can learn
this practical, magical art. Here are methods, tips and
resources to enable you to: create a listening space; use
the day's events to make stories; transform old stories and
make up new ones; bring your personal and family stories
to life; learn stories by heart using pictures, inner theatre,
walk-about, singing the story and other methods.

192pp; 234 x 156mm; paperback;
ISBN: 978-1-907359-26-2

ORDERING BOOKS

If you have difficulties ordering Hawthorn Press books from a bookshop, you can order direct from our website www.hawthornpress.com, or from our UK distributor BookSource: 50 Cambuslang Road, Glasgow, G32 8NB: Tel: (0845) 370 0063, E-mail: orders@booksource.net.

Details of our overseas distributors can be found on our website.

Hawthorn Press
www.hawthornpress.com